D0819433

GENDER AT WORK

GENDER AT WORK

ORGANIZATIONAL CHANGE
FOR EQUALITY

Aruna Rao
Rieky Stuart
David Kelleher

KUMARIAN
PRESS

Gender at Work: Organizational Change for Equality

Published 1999 in the United States of America by Kumarian Press, Inc.,
14 Oakwood Avenue, West Hartford, Connecticut 06119-2127 USA.

Production and design by The Sarov Press, Stratford, Connecticut.
Index by Barbara J. DeGennaro.
The text of this book is set in New Baskerville 10/14.

Printed in Canada on acid-free paper by
Transcontinental Printing and Graphics, Inc.
Text printed with vegetable oil-based ink.

∞ The paper used in this publication meets the minimum requirements
of the American National Standard for Information Sciences—Permanence of
Paper for Printed Library Materials, ANSI Z39.48–1984.

Library of Congress Cataloging-in-Publication Data
Rao, Aruna.
    Gender at work : organizational change for equality / Aruna Rao,
Rieky Stuart, David Kelleher.
        p.   cm.
    Includes bibliographical references and index.
    ISBN 1–56549–103–3 (cloth : alk. paper). — ISBN 1–56549–102–5
(pbk. : alk. paper)
        1. Women—Employment—Developing countries. 2. Women—Developing
countries—Social conditions.   3. Sex discrimination against women—
Developing countries. 4. Sexism—Developing countries.
I. Stuart, Rieky, 1945–   II. Kelleher, David, 1944–
III. Title.
HD6223 .R36   1999
331.4'133'091724—dc21   99–33624

08 07 06 05 04 03 02 01 00 99   10 9 8 7 6 5 4 3 2 1

First Printing 1999

DEDICATION

TO F.H. ABED for his belief that gender equality is integral to human happiness and progress, his courage in opening the doors of BRAC to new ideas and explorations and questioning of established practices, his inspiring personal example, and his unstinting support and collaboration.

RECALL THE FACE of the poorest and most helpless person you have ever seen and ask yourself if the step you contemplate is going to be of any use to them. Will they be able to gain anything by it? Will it restore them to a control over their life and destiny?

Gandhi

CONTENTS

LIST OF FIGURES

ACKNOWLEDGMENTS

THE IDEAS AND APPROACHES in this book have been shaped in many discussions during the past three years—at conferences and kitchen tables, on field trips and in hotel rooms, face to face and by e-mail, as well as by reflection on writings; others' and our own.

F.H. Abed, the founder and Executive Director of BRAC, gave us our first serious opportunity to explore the connections between gender and organizational change in the context of a large, vibrant NGO working for poverty alleviation and women's empowerment in Bangladesh. We owe a debt of gratitude to him, the senior managers of BRAC, and the BRAC Core Gender Team, Sheepa Hafiza, Habibur Rahman, Sadequr Rahman, and Naheed Sultana.

The 1996 Canada Conference was an early step in developing this book of cases and the concept of the deep structure of organizations that hinders a gender-equality agenda. It was also crucial to the building of a global network of people who worked together to further our understanding of these issues.

During 1997–98, the case conferences at the Simmons Institute for Leadership and Change in Boston offered us an opportunity to deepen both our analysis of gender and organizational change interventions and our reflections on power. We are grateful to Debbie Kolb, Deborah Merrill-Sands, and Joyce Fletcher for their rich insights.

This writing endeavor has been a knowledge discovery between us and our case contributors—Michelle Friedman, Debbie Kolb, Debra Meyerson, Deborah Merrill-Sands, Joyce Fletcher, Anne Acosta, and Rebecca Tripp. Our differences as much as our shared visions have made for new understandings and have generated difficult questions. Bringing everyone together has been no mean feat, but we have moved our thinking and the case writing along at small meetings held in Canada and Boston, and at a large international conference held in South Africa. We have built lasting friendships and respect for our differences. We are thankful for the wonderful contributions of all the case writers and are grateful to them for sticking it out and coming through.

By asking tough questions and making invaluable suggestions for improvement, our readers—Kathy Staudt, Rhona Rapoport, Kate McLaren, Betty Plewes, Beth Woroniuk, and Reidar Kvam helped us to clarify our ideas, our voice, and the scope of this book. We are grateful to all of them for making this a better book. Our splendid editor, Charis Wahl, asked probing questions about meaning, reflected with us on key ideas and the shape of this book, worked closely with all the case writers, and corrected our convoluted prose. To her, we owe many thanks. Elizabeth Ballard formatted and scrutinized the manuscript, tracked down references, and added consistency.

We wish to thank the Ford Foundation for its support of our work with BRAC, our Canada conference, and this book.

Finally, we wish to thank our families—Colin, Netami and Beth, Holly, Reidar, Priya and Sarita— for their support and constant encouragement, for putting up with our debates that often overflowed into lunches and dinners, and for believing in the value of this work and in us.

INTRODUCTION

THIS BOOK IS INTENDED as a reflective moment in an ambitious, collaborative process intended to develop and share knowledge about gender and organizational change.[1] As the use of these terms is neither self-evident nor universally agreed upon, we set out our understanding of these terms as the self-conscious use of organizational/learning and change principles for the particular purpose of affecting organizational norms and practices that prevent equitable gender relations—both in the organization and in how it serves its clients.

When we use the word "gender" we mean the socially constructed roles, status, expectations, and relationships of women and men. Similarly, when we use the terms "gender equity" and "gender equality" we are not suggesting an equality based on sameness but rather one based on difference. The process of achieving gender equality is a striving for justice through the transformation of constraining gender roles and ideologies that influence organizational structures, values, behavior, and outcomes.

So, is this book about workplace gender equity? Yes, but not solely, and certainly only as a means toward a greater end, that of organizational effects that benefit women as well as men. Our book title encompasses both the means and ends of our work—it is about both gender at the worksite and how the gendered organization affects the external environment—the public and private space where women and men live their lives. We believe that gender exclusion is both all pervasive and insidious, and that working to uncover gender-biased ideologies and value systems is difficult and often painful. Gains are possible but fragile.

We believe that gender-inequitable organizations produce gender-inequitable effects. Inviting more women to participate in existing organizations as workers or even as leaders, while maintaining existing values and ways of working, will not equalize the inequitable impact of organizations on the lives of women and men clients. Looking at gendered organizational impact without examining the embedded patriarchal values and practices of organizations will not create sustainable change.

This does not mean that we think gender-inequitable organizations cannot produce outcomes that can aid in the empowerment of women—credit schemes for women and innovative education for girls can be delivered by patriarchal models of organization. However, we believe that re-shaping social institutions and organizations so that they include women and men's varied perspectives to the benefit of both, is of a different order. How do we describe the transformed institution? In trying to do so we thought of the Buddha's attempt to describe nirvana adequately to a "rational" mind by describing some of its characteristics and principles of practice. With far less eloquence, we shall attempt to do the same for our more modest vision.

At the very least a "transformed" organization would have women and men in equal numbers at all levels and in all functions, with equal benefits. Where necessary it would re-distribute resources across gender, class, and race within and outside organizations. It would be community- and client-centered and would work toward women's empowerment and transformation in gender relations. It would value productive and reproductive labor, and diminish the split among work, home, and community. It would decrease oppressive hierarchy in organizations, and include those voices that are currently marginal in decision-making. It would ensure empowerment and accountability at all levels in organizations and value the different perspectives formed by gender, racial, ethnic, age, class, and sexual orientation differences. These individual viewpoints, however, coalesce in a whole larger than its parts; for our aim is to build organizations in which women and men both thrive and in which women are not systematically disadvantaged because of organizational, cultural, or societal norms. In order for this to come about we must change the constraining gender roles and ideologies that influence organizational structures, values, and behavior; we must redefine power on a foundation of valuing difference.

What does this mean for Monday morning? It might mean a change in what organizations focus on, how they get the job done, how they allocate resources, how they are structured, and how they enhance the quality of the worklife of their members. Such change is important because we expect that, by changing in these ways on the inside, organizations will also change in desired ways on the outside: what and how they deliver, how they measure progress, whom they include, and what impact they have. That's the important part for us.

What do we offer in this book? This book is aimed at practitioners. It shares ways of thinking and methods of acting that hold promise of movement and gains, however fragile, in transforming organizations and their effect on people's lives. This book tells stories and aims to generate conversations about gender and organizational change. We don't offer road maps but we do offer promising new directions based on current thinking and experience.

The contributors to this book bring a range of backgrounds and motivations to this work, and emphasize different elements. Some of us work in development and/or social-change organizations; some are primarily researchers, based at academic institutions. Some are external consultants, others work inside organizations. Each case holds its own world view, which has shaped the interventions and practice; the skills, interests and position (internal or external) of the intervenors; and the organizational and larger political contexts in which the organization sits. Similarly, each case speaks in its own voice. What the cases share—and this is the reason we included them—is that they dare to imagine a better way of doing things, delve into the heart and soul of organizations, and aim to change inequitable work practices.

The three principal authors came together in 1994 to work as part of a team at BRAC (Bangladesh Rural Advancement Committee), a large NGO in Bangladesh, to improve both BRAC's capacity to deliver gender-sensitive programming and its gender relations within the organization. Rieky has been a development worker since the 1960s and since 1985 she has worked as a trainer, writer, consultant, and manager concerned with gender and organizational change around the world. Currently, she is Executive Director of Oxfam Canada. She also knits spectacular sweaters and makes a good pot of soup. David is an independent organizational consultant specializing in public and non-profit organizations in Canada and internationally. He also plays jazz guitar. Aruna, for whom the path not taken is the Streisand route to fame, has been working on gender and development issues in Asia and internationally since 1979; she now writes and consults on gender and organizational change. Together, we have been involved for the past five years in building a global network of theorists and practitioners in this newly emerging field.

The contributors to this book are women and men who work on the promotion and sustenance of a vision of change, and on the role of organizations in that process. In the early 1990s, a number of change agents began to combine organizational-change theory and feminist theory, using our experience and these bodies of knowledge to create new approaches to organizational change. Governments, for-profit companies, and voluntary organizations in North America, Asia, Europe, Africa, and Latin America have worked with us in these experiments. Although our efforts began independently, in very different locations, when we first compared notes—at the fourth United Nations World Conference on Women, in Beijing in 1995—we found, to our pleasure and surprise, a great deal of convergence in our approaches and methodologies. Subsequently, a number of us continued to share and develop our analysis and reflections on the interventions at a conference organized in Canada in 1996, at case conferences sponsored by the Simmons Institute for Leadership and Change in Boston, and at a conference in Cape Town, South Africa, in 1998, sponsored by the African Gender Institute and the Association for Women in Development.

Now, on to how this book is organized. The first chapter describes the origins of this work. It presents our analysis of the institutional barriers to gender equality and our thinking on organizations and how they change— or resist change efforts. We also discuss uncovering dimly understood but defining aspects of organizations, and the need to think in very new terms. Just as the Newtonian conception of a mechanical universe is being superseded by more complex theories of "new science," especially quantum physics, so we can re-model organizations in ways that break from Weberian hierarchies built on particular notions of rationality, linearity, control and efficiency. Chapter One outlines elements of a gendered organizational "deep structure," which help to frame the interventions described in the case studies. Chapter Two sets out approaches to work on organizational change and gender equality, and serves as an introduction to the ideas pursued in the cases.

Next, we provide five case studies, the stories of interventions. We have deliberately chosen cases that involve diverse organizations—BRAC, a Bangladeshi social development NGO; CIMMYT, the international agricultural-research institute for maize and wheat based in Mexico; The Body Shop, a multinational beauty-products company; The National Land Committee (NLC), a South African NGO working for majority land rights, and Urban Housing (UH), the pseudonym of a Canadian social-housing organization.

Although the cases share an approach, they are different in important ways. Four are organizations whose primary mission is a social one; one is a multinational corporation with a strong interest in social causes. They also vary in the extent to which they engage the organization's deep structure and question the rules of the game. Several interventions were intended to improve the position of women as staff; others address a concern for women as clients or beneficiaries. The common elements are equality linked to key organizational goals, and a participatory approach grounded in work practice.

In a postscript, we describe and discuss dilemmas we face as we work to uncover and engage the deep structure of organizations. These dilemmas are common to many of the cases. We hope that our collective thinking and practice can move us through these dilemmas to the challenges that lie ahead.

NOTES

1. We use the word gender to mean the socially constructed roles, status, expectations, and relationships of women and men.

1

ROOTS OF GENDER INEQUALITY
IN ORGANIZATIONS

LIKE MANY OTHERS, we are concerned with improving people's lives in gender-equitable ways. Our focus on organizations, as instruments in that process, is one of many efforts to similar ends, from grassroots organizing and advocacy to changing legal frameworks, policy analysis, and program implementation. Our analysis begins with the premise that the problem of gender inequality is rooted in the institutional arrangements of organizations, which in turn produce gender-inequitable outcomes.

This insight has been put forward persuasively by others before us. Nuket Kardam[1] was one of the first to point out the importance of understanding the gendered nature of development organizations and their broader institutional environment. Without such an understanding, she argued, change efforts and policies aimed at achieving women's empowerment stall, not only in the quagmire of bureaucracy but, most important, in the gender-biased assumptions on which organizations are founded. Kathy Staudt, a prolific writer on gender and institutions, identifies institutionalized male privilege as a fundamental principle of organizations.[2] Anne Marie Goetz, in her first article on gender and administration, analyzed ways in which organizations were gendered and how that affected their ability to produce outcomes beneficial to women.[3]

Advocates of organizational gender equity often have focussed on employment-equity issues, that is, on reducing barriers to women in the workplace and improving the representation of women at higher levels of organizations.[4] They have also focussed on the programs or services provided by organizations. For example, gender specialists have demonstrated that in development and other international organizations, such as the UN, not only that the work discriminates against women but also that a more equitable approach would better fulfill the mandate of the organization.[5]

THE DEEP STRUCTURE OF ORGANIZATIONS

Both psychotherapy and organizational theory recognize those deeply felt but hidden aspects of consciousness—individual or organizational—that shape meanings and understandings, actions and reactions. Edgar Schein, one of the first organizational theorists to identify the importance of organizational culture in shaping organizational outcomes, saw culture as hidden, and needing to be uncovered.[6] (Schein, however, does not deal with gender, and his conception of culture is organization-specific.) Itzin and Newman, taking a broader view of culture, describe the ways culture blocks change toward gender equity in municipal governments.[7] Goetz[8] and Kabeer[9] have also written about this hidden aspect of organizations.

Our explorations focus on the institutional arrangements of organizations, on what Joan Acker calls the "gendered substructure" of organizations. This she characterizes as being built on a fundamental separation, and consequent devaluation, of "life" from "work."[10]

We call this the "deep structure" of organizations, that collection of values, history, culture and practices that form the unquestioned, "normal" way of working in organizations. We shall specify four elements hidden in this "deep structure," that we believe are both common to most organizations and critical determinants of the gender-biased organization. This analysis leads first to an exploration of how these unexamined assumptions and values of organizations are reflected in the way work is done. Next, it leads us to look at core organizational processes such as decision-making, allocation of power, use of staff time, rewards and incentives, and measures of success. Making organizations gender-equitable internally is not our sole aim. The most important question for us is: how can making change happen in ways that will make organizations more gender equitable on the inside *and* bring about gender-equitable outcomes on the outside?

Much of the current literature on gendered organizations and gender-biased outcomes stresses the importance of accountability to a constituency, incentive structures, outside pressure to keep the organization's feet to the fire, bureaucratic entrepreneurship, and making the intellectual case for gender equality. The assumption is that if we had more power we could compel compliance to a more equitable regime. Goetz, for example, concludes that "in the end it's a matter of political struggle."[11] Miller and Razavi advocate feminist engagement with institutions that tries to promote change within existing bureaucratic structures. They describe the "policy entrepreneur," who uses a mixture of bureaucratic politics and intellectual efforts to demonstrate how paying attention to women can benefit the accomplishment of organizational goals.[12] Kathy Staudt supports this approach but, like Goetz, emphasizes the political struggle.

Our approach is different in two important ways. First, our understanding of organizational change marries insights from feminist and organizational change theory. Although power and accountability are important, we believe that change requires more than getting power and then telling people what to do or training them to do it. It requires both power and participation. We describe a change process to do this, elements of which underlie the five cases.

Second, our goal is not simply to improve existing structures. We don't want to play by the rules; we want to change them fundamentally and contribute to the evolution of a new way of thinking about organizations. We aim for "transformation," not just change.

Organizations will not become gender equitable without such transformation. Even if powerful leaders wanted equity, the staff were in agreement, and outside constituents were demanding it, current ways of understanding organizations will entrench the status quo. Trying to "add gender" into the structure and work of organizations is like trying to add the idea that the world is round to the idea that the world is flat. Rather, we must rethink the whole matter. We need first to re-conceptualize what an organization is, then we can re-invent organizations and institutions of all kinds in line with our vision of gender justice and racial equality integrated with sustainable development.

This is as radical as the development of bureaucracy in the last century. At that time, new forms of organizing were needed, as those that had been sufficient for family-based or craft organizations were incapable of managing complex industrial organizations, such as large factories and railroads. Similarly, our task is to imagine and invent new forms of organization that can respond, not only to the complex nature of the problems modern organizations must address, but also to the inequities faced by women and other groups excluded on the basis of difference. The cases are examples of steps towards this transformation.

Our approach to change encourages organizations to engage with these ideas in their own context. It helps them to examine ways in which hidden assumptions and values inhibit gender equality, thereby affecting the organization's ability to pursue a social-transformation agenda. Key to this process is finding the levers in the substructure of organizations that control the assumptions, values and deeply-held beliefs about the "way we do things." We must change organizational practice to reflect gender-equitable assumptions and construct a way to understand and internalize the change dynamic and its outcomes. We call this task "working with the deep structure."

Reflecting upon our experience and the analyses of others, we have come to believe that at least four aspects of the deep structure of organizations stand out as perpetuating gender inequality: the valuing of heroic individualism, the split between work and family, exclusionary power, and the monoculture of instrumentality.

Valuing Heroic Individualism

As organizations were founded and, until recently, peopled largely by men, it is not surprising to find them designed and maintained in ways that express men's identity. Much of that identity is fuelled by the myth of heroic individualism, expressed in images, language and behaviors that have become part and parcel of everyday organizational conversation: business travellers are "road warriors"; traders require a "killer instinct"; salesmen must "penetrate markets."

This myth of the crusader is behind a variety of gendered organizational behaviors. For example, organizations tend to value the "hero" who works day and night against tremendous odds to solve a crisis. The person who manages her work smoothly, thereby avoiding such crises, is invisible and undervalued. The end product and its producers are visible and valued; those who play a support role in the production process are neither. (This phenomenon is discussed in detail in the CIMMYT case study.) Other important aspects of the myth are competition and individual accomplishment. The rewards of the hero are status, power and, (as Hollywood would have us believe), the girl.

The Split between Work and Family

For most of human history, work and the rest of life were completely integrated. Artisanal work took place in the home; both adults and children were engaged in work, household maintenance, and celebration. Women, men, and children were engaged in crop production and processing for subsistence and sale; and in festivals to mark the turning of the seasons and the rituals of birth, death, and marriage. With the industrial revolution, the "workplace" moved out of the family, home, and community—both literally and metaphorically. The workplace became men's domain; so its organization conformed to their needs and interests. Women came to bear the responsibility for supporting the health and productivity of men in the workplace by domestic cooking, washing, and cleaning; raising children; and supporting the community through unpaid, and therefore, undervalued work—often in addition to undertaking paid work. Increasingly, home and community subsidized the workplace and the "privileging of economy over life" became institutionalized.

The challenge of re-balancing work and family has its academic beginnings in the work of Rhona and Robert Rapoport[13] in the 1960s; it has continued in that of Rosabeth Moss Kanter,[14] Lotte Bailyn,[15] Arlie Hochschild,[16] and Joan Acker. From Acker's work it is clear that the gendering of organizations—in the patterning of jobs, the creation of symbols and myths, interactions that enact dominance and subordination, and the determination of gender-appropriate behaviors and attitudes—is built on and reproduces a gendered substructure. This foundation comprises the spatial and temporal arrangements of work, rules prescribing workplace behavior, and the relation of workplaces to living places. It is supported by the assumption that work is separate from the rest of life, and that work has the first claim on the worker. From this is developed the notion of the ideal worker, who fulfils these demands. Women, who irrespective of their participation in the paid workforce are still primarily responsible for family and reproductive activities, tend not to be that "ideal" worker.

Moreover, these gendered assumptions, Acker points out, are reinforced by organizational processes focussed on power and control—the textual tools of management such as job evaluations that although seemingly neutral favor those who can minimize obligations apart from the job. Acker concludes that the ideal worker "excludes and marginalizes women who cannot, almost by definition, achieve the qualities of a real worker because to do so is to become like a man."[17]

This is an important element in several of the case studies. For example, in BRAC, working conditions in the field make it difficult for female staff to be married. In CIMMYT, the ideal worker is one who will travel great distances and work long hours, even at the expense of family life. At The Body Shop, a supervisor's job description is less a description of the work than a description of a male worker. These are some subtle ways in which organizations perpetuate inequality. These and innumerable other work "norms" function as an interlocking system that perpetuates not only inequality, but also the belief that there are no viable alternatives.

Exclusionary Power

Power, like technology, is neither inherently good nor bad; it just is. Our interest is in institutionalizing ways of thinking about and exercising power that do not reinforce sexist exploitation, but resist it and facilitate gender equality.

Simply put, there are two views of power. In one, power is a limited commodity—if I have more you have less. In the other view, power is infinite—the more we have the more there is. The former view corresponds to Lukes's first dimension of power[18]—A makes B do something he or she would not otherwise do. This assumes a win-lose situation in which there are a limited number of options: and if my option wins, yours has to lose. The second world view draws on Margaret Wheatley's view of the implications of twentieth-century science for twenty-first-century organizations: "power in an organization is the capacity generated by relationships."[19] In this view, power-as-energy is the product not only of position but also of information, relationship, and spirit. It assumes a win-win situation, focussed on building relationships and the capacity of both individuals and groups to respond to changing organizational and external realities.

Neither of these views about power is true or untrue. Each represents a set of assumptions that tends to evoke the behaviors implicit in the world view. In other words, each is a self-fulfilling prophecy. We believe that power viewed as empowering and infinite, and practiced as inclusionary is conducive to a gender-equality agenda. We think there are at least five sometimes overlapping ways of exercising power: positional power, agenda-setting power, hidden power, power of dialogue, and power of conflict.

Positional Power   Positional power is the authority derived from an office or title in an organization. It can be used, for example, either to release or to limit money, time, information, or other material resources. It can be used to bring people into the organization or to expel or exclude them. It can be used to create space for organizational change and to put gender justice on the agenda. It is needed to legitimate change. When used to expand an agenda through influence, we may call it persuasion: your knowledge, authority, or perspective may influence me to agree with you and do as you ask. When it is used to control or limit the power of others, positional power can be coercive or even abusive.

Positional power resides in every position in an organization, not only at the top. Although we may see the power of management to be hegemonic, workers have and exercise their own power. Each position in an organization has power over the function entrusted to it: to do it, not to do it, or to do it in ways that increase the probability of certain outcomes. For example, secretaries of senior executives in large organizations are famed for their power to set agendas by who they let in to see the boss, how they schedule the boss's time, and how they assign priorities. Most positional power is far from absolute, however, as its exercise can generate covert and overt resentment and resistance—passive withdrawal, non-cooperation, or sabotage.

The potential of positional power as domination is entrenched in the hierarchy and control structure of organizations and becomes manifest in the male-dominated, authority-based cultures that Itzin and Newman identify as the "Gentlemen's Club" and "The Barrack Yard." Not surprisingly, both are very unfriendly to gender equality.

Agenda-Setting Power   A more subtle exercise of power is agenda-setting power, which corresponds to Lukes's second dimension of power. For example, some NGOs have cultures that value hard work for social change. In these organizations, it is inappropriate to question long hours or low pay; staff may feel these concerns, but they are not to be discussed.

In organizations, as in families and societies, there are clear, unspoken rules that determine what can and cannot be discussed openly. (Sexual harassment and abuse of power are examples of "taboo" topics.) Restricting the agenda can often protect abuse or hide problems. Because organizations are gendered, what is not on the agenda is often what is not important to men, although it may be important to women. Understanding and working with agenda-setting power can often help an organization to democratize power relations. Equally important, thinking in new ways or, as Rebecca Tripp says, "thinking against yourself,"[20] is often key to understanding and change. The view of "power-as-energy" requires that agenda-setting becomes transparent.

Hidden Power   Hidden power corresponds to Lukes's third dimension of power, which he calls the unobtrusive exercise of power. As explained by Joyce Fletcher, "people do not realize that power is being exercised at their expense; therefore there is no resistance or conflict."[21] Not only is your issue not on the agenda, you are not even aware that it is an issue. Power is exerted to ensure that certain ideas are accepted as normal, and therefore people don't question them. It's just the way things are. The "oppressed" don't conceive of themselves as victimized. In the view of power as a limited commodity internalized subordination is right and proper. For those who see power-as-energy, what is required is what Paolo Freire has called a "conscientization process"—making the possibility of internalized subordination and superiority a topic for exploration and discussion.[22] (One must note, however, that each individual makes the final determination about his or her own level of consciousness: it can be both risky and presumptuous to judge another's level of internalized subordination or superiority.)

Bailyn, Kolb, Merrill-Sands, and others associated with the Center for Gender and Organizations have shown how hidden power—in the form of unquestioned assumptions about work practices—are very powerful ways of maintaining inequitable systems.[23] For example, in a high-performing, software-engineering group, no one questioned the inequity of all-night work sessions expected of female staff with childcare responsibilities. At CIMMYT, no one questioned the belief that in order to do good science, one had to work extremely long hours at far-flung field research sites and to place work ahead of all else. Nor did they question the gendered impact of such assumptions.

Perhaps the most deeply hidden aspect of how power supports gender inequality is historian Joan Scott's conception that gender itself is a signifier of power.[24] "Gender is a primary field within which or by means of which power is articulated. . . . Established as an objective set of references, concepts of gender structure perception and the concrete and symbolic organization of all social life. To the extent that these references establish distributions of power (differential control over or access to material and symbolic resources), gender becomes implicated in the conception and construction of power itself."[25] She illustrates this point with examples of how rulers have legitimized domination, strength, and central authority as masculine; and enemies, outsiders, subversives, and weakness, as feminine.

Power of Dialogue   Through dialogue we uncover the exercise of power and expose how it builds or prevents equity. At the 1996 Canada conference, we focussed on the work of a number of organizations that were using the power of dialogue to move organizations toward gender equity.[26] Common to many of these change efforts were the surfacing of silent voices and finding ways to link the concerns of unempowered staff with the issues of the organization. This touches what Lukes calls false consciousness. By excavating other perspectives, we take the first step toward facilitating informed choice and action. In BRAC, groups of staff in area offices analyzed gender issues in the office and in the program, and designed small-scale changes that would produce greater equality and enhance program effectiveness. When women in one office realized that they had far more experience than the men but less information, because they did not write the reports, they learned how to write the reports, and took over a share of report production. This resulted in more flexibility in work-sharing, the elimination of some backlogs as well as more equitable power relations.[27] Similarly at Xerox, after discussion revealed that the pressure to produce resulted in long hours, late nights, and difficulties for staff trying to care for children, staff invented new ways of working that were both family-friendly and increased productivity.[28]

Power of Conflict   The dialogic tone of this book is in sharp contrast to the work of many intervenors who have utilized more confrontational or "guerrilla" strategies to get gender equality on the agenda, and to harness the power of outside pressure and legislation to re-shape the organization. These intervenors use a mixture of alliance building, dialogue and pressure tactics. Chesler[29] contrasts consensus-based approaches with conflict-based ones; he asserts that, if change is to produce socially just and anti-sexist/anti-racist organizations, power and norms must be confronted. Jackson and Holvino[30] also found that purely consensus-based strategies are not effective.

The apparent choice between conflict and compromise is not a real choice at all. Both are needed to make change happen. For example, the Women's Budget project in South Africa is a kaleidoscope of aspects of power: working with women in civil society to build a dialogue on the budget; marshaling the power of large numbers of women to maintain pressure for equity; building alliances inside government; developing the best possible information through research and networking; and, finally, paying careful attention to bureau-cratic politics to build a platform for implementation.[31]

We began this discussion of power acknowledging that it exists, it flows, or as Foucault would say, "is always at interplay."[32] We then identified exclu-sionary power operating through rigid hierarchy in ways that limit participa-tion and voice as an important aspect of the deep structure of organizations that hinders a gender equality agenda. Like Foucault, we believe that power exercised to dominate or exclude needs to be effectively countered and struc-tures and practices built to allow "transgressions."

Our beliefs about power are one of the key "fields" we create in an orga-nization—the invisible non-material structures, like gravity or magnetism, that shape and bound the behavior of related particles within them. These fields tend to become self-fulfilling prophecies, the Heisenberg principle in organizational practice. Exploring how different people in the organization understand and work with these beliefs and practices—the stuff of all five interventions in this book—can lead to re-interpreting and recreating organizational culture and practice and the appropriate exercise of power in the organization. Part of that re-interpretation is building accountability to the organizational mission rather than exercising power as a mechanism of control aimed at the achievement of narrow organizational objectives.

Monoculture of Instrumentality

We define instrumentality as a narrow focus on the accomplishment of quantitative goals. In thinking about this we have been inspired by Indian feminist ecologist, Vandana Shiva's concept of "monocultures of the mind."[33] Shiva uses scientific forestry to illustrate this concept, showing how western, capitalist knowledge is valued, and local knowledge "disappears." Western forestry sees the forest as timber to be cut and sold; local knowledge knows that the forest is a source of water, fodder, fertilizer, medicine and food. When western knowledge and business triumphs, the forests become a monoculture with the sole goal of profit from timber.

The tropical forests when modeled on the factory and used as a timber mine become a non-renewable resource. Tropical peoples also become a dispensable and historical waste. The diversity must be weeded out. . . . Those that do not fit into the uniformity must be declared unfit.[34]

Organizational monocultures of the mind focus on narrow goals at the expense of broader goals such as sustainability, justice, and other less evident requirements for organizational health and equity. This focus excludes people, perspectives, and processes not directly related to the accomplishment of the narrow goal. In other words, quantitative targets capture organizational attention to the detriment of the larger mission. For example, development agencies need to disburse funds on a schedule; indeed they, and their project officers, are often judged on how much money they can move on time. Meeting disbursement targets can overwhelm consultative and organic program management needs that take the involvement of local women and men seriously.

A narrow, quantitative target focus has additional implications. First, in non-profit and government organizations, instrumentality can lead to the implementation of performance- or results-based management systems that include quantitative targets to which managers (and the organization) are held accountable. Much of this is laudatory; but the focus on quantitative measures tends to de-value qualitative aspects of the work, including such "invisible" and "relational" activities as building teams, agreement, and part-nerships.[35]

Second, although efforts are underway to marry results-oriented man-agement with the more complex and harder-to-measure requirements of so-cial development, the emphasis on targets can lead to gender-biased deci-sions to provide certain services and not others. Third, the organization is likely to be more careful about devoting staff time to new initiatives not di-rectly related to meeting targets. It will be less likely to spend time and re-sources on exploring new ways of working that might benefit the organiza-tion and its clients in the longer run. An organization that pays insufficient attention to innovation runs the risk of becoming irrelevant.

HOW IS DEEP STRUCTURE CONNECTED TO ACHIEVING GENDER EQUALITY?

Our belief is that an organization that is gender-biased on the inside is incapable of producing gender-equitable outcomes. Peters and Waterman have documented numerous examples from the corporate sector of how organizational culture determines the ability of the organization to accom-plish excellence goals such as customer service and quality production.[36] As well, Hampden-Turner has shown that the top-down militaristic culture of British Airways had to be changed in order to develop a capacity for quality customer service.[37] Similarly, we contend that the four aspects of deep struc-ture described above need to be changed in order for organizations to pur-sue a gender-equality agenda.

We should be clear from the outset how these aspects of deep structure hinder the accomplishment of gender-equality outcomes. *Heroic individual-ism* does so in two important ways: first, it encourages a culture of winning, which sidelines a focus on the client. Winning, being goal oriented, demands a focus on clear outcomes rather than on the largely processual and some-what murky business of uncovering gender inequity in social relations and institutions. Second, given stereotypic gender roles, the heroes tend to be men, as the organizational culture they have created has been unfriendly and uninviting to women. As such, women's interests are under-represented; and therefore, there is no pressure or constituency for challenging existing gender-biased relations and ideologies. After all, the idea that women's rights are human rights came not from the human-rights movement but from the women's movement.

The *work-family split* element of deep structure also devalues women's interests within organizations and women's work outside them. As women are still largely responsible for care of the family, this deeply held value largely limits women's participation in public organizations and does not support re-organizing responsibilities within families.

The third aspect of the deep structure, *exclusionary power*, blocks organizational learning particularly with regard to core organizing values. Exclusionary power regimes devalue participation and silence the voices that would bring the alternative perspectives and knowledge required for gender-equal outcomes.

Finally, the *monoculture of instrumentality* confuses the accomplishment of narrow objectives with social change. For example, holding nutrition-education sessions at which poor rural women in Bangladesh are exhorted to eat green leafy vegetables should not be confused with improving the nutrition of those women, which can come about only if nutrition programs are sensitive to women's unequal access to food and other family-based resources.

Moreover, the point is not merely to understand gender inequality but to change it. In the next chapter, we describe an approach to uncovering and changing deep structure.

NOTES

1. Nuket Kardam, *Bringing Women In: Women's Issues in International Development Programs* (Boulder: Lynne Rienner, 1991).

2. Kathy Staudt, *Policy, Politics and Gender: Women Gaining Ground* (West Hartford, Conn.: Kumarian Press, 1998).

3. Anne Marie Goetz, "Gender and Administration," *IDS Bulletin* 23, no. 1 (1992).

4. See for example, Carol Agocs, Catherine Burr, and Felicity Somerset, *Employment Equity: Co-operative Strategies for Organizational Change* (Toronto: Prentice Hall, 1992).

5. See for example, Carol Miller and Shahra Razavi, *Missionaries and Mandarins: Feminist Engagement with Development Institutions* (London: Intermediate Technology Publications, 1998).

6. Edgar Schein, *Organizational Culture and Leadership*, 2nd edition (San Francisco: Jossey-Bass, 1992).

7. Catherine Itzin and Janet Newman, eds., *Gender, Culture and Organizational Change: Putting Theory into Practice* (London: Routledge, 1995).

8. Anne Marie Goetz, ed., "Introduction: Getting Institutions Right for Women in Development," *Getting Institutions Right for Women in Development* (London: Zed Press, 1997).

9. Naila Kabeer, *Reversed Realities: Gender Hierarchies in Development Thought* (London: Verso, 1994).

10. Joan Acker, "Gendering Organizational Theory," in Albert Mills and Peta Tancred, *Gendering Organizational Analysis* (Newbury Park: Sage, 1992).

11. Goetz (1997), 28.

12. Miller and Razavi (1998).

13. Rhona Rapoport and Robert N. Rapoport, *Dual Career Families* (Harmondsworth: Penguin, 1971).

14. Rosabeth Moss Kanter, *Men and Women of the Corporation* (New York: Basic, 1979).

15. Lotte Bailyn, *Breaking the Mold: Women, Men and Time in the New Corporate World* (New York: Free Press, 1993).

16. Arlie Hochschild, *The Time Bind: When Work Becomes Home and Home Becomes Work* (New York: Metropolitan Books, 1997).

17. Joan Acker, "Hierarchies, Jobs, Bodies: A Theory of Gendered Organizations," *Gender and Society* no. 4, 1990, 150.

18. See Stephen Lukes as discussed in Joyce Fletcher, "A Radical Perspective on Power" in Aruna Rao and David Kelleher, ed., *AWID Trialogue on Power* vol. 2, no. 2, Spring (1997).

19. Margaret J. Wheatley, *Leadership and the New Science* (San Francisco: Berrett-Koehler, 1992).

20. Rebecca Tripp, "Tank Girls, Trouble, and the Empire Strikes Back: A Case Study," this volume (1999).

21. Fletcher (1997a), 6.

22. Paolo Freire, *Pedagogy of the Oppressed* (New York: Herder and Herder, 1971).

23. Lotte Bailyn, Rhona Rapoport, Deborah Kolb, Joyce Fletcher et al., *Re-linking Work and Family: A Catalyst for Organizational Change*, Working Paper, Sloan School of Management, April, 1996.

24. Joan Scott, "Gender: A Useful Category of Historical Analysis" in Aruna Rao, ed., *Women's Studies International* (Feminist Press, New York: 1992).

25. Scott (1992), 28.

26. David Kelleher, Aruna Rao, Rieky Stuart, and Kirsten Moore, *Building a Global Network for Gender and Organizational Change*, Conference Report (Ottawa: CCIC, 1996).

27. For a full description of the BRAC gender program see Aruna Rao and David Kelleher, "Gender Lost and Gender Found," *Development in Practice* 8, no. 2, Oxfam UK, Oxford, May 1998.

28. Bailyn, Rapoport, Kolb, Fletcher, et al. (1996).

29. Mark Chesler, "Organizational Development Is Not the Same as Multicultural Organizational Development," in Elsie Cross et al., ed., *The Promise of Diversity* (New York: Irwin, 1994).

30. B.W. Jackson and Evangelina Holvino, "Multicultural Organizational Development," Working Paper 11, Ann Arbor, Program on Conflict Management Alternatives, quoted in Chesler (1994).

31. See Pregs Govender in Rao and Kelleher (1997).

32. Michel Foucault, in Paul Rabinow, ed., *The Foucault Reader* (New York: Pantheon Books, 1984).

33. Vandana Shiva, *Monocultures of the Mind: Perspectives on Biodiversity and Biotechnology* (New Delhi: Natraj, 1993).

34. Shiva (1993), 19.

35. Joyce Fletcher, "Relational Practice: A Feminist Re-construction of Work," *Journal of Management Inquiry* 7 (1997b).

36. Thomas Peters and Robert Waterman, *In Search of Excellence: Lessons from America's Best-Run Companies* (New York: Harper and Row, 1982).

37. Charles Hampden-Turner, *Creating Corporate Culture* (Reading, Mass.: Addison-Wesley, 1992).

2

STRATEGIES FOR
GENDER EQUALITY AND
ORGANIZATIONAL CHANGE

AS WE STATED in Chapter One, in order for organizations to effect gender-equitable outcomes, we need to change the way they work: because seldom examined day-to-day practices and ways of thinking prevent them from delivering services in a way that is gender equitable, we need to change the "deep structure" of organizations. We are beginning to accumulate a number of promising ideas on how to do this, ideas distilled from experience, the writing of others and recent conferences focussed on gender and organizational change.

In this chapter we will discuss those promising ideas and their implementation. Drawing on our understanding we will speculate on what it will take to keep the change process alive and vibrant so it can have a transformative impact on the deep structure. The cases described in this book illustrate how these ideas look in practice. These interventions are important first steps in changing the deep structure of organizations. Yet their gains could be easily lost unless new gender-equitable practices are systematized, new meanings of gender in the organization are widely shared, new priorities acted upon, appropriate structures developed to house new processes, and leadership evolves both to give direction to the change process and to share power.

The first case describes a change process in BRAC, a large development organization in Bangladesh. Over a period of several years, a team of three external consultants—one based in Dhaka and two traveling from Canada—helped an internal-change team at BRAC to carry out a pilot project. Its goal was to change how staff both thought about and did their work, and how they related to one another and to the women BRAC serves.

The second case was an intervention at CIMMYT, the international wheat and maize research organization based in Mexico. A team of action-researchers helped CIMMYT management to examine how existing "mental models" prevented women from attaining senior positions, and to begin a series of experiments in new ways of working.

The Body Shop is the site of the third case. Again, action-researchers worked with managers and the staff at several work sites to examine how they thought about and practiced ways of working that excluded women.

South Africa's National Land Committee responded to pressure from women leaders in the organization to hire a staff coordinator of the efforts by the organization to include women as landholders in their struggle, as the focus of the organization shifted from fighting against removals and documenting claims to advocating new land policies in a rapidly democratizing South Africa.

The final case tells the story of a large, urban, Canadian social housing organization where a small team of change agents worked with the general manager to improve service equity in a political and organizational environment that became increasingly hostile.

HOW THE CHANGE PROCESS AFFECTS DEEP STRUCTURE

This section discusses two promising ideas—surfacing multiple perspectives and developing new work practices—as the anchors of the change process. We then describe ways to create the power-as-energy needed to start and sustain the process. We also consider what is required to keep the process ongoing, so it results in change to the deep structure and in gender-equitable outcomes.

Surfacing Multiple Perspectives

Surfacing and engaging with multiple perspectives, the first anchor of our change process, takes many forms—a needs assessment at NLC and BRAC; interviews and feedback at CIMMYT and The Body Shop; and an action-learning focus of the teams at BRAC. Central to each was giving voice to those who had been silent, valuing and engaging with their perspectives; and starting discussions and action from where people are—their particular understandings and what they are willing to work on. The process considers a variety of factors: what the issues are; how they are related to the work of the organization; where change should start, and at what level; which strategies might work; and what needs to be negotiated with the groups involved.

The term "gender" has particular implications for different organizational contexts, and for different people. Elegant formulations and theories of gender relations and women's disadvantage (even useful ones) may need to be modified to focus on a particular organizational context. Therefore rather than trying to impose a particular view of gender, the change agents in these cases structured discussions that allowed a wide cross-section of members of the organization to raise the gender-related issues they saw as important. The development of a genuinely new conception of the place of gender in the organization was dependent on the inclusion of marginalized voices as well as mainstream ones: men as well as women; people of minority ethnicities and races; and people in different departments and levels of the organization and, in some cases, their families.

Giving voice to multiple perspectives can unleash cacophony. Therefore, an important part of the work is to harmonize the information received into a few important and generative themes that will resonate with the organization and offer potential for change. (A good example is the idea of "mental models" discussed below and in the CIMMYT case.)

In the course of carrying out their work, the change agents in the cases developed a number of conceptual and operational tools to aid in this multi-dimensional conversation. These tools are described briefly below and in more detail in the cases themselves.

Needs Assessment   The purpose of a needs assessment is to build broad-based knowledge about the organization and how it is gendered, by raising and engaging with a multitude of perspectives. However, an equally important function is to signal to the organization that the change team does not have a predetermined solution that can be imposed. On the contrary, each organization is unique, needs to be understood in its own terms and requires its own solutions.

The different change teams conducted the needs assessment in different ways; but in each one, previously silent voices spoke on important organizational matters. At BRAC the internal team met groups of staff in a series of one and two day workshops. At CIMMYT and The Body Shop, the external action-research teams combined observation with individual interviews and discussions with staff. At NLC, the needs assessment was undertaken with representatives of the affiliates in workshops.

Mental Models   This term is used by Peter Senge and his colleagues at the Massachusetts Institute of Technology to describe the deeply held assumptions and beliefs people carry regarding how the organization works.[1] Often these mental models are not discussed openly yet they are important organizing principles.

The key mental models of a particular organization and how they are gendered provides a very helpful way to understand that organization. The CIMMYT case contains a valuable description of how to use mental models not only to understand an organization but also to shape an intervention and keep it on track. For example, one of CIMMYT's mental models was, "Default to Hierarchy," the largely unquestioned assumption that a strong hierarchy was the best way to organize. All management systems, such as planning, budgeting, and performance review were ordered vertically, with little lateral communication. The action-research team brought to light how defaulting to hierarchy hindered CIMMYT's ability to respond to its changing environment and also its effects on gender equality. Because women were not well represented at senior levels, their perspectives, experience, and skills were not used effectively; as a result they felt distanced, less connected, and less valued.

Holding up the Mirror   Three of the cases in this book used this tool to build broad ownership of a particular definition of the gender- and organizational-effectiveness problem facing these organizations. We define "holding up the mirror," as the practice of building knowledge about an organization and then feeding this information back to organization members. The feedback discussion can be quite heated, but it can also lead to agreement on the critical gender issues facing the organization. At BRAC, after a needs assessment that worked with four hundred staff at all levels, the gender team presented the findings to a two-day retreat for senior management. At CIMMYT, after interviews with fifty-eight staff members and a number of spouses, the team presented their findings in meetings open to all staff. At these meetings, issues that people had spoken of only informally were legitimated in a public forum that occasioned a great deal of spirited discussion. In both organizations, these meetings resulted in a particular set of problems being accepted as a basis for the interventions that followed.

The Fourth Frame   The Body Shop team has developed a framework to help organization members identify the various ways their organization is systemically biased against women's participation. The first frame is a Liberal-Individualism or "Fix the Woman" way of thinking, in which the problem is seen as a woman's lack of skills; the remedy is training women in those skills. The second frame is an Equal-Opportunity way of thinking that focusses on policies such as affirmative action to level an "uneven playing field." The third frame looks at "masculine" and "feminine" ways of being, in an effort to value such considered traditional "female" attributes as listening, collaborating, and relationship building. The fourth frame looks deeper, at how gender is "an organizing category that shapes social structure, identities, and knowledge." (See Kolb and Meyerson, this volume.) In their work at The Body Shop, the external research team used this framework to help the internal change team see how formal, informal, symbolic, and interactive processes combined to make gender inequality not only an important part of a wide variety of interactions, but also very difficult to see.

Seeing Invisible Work   Seeing issues from a variety of perspectives and thereby breaking the hegemonic power that legitimizes some things and devalues others makes visible "invisible work." This term is used by Joyce Fletcher to describe work traditionally associated with "the feminine" within organizations. She believes, as do we, that organizations value what have been seen as "masculine" traits and devalue "feminine" ones. Creating a team, facilitating decisions, and other behaviors that could be termed "relational" are ignored, undervalued, and made invisible. In contrast, "autonomy, self promotion, and individual heroics [are] highly prized . . . technical competence [is] highly valued and seen as the route to power. . . ."[2]

As we look at organizations, it is important to see not only the "heroes" but the supporting contributions of women and men to the accomplishment of organizational goals.

All of these tools—needs assessment, mental models, holding up the mirror, the fourth frame, and seeing invisible work—allow organization members to "see" the organization in ways previously unimaginable. For example, at The Body Shop, a supervisor doesn't need to be the authoritative disciplinarian set out in the job description (thereby implying that it was a job for men). When workers looked at what the supervisor really did, they realized the job was about motivating people, resolving conflicts, and liaising with other parts of the factory. Such a description would attract women to the job. Similarly, BRAC staff discovered that problems don't necessarily need to be solved only by Area Managers; it is possible to visualize the staff solving problems together.

Developing New Work Practices

After the dialogues described above have built some understanding of the issues and an approach to change, the next step is to design new ways of doing the work. This brings us to the second promising anchor in the change process—"developing new work practices." Translating new perspectives into action requires new ways of working that challenge taken-for-granted assumptions about basic aspects of organizational life: hierarchy, work-family balance, the gendered division of labor, the belief in individual achievement, and the connection between work practices and gender-equitable outcomes. An example of such an intervention was the Gender Quality Action Learning process (GQAL) at BRAC, the way local office groups analyzed their work and office environment to identify gender issues and to take action on them.

Office groups worked with a facilitator for several months. The process began with an orientation to gender relations; then the facilitator led a discussion to surface issues in their work together that the group thought were related to gender. The group then selected an issue to work on, analyzed its causes, isolated causes amenable to action by the group and built an action plan. After implementing their plan they evaluated its effect.

At CIMMYT, the change team used a different approach. The coordinating group managed a set of "experiments" designed to get at the issues agreed to in the discussion of mental models. For example, in order to moderate hierarchical decision-making, the team designed and implemented an experiment involving 360° evaluation. (In this type of evaluation a manager is evaluated by peers and subordinates as well as by his or her boss.) At The Body Shop, the team developed self-managed work groups that re-organized production-line work in a cosmetics factory. At UH, the planning document spelled out how staff would work in a more gender- and race-sensitive manner and in a new de-centralized structure. At BRAC the action-learning process resulted in such local innovations as male staff talking with husbands of BRAC members about domestic violence.

It is this focus on work practice that makes our approach crucially different from those that develop gender policy or do gender training. Even efforts at cultural change, such as high-profile announcements and getting the leadership to take on the issue do not change the way people work in ways that alter the deep structure. This last point is key. It is possible to effect seemingly gender-equitable organizational changes that turn out to have little to do with gender. Team work introduced to break down gender hierarchies can end up as simple team building that leaves gender hierarchies in place. To change deep structure, new work practices need to undermine heroic work styles, or change how power is exercised (toward power-as-energy) or enable staff to better manage family responsibilities or focus clearly on affecting the lives of women. It is critical that those involved in the change process continuously make the links between new work practices and gender equality. (The Body Shop case discusses this last point in some depth.)

In summary, the two "anchor" ideas in working with deep structure are first, that multiple perspectives challenge gendered ideas of organization, such as the place of hierarchy, the gendered division of labor, work-family balance, the place of heroic individualism, and gendered outcomes. Second, this challenge to existing ways of work must ultimately build a more gender-equitable organization. However, as none of this is possible without the power to begin and sustain the process, we now turn to the question of working with power.

Working with Power to Support Dialogue and New Work Practices

Change in organizations is dependent upon *pressure*—from powerful insiders, from donors, from board members, or from the broader cultural and political context, such as the current pressure for transformation in South Africa. However, pressure alone does not create change. The Hawthorne studies of Northern Electric in the 1930s, Allison's study of the US Navy's blockade during the Cuban missile crisis[3] and countless studies of "resistance to change" teach us that clear direction from the top does not necessarily drive organizational behavior. In fact, Michael Beer, in a study of change efforts in six companies found that "programmatic change" implemented to counter clearly recognized problems and having the enthusiastic support of senior management and adequate financial and consulting resources, had little effect in changing these organizations.[4] Karl Weick's concept of "loosely coupled systems"[5] (which shows how orders from the top may not reach the bottom), Nuket Kardam's analysis showing that accountability is generally missing in development projects,[6] and Anne Marie Goetz's analysis of the discretion of field level staff whether to implement policy or not[7] help us understand why policy doesn't necessarily become programs, and programs don't become behavior.

During the past thirty years a set of change practices has been developed that has attempted to overcome these difficulties by stimulating change using participative and educational methods. These approaches grow out of organizational-change practice,[8] and are an important part of the change strategies we are proposing. The change agents represented in this book have drawn on that work but have gone beyond it. Much organizational-change work claims to be "transformational"—cultural change in relation to customer service, better quality, or faster time to market. Such changes have certainly been difficult to accomplish, but changing the deep structure is a challenge to something more fundamental.

Organizational-change literature and practice is helpful, but it is only the beginning. Consultant Evangelina Holvino points out that "we must help organizations push the limits of what can be said, what cannot be said and what is not even thinkable because of our usual ways of thinking about what is and is not possible in organizations."[9] While changes toward customer service or manufacturing quality have become part of business culture, gender equality is so deeply counter to the culture that most organizations have neither the interest nor the capacity to think about it.

Therefore, we must capture and hold the attention of the organization and help to maintain its focus on gender. In order to do so, we need to use all the power available to us. However, we need to balance the exercise of power with that of participation which allows those in the organization to bring their issues and meanings to a discussion of gender and to take action based on informed choice. Finally, beyond such facilitation, we get to the crux of the process, pushing organizations to examine deeply held and often dimly understood ideas about gender, organizations and programs.

The change process described in this book starts at the point where sufficient power exists to focus the attention and resources of the organization on change toward gender equality. In a world in which much power is focussed on maintaining gender *inequality,* what is needed is an "alternative power base" from which to challenge existing ways of working. The factors that comprise this power base include: pressure from inside and outside the organization, management and organizational trust in the change agents, and the relation of the process to management's own interests.

This last point needs elaboration. The change agents in these cases did not tell management they needed to work on gender because it was the right thing to do. Each case tied gender equality to already-valued organizational outcomes. We believe that positive change will not come about without direct, articulated connection between gender equality and the values of the organization (or the agenda of powerful insiders).

One way of expressing this is the concept of the "dual agenda," pioneered in a Ford Foundation project studying gender, family, and work in three corporations.[10] At Xerox Corporation, more flexible scheduling to permit better integration of work and family responsibilities was successfully shown to result in less absenteeism and higher productivity. It demonstrated that better attention to the needs of families is not incompatible with organizational effectiveness.

The idea that attention to gender equity would enhance other aspects of organizational effectiveness was an important selling point in beginning The Body Shop and CIMMYT projects. Maintaining this dual agenda in the thinking of organization staff is extraordinarily difficult, however, as organizational issues can overwhelm gender discussions. (See in particular, the discussion in The Body Shop case.)

In the other cases, the term "dual agenda" is less applicable. All three— NLC, UH, and BRAC—have an overt social development agenda in which gender equity is integral. In NLC, the constituency demanded that the mandate shift from "land" to "land for men and women." In UH, the new management introduced "service equity," a term that implied a new emphasis on racial and gender equality. At BRAC, the focus was on bringing a deeper understanding of gender equality to the existing organizational goals of poverty alleviation and women's empowerment.

All the change projects described in this book began with a broad—and nebulous—mandate: to "do something" that would promote gender equality without sacrificing organizational effectiveness. This enabled the change agents to begin the process of change with a problem rather than a solution. This is important in several ways: first, pre-identified solutions are often wrong or inadequate. Second, change agents who begin with a situation or problem can enhance the potential for change by negotiating a broad mandate. The process of consulting widely to determine the scope of the problem, analyzing it, and generating proposals for action and change builds both readiness for change and ownership of agreed-upon changes. This is essentially different from being asked to create a predefined solution—"write a gender policy" or "develop a gender training course"—it is also potentially more useful, a variation of "process consulting," in which the change agent takes on the role of co-diagnostician and facilitator.[11] However, there is often an instinct within the organization to circumscribe the intervention before it starts— terms of reference, benchmarks, phases. In such cases, change agents try to negotiate the broadest possible initial mandate and an agreement to re-visit that mandate periodically.

Establishing an alternative power base does not give the change agent a license to make change. It is merely a ticket into the game. "Power-as-energy" needs to be tended, increased by what we call "political knitting" and invested in a dialogue on gender equality. The main purpose of political knitting is to come to know the organization's people, their power relations, and their issues well enough to be able to weave an intervention into the life of the organization, while building respect and trust. When trying to promote gender equality, we need to build and maintain a broader range of allies and relationships in the organization than would be available either to an insider (whose position would be bound by hierarchical, departmental, and professional lines) or to an external consultant (who is viewed as the creature of its contracting client).

Political knitting involves creating opportunities for meeting and getting to know a wide range of organizational actors. Central to this activity is an analysis of power relations—who has what kinds of power; what are their interests; and who are allies, enemies, and fence sitters. (See Tripp, this volume, and Peter Block[12] for ways of thinking about power relations.)

Political knitting also involves staying in touch with these various groups, confronting issues as they come up, and shaping the intervention on an ongoing basis. Such activity is essential to maintaining and enhancing trust and to increasing the power-as-energy available to the process.

Also critical to increasing power-as-energy is ownership. If change is to be lasting, it must be owned by the organization—by workers and management, by women and men, by all departments. In order to generate this ownership, people need to be informed and involved. If there are choices, the organization needs to debate them and decide among them. The entry points and strategies to be used must be discussed with organizational insiders and leaders. Gender and organizational-change work often gets "stuck" in human resources or training departments, which can marginalize the process.

If there is a representative internal team, it is helpful to have it mandated by the groups it represents, and to report back regularly. In the work at BRAC we made it a rule that there would be "no surprises." When we planned a presentation, we made sure that the people responsible for the session knew what we were going to say, and had a chance to comment on it ahead of time. The gender-team members briefed and debriefed one another frequently, and regularly met with senior managers and the Executive Director. When there were problems, we made sure the relevant employees and managers knew of them. Sometimes this resulted in us not being able to go as fast as we would have wanted. For example, BRAC took four months to agree to a particular program design.

Sometimes the intervention that would be most strategic is not possible, and the change agent group needs to reformulate its expectations. Settling for less can accomplish the difficult task of keeping the ownership of the process and the outcomes with the organization.

Finally, the multilevel conversation that is political knitting makes possible the enlargement of the original power base through alliances and constituencies that see their interest served by the evolving discussion. For example, the process in both BRAC and CIMMYT included issues of interest to men, such as family leave and more democratic decision-making. In some cases power-as-energy is also built by challenging the unobtrusive power that prevents people from seeing the inequalities they live with. In others it is boosted by opening up a sanctioned channel to voice felt needs. In either event, if the process changes what it is possible to talk about in the organization, the power of the process can be enhanced.

Figure 2–1 summarizes a complex, recursive process to challenge organizational deep structure. Progress toward change is neither certain nor easy. The diagram represents a "best possible scenario." Beginning at the left, we believe that a configuration of factors generates the power and energy for the change process. The stock of "power-as-energy" can be increased by the interaction of such factors as political knitting, building allies and an internal constituency, more women in senior positions, and the growing understanding of how attention to gender can lead to a more effective accomplishment of the organization's mandate. Critical to all of this is maintaining the trust of the various factions in the organization.

How new practices add up to sustainable, transformative change is less clear. It may be that there is a threshold analogous to the belief that when more than 30 percent of parliamentarians are women, policy becomes more responsive to women's interests. Management theorist Karl Weick[13] believes that carefully chosen "small wins" lead to change. Others believe that widespread and varied changes interact both with one another and with outside changes to drive evolution to a new level.

Our belief is that the change process is recursive and self-reinforcing: a number of factors influence one another and set up a "virtuous cycle."[14] Once experiments that depart from the traditional deep structure begin to accumulate, the organization can become more amenable to women's participation, a site where women and men are likely to be able to work more effectively. This, in turn, can lead to women's perspectives having more currency in the organization and to making more likely the provision of services that are gender equal. This ultimately, can lead to more power-as-energy devoted to transforming gender relations and enhancing gender equality.

An important caution is needed: the virtuous cycle can turn into a vicious

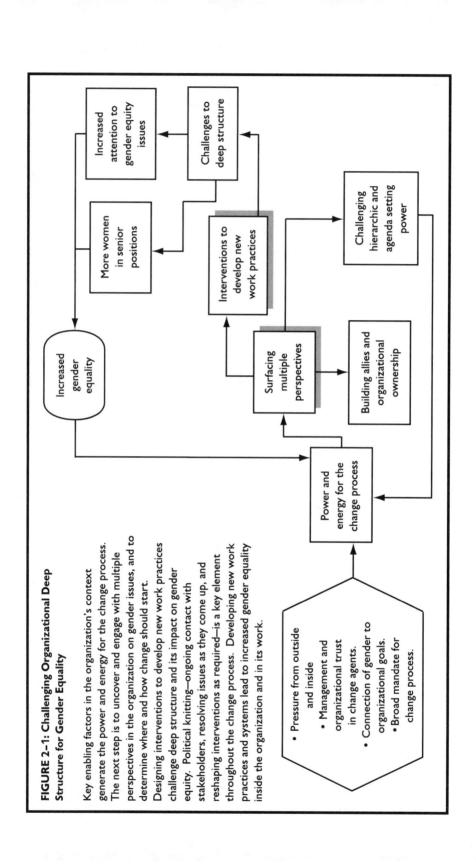

FIGURE 2-1: Challenging Organizational Deep Structure for Gender Equality

Key enabling factors in the organization's context generate the power and energy for the change process. The next step is to uncover and engage with multiple perspectives in the organization on gender issues, and to determine where and how change should start. Designing interventions to develop new work practices challenge deep structure and its impact on gender equity. Political knitting—ongoing contact with stakeholders, resolving issues as they come up, and reshaping interventions as required—is a key element throughout the change process. Developing new work practices and systems lead to increased gender equality inside the organization and in its work.

Increased attention to gender equity issues

Challenges to deep structure

More women in senior positions

Interventions to develop new work practices

Challenging hierarchic and agenda setting power

Increased gender equality

Surfacing multiple perspectives

Building allies and organizational ownership

Power and energy for the change process

- Pressure from outside and inside
- Management and organizational trust in change agents.
- Connection of gender to organizational goals.
- Broad mandate for change process.

circle and gains can be reversed in relatively short order. Therefore, nurturing a sustained and sustainable process must be a long-term endeavor. Yet, many organizations see work on gender equality as something they can "do" once, achieve some measurable outcome, and move on to other issues; thus they have a tendency to want as little "process" as possible. But organizational excellence and gender equality need on-going processes with intended outcomes, just like accounting or leadership. (We don't hear organizational insiders say, "We did accounting last year, so we don't need to do it again.") We need to pay attention, to work on them all the time—and we need to expect results.

One way to maintain momentum in the change process is to "take stock," as was done at CIMMYT. There, one year after the project had begun, the action-research team returned to analyze progress. They interviewed a broad sample of staff and management to assess their perceptions of change, asking particularly whether the situation of women within CIMMYT had improved. Their findings were discussed with senior management and the change team. Later, the results were published in the organization's newsletter. This exercise not only celebrated successes and re-focussed efforts but also re-energized the process and provided a platform for discussion between the action-research team and management. The process was repeated after the second year.

When the follow-up relies primarily on energy from outside the organization, as in the case of taking stock at CIMMYT, it raises the question: how does one build enough internal momentum in the process to affect deep structure? One way to do this is building capacity for gender equality. This means, in part, that leadership must move beyond a predominant focus on counting services provided to clients toward a more serious grappling with their impact on social improvements, including gender equity. For example, in our discussions at BRAC, managers realized that the leadership required of the field-level managers is very complex. It needs to focus on "soft" elements, such as staff relations, empowerment, social analysis and gender equality as well as on such "hard" elements as loan repayment, credit discipline, and ensuring accomplishment of quantitative goals. If the organization is going to move toward using power in an inclusionary way, managers also need to re-think their roles. While some may see it as a simple loss of control, it is, in fact, putting in place the potential for a different kind of order and is revealing the glimmerings of a different form of accountability. This, in turn, will necessitate the re-evaluation of systems in which traditional views of power and leadership are embedded, such as planning, evaluation, and performance appraisal.

Too often capacity building is taken to mean only leadership development or staff training. The problem is building the capacity not of *individuals*, but rather building the *organization's* capacity to continually address gender equality. This requires that the organization build a cadre of well-trained, committed and well-placed people; it must build organizational structures that nurture and sustain efforts toward gender equality; it must be permeable to ideas from outside but able to adapt them to the particular realities of the organization; and finally, the organization needs to develop a focus on achieving gender equality, not just on process.

These change strategies, at their best, build new practices and a new collective imagining of how the organization can be different; it is from this new collective imagination that the future emerges.[15] The cases that follow are efforts to build that just and equitable future.

NOTES

1. Peter Senge, *The Fifth Discipline: The Art and Practice of the Learning Organization* (New York: Doubleday, 1990).

2. Joyce Fletcher, "Relational Practice: A Feminist Re-construction of Work," *Journal of Management Inquiry* 7, no. 2 (1998), 175.

3. Allison Graham, *Essence of Decision: Explaining the Cuban Missile Crisis* (Boston: Little Brown, 1971).

4. Michael Beer, "The Critical Path for Change: Key to Success and Failure in Six Companies," in Ralph Kilmann, et al., *Corporate Transformation: Re-Vitalizing Organizations for a Competitive World* (San Francisco: Jossey Bass, 1989).

5. Karl Weick, "Educational Organizations as Loosely Coupled Systems," *Administrative Science Quarterly* 21 (1976).

6. Nuket Kardam, in Anne Marie Goetz, ed., *Getting Institutions Right for Women in Development* (London: Zed Books, 1997).

7. Anne Marie Goetz, "Local Heroes: Patterns of Field Worker Discretion in Implementing GAD Policy in Bangladesh," IDS Discussion Paper no. 358, University of Sussex, 1996.

8. See Marvin Wiesbord, *Productive Workplaces, Organizing and Managing for Dignity, Meaning and Community* (San Francisco: Jossey-Bass, 1991), and Ralph Kilmann, et al., *Corporate Transformation: Revitalizing Organizations for a Competitive World* (San Francisco: Jossey-Bass, 1989).

9. Holvino, Evangelina, "A Vision: The Agitated Organization," in Elsie Cross et al., eds., *The Promise of Diversity* (New York: Irwin, 1994).

10. Lotte Bailyn, Rhona Rapoport, Deborah Kolb, Joyce Fletcher et al., *Re-linking Life and Work: Toward a Better Future* (New York: Ford Foundation, 1996).

11. Edgar Schein, *Process Consultation: Lesson for Managers and Consultants, Volume II* (Reading, Mass.: Addison-Wesley, 1987).

12. Block Peter, *The Empowered Manager: Positive Political Skills at Work* (San Francisco: Jossey-Bass, 1987).

13. Weick, Karl, "Small Wins: Redefining the Scale of Social Problems," *American Psychologist* 39, no. 1 (1984).

14. Charles Hampden-Turner, *Charting the Corporate Mind: Graphic Solutions to Business Conflicts* (New York: Free Press, 1990).

15. Susan Griffin, "To Love the Marigold: The Politics of Imagination," in Aruna Rao and David Kelleher, eds., *AWID Trialogue on Power* 2, no. 2, Spring (1997).

3

BUILDING GENDER CAPITAL AT BRAC: A CASE STUDY

Aruna Rao, Rieky Stuart, David Kelleher

THE BRAC[1] GENDER Quality Action Learning Program (GQAL) involves male and female field staff and managers of the largest rural development NGO in the world. It utilizes a process of issue-analysis, action planning, and implementation to address organizational-change and program-quality concerns in a way that is informed by an understanding of gender. Since 1994, the program has been building organizational capacity to co-design, carry out, and subsequently lead the change effort. By 1999, the GQAL leadership team had grown to over forty-three headquarters-based supervisory personnel and field-level facilitators; about six thousand BRAC staff—close to 30 percent of the total—have been involved in the GQAL program. How we built and sustained this capacity within different levels of BRAC to challenge gender injustice and the problems we faced along the way are the focus of this study. Our story centers on a series of meetings held during the course of three years, starting in January 1994.

THE GENDER TEAM'S FIRST MEETING

The slanting rays of the morning winter sun brightened the edges of the green handloom curtains. They had been drawn back to warm us up, as we sat around a large table in the conference room of the BRAC Donor Liaison Office (DLO) in Dhaka. We were meeting for the first time as a full working team of seven members—the BRAC Gender Team. It was late January 1994, and we were in Bangladesh.

Bangladesh

Amar Sonar Bangla ("our golden Bengal"). The poet Tagore's words, captured in the national anthem, describe a land of beauty. But the golden sunsets over the delta and the cool, translucent green of newly transplanted paddy coexist with the "quiet violence" of poverty. With a population close to 120 million, and the highest population density in the world, about half still live below the poverty line. Because of population pressure, more and more people are occupying land prone to flooding and have no recourse when their shelters and meager goods are washed away. The economy of Bangladesh is primarily agrarian: 46 percent of GDP comes from agriculture, which employs 65 percent of workers; rice and jute are the main cash crops. About 70 percent of the population are landless laborers, and the extremely uneven distribution of resources is the chief cause of chronic poverty. However, there has been a steady growth in GDP, fueled by the ready-made garment sector, which primarily employs women.

The difference in position and condition of women and men in Bangladesh is greater than in many other countries. As stated in *Towards Gender Equity*, BRAC's Gender Policy document:

Women worldwide are discriminated [against], but in Bangladesh it is institutionalized in patriarchal ideologies, repressive laws, and age-old customs; and its manifestations can be seen in the gradual trend towards the feminization of poverty, high rate of female mortality, and increase in violence toward women.[2]

In Bangladesh, women's mobility is restricted, and there is a rigid division of labor by gender. Differences between women's and men's education and literacy levels are among the highest in the world in favor of men. The ratio of women to men is lower than the worldwide norm, indicating that statistically significant numbers of women die from female infanticide, malnutrition, overwork or lack of access to health care. Men control almost all aspects of women's lives and "sexism not only affects women's personal lives; it is reflected in all public institutions . . . and it is formalized in law and custom."[3]

Despite these obstacles, Bangladesh and its women have made substantial progress in its first twenty-five years of independence: it is virtually self-sufficient in food grains; 70 percent of new-born children are now immunized; life expectancy has risen by eight years; fertility rates have fallen; early-warning systems and preparedness have dramatically lessened loss of life caused by natural disasters; and women are increasingly gaining access to credit, education, and jobs, as well as organizing to fight for their legal rights through innovative development institutions.

BRAC

BRAC, now one of the largest NGOs in the world, was born shortly after Bangladesh itself, in response to the human devastation of the Liberation War of 1971. BRAC has two major goals: poverty alleviation and the empowerment of the poor. Initially focussed, in 1972, on relief and rehabilitation, BRAC has taken a community-development approach to poverty alleviation. It began a women-specific program in 1975, simultaneously experimenting with credit delivery and building village organizations with a political voice. In the 1980s, BRAC moved toward a more economically focussed, target-oriented approach to sustainable development and empowerment.

During the last decade, the credit program has predominated, although BRAC has also taken on a host of supplementary social services: income-generation skills training, human-rights and legal education focussed on women's legal rights, a family-planning and women's-health program, the non-formal education of BRAC members' children; and higher-order economic enterprises. In 1998, BRAC had more than twenty-thee thousand staff and thirty-three thousand part-time teachers in villages throughout Bangladesh. Close to two million women who own less than 0.5 acres of land are BRAC members, organized in about fifty-four thousand village organizations. In total, they had saved over one billion taka (US$30 million). BRAC is running close to thirty-five thousand non-formal primary-education schools; its health and population program is reaching an estimated twelve million people. More than 80 percent of BRAC's credit recipients are women, and more than 70 percent of the children in its rural schools are girls.

In the late 1980s, BRAC founder and Executive Director, F.H. Abed's commitment to gender equity was substantial. (This direction, had also been encouraged over time by donors and numerous evaluation and appraisal missions.) At that time, BRAC began actively recruiting women staff. At its highest, the ratio of female to male staff was 1:4; at the end of 1998 women comprised approximately 23 percent of all full-time BRAC staff. Women staff are concentrated in the health and non-formal education programs, and in junior positions at headquarters.

BRAC's rapid expansion in the early 1990s, its interest in recruiting more women staff, and its commitment to women's empowerment posed considerable challenges organizationally and programmatically. BRAC had developed policy incrementally, in response to specific women-staff-related issues and problems. In 1991, it appointed a Women's Advisory Committee to advise the Executive Director on women-staff issues. At this time, while only about 20 percent of staff were women, two of the seven directors were women, the number of women area managers was growing, and there was a fast track to develop women managers. Most important, the Executive Director was committed to gender equality within the organization and to women's empowerment in BRAC's work.

In 1991 BRAC began its first gender awareness program, Men and Women: Partnership in Development, as a one-day seminar for staff. The initiative to launch a broader Gender Program came from BRAC's Executive Director. In October 1991, after observing a gender training session conducted by Aruna Rao, he expressed his interest in having BRAC professional staff trained in gender analysis. During the next year, through a series of informal discussions, the broad outline of the gender intervention best suited to BRAC was developed. In July 1993, BRAC introduced its gender awareness and analysis course for all BRAC staff. Before the Gender Team began its work six months later however, a broadened brief for the Team was negotiated with senior management. Originally intended to further develop training center-based courses for staff in gender analysis, the Team's role was expanded to:

1. building staff capacity to plan, deliver and monitor gender-equitable programming; and

2. working with managers and staff to strengthen organizational systems, policies, and procedures in support of BRAC's gender goals.

This approach was grounded in the belief that training alone was insufficient to integrate a gender perspective in organizations, and that individual-focussed strategies need to work hand in hand with strategies to examine and change systemic gender inequities. Implicit in this approach is the need for BRAC to evolve an organizational culture, systems and procedures that attract and retain high-quality women and men staff and allow them to be their most productive. This went beyond the issue of gender parity to that of gender relations within the organization, itself a determinant of female staff retention.

Team Members and Team Norms

Who were we, sitting around that conference table in January 1994? There were four BRAC staff members of the Gender Team—two women and two men. All were senior trainers and three had many years of field experience with BRAC. All were assigned by BRAC to the Gender Team full-time. Sheepa Hafiza was a faculty member of the BRAC Management Development Program (MDP); she is currently the Program Director of the GQAL Program. Naheed Sultana started her career in BRAC's first women's program in Jamalpur and had worked for many years as a manager and trainer. At the time of our meeting, she was an associate faculty member in the Management Development Program. Habibur Rahman had been working in BRAC's multi-dimensional development programs for sixteen years, most recently as an associate faculty member in the MDP. Sadequr Rahman had been working for more than thirteen years in BRAC's Rural Development Program and in the Training Division.

There were also three outside consultants hired by BRAC on the Gender Team: Rieky Stuart, a Canadian, had worked in international development, particularly on gender and development issues, as a manager, programmer, and trainer. David Kelleher, also a Canadian, was an experienced consultant in organizational learning and development with NGOs and government, and had taught and published on organizational change. The Gender Team leader was Aruna Rao, a citizen of India resident in Bangladesh for a number of years. She had worked in international development, particularly in gender and development, and had published widely. In 1992, she had participated as a member of the appraisal team for the third phase of BRAC's Rural Development Program. The BRAC Gender Program—what came to be known as the GQAL (Gender Quality Action-Learning) Program, which we worked on; the Gender Resource Center; and a gender-perspective component of BRAC's research program—was financially supported by the Ford Foundation.

Early in our four weeks together as a full team in January–February 1994, we established a set of team norms to guide our working relationships. While BRAC is structured hierarchically and authority rests with line managers, the BRAC Gender Team was led by an outsider who had no line authority over team members. (BRAC Team members were accountable to the senior staff of the Training Division, where this program was based.) We hoped to operate in a non-hierarchical and gender-equal manner in accordance with the objectives of the program, responsible to the work and to one another. In the course of our two years together, this became a very difficult process to sus-

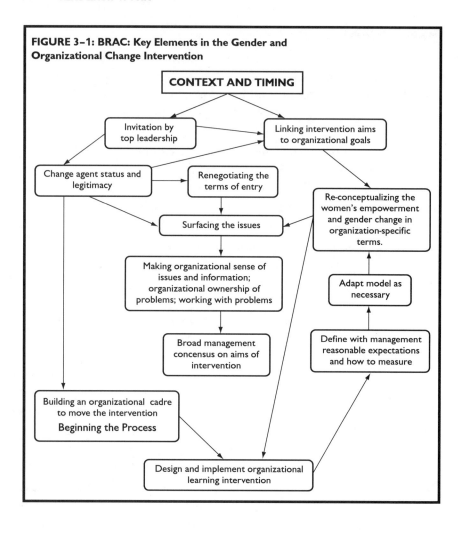

FIGURE 3–1: BRAC: Key Elements in the Gender and Organizational Change Intervention

CONTEXT AND TIMING

Invitation by top leadership

Linking intervention aims to organizational goals

Change agent status and legitimacy

Renegotiating the terms of entry

Re-conceptualizing the women's empowerment and gender change in organization-specific terms.

Surfacing the issues

Making organizational sense of issues and information; organizational ownership of problems; working with problems

Adapt model as necessary

Broad management concensus on aims of intervention

Define with management reasonable expectations and how to measure

Building an organizational cadre to move the intervention
Beginning the Process

Design and implement organizational learning intervention

tain. We set out to consider the family responsibilities of individual team members; but this, too, was later violated under pressure of work. We undertook to value a level of openness regarding personal feelings, and encouraged a collaborative effort in the creation of knowledge and its application to our work. To this we remained faithful: no aspect of the program was designed from the outside to be merely implemented in BRAC.

Figure 3–1 sets out an overview of the complex, recursive process used by the gender team: We continued to refine the change intervention as we gained new information and shared it with BRAC.

Beginning the Process

At that first meeting, the Gender Team had little clarity about what was needed and what we would do. We worked to develop our collective understanding about what women's empowerment and gender equality meant in the BRAC context. We observed BRAC's work with rural women in the field, and tested our understandings with senior staff and regional managers of BRAC's field programs. We also designed a needs-assessment exercise which we describe in detail below.

The managers agreed that the Gender Team should consult with a cross-section of staff, in order:

1. to determine how BRAC staff felt about women's empowerment and gender equity, and what they understood;

2. to determine whether there were differences in awareness and behavior among different kinds of staff (men/women, senior/junior, in different programs); and

3. to inform BRAC staff widely that BRAC was trying to improve in the area of gender equity.

During this period we also developed a number of procedural principles or guidelines for the Gender Program:

1. *transparency:* We felt it was important that information be shared both within the gender team and also among the team, managers, and BRAC staff. We did not position ourselves as brokers, or as advocates of one group or another. We developed a term, "political knitting," to describe this information sharing and feedback seeking, as well as problem-solving that we did.

2. *holism:* We felt that we needed to address both program-related and personnel-related issues; and that all levels of BRAC staff should be included in our interventions. We felt that we needed to address attitudes and perceptions, not just knowledge and action. This desire for holism affected both the pedagogy and the complexity of our work.

3. *ownership:* Decisions would be made by those who were responsible for them. Managers had to be prepared to approve of or decide on proposed interventions. If there was no agreement, the work could not advance. We also framed the action-learning sessions to encourage staff

to opt into the process; for without their active participation, there could be no progress.

4. *linkage:* We felt that if we could link the gender improvement efforts with other organizational-change issues BRAC was interested in, we would have a greater likelihood of an impact. At the time, BRAC was planning a strategic review and was interested in quality issues.

Understanding Women's Empowerment and Gender Transformation in the BRAC Context

Our definition of women's empowerment was grounded in BRAC's major programmatic directions: rural development, with credit and employment as key anchors; education and legal awareness; and the development of village organizations for collective action. We saw women's empowerment, then, as the capacity of women to be economically self-sufficient and self-reliant, having control over decisions affecting their life options, and free from violence. Thus, we conceptualized programming for women's empowerment goals having three broad strands:

1. increasing women's ability to be economically self-sufficient (that is, to earn an income, own assets. and manage their own finances);

2. increasing women's confidence and ability to know and negotiate for their rights, in the household and the community; and

3. increasing women's control over their bodies, their time, and their movement, including freedom from violence.

We conceptualized working toward gender transformations in terms of:

1. increasing women's and men's ability to analyze and reshape socially constructed gender relations in order to transform power relationships;

2. equitable access and control over both public and private resources; and

3. equitable participation in household, community, and national decision making; and reshaping social institutions and organizations to include women's and men's varied perceptions and to benefit both women and men.

We intended that our work would provide a means of women's empowerment and of moving beyond the male/female power nexus toward gender transformations. Engagement with issues of class, which both unite and divide men and women was implicit.

Key to our dialogue with BRAC was that gender does not mean "women." Moreover, we were not concerned simply with empowering women; we were also trying to alter the relationship between men and women so that it became characterized by more equity and an ability to negotiate to agreement on the needs of both. This may seem ambitious enough, but we were aware that Joan Acker,[4] among others, challenges one to deal with larger and more systemic issues:

Long term strategies will have to challenge the privileging of "economy" over life and raise questions about the rationality of such things as organizational and work commitment as well as the legitimacy of the organization's claim for the priority of their goals over more broad goals. The gendered structure of organizations will only be completely changed with a fundamental reorganization of both production and reproduction.

Nevertheless, we chose to define "gender" in terms that made sense to BRAC: our normative change strategy demands that the issue be defined in the client's terms. (Throughout the process, we engaged in a dialogue with BRAC to build a joint agreement as to what is a gender issue.) However modest, our problem definition is quite wide ranging and allows a broad spectrum of intervention targets. Once you are convinced that a gender issue is anything that hinders, prevents or restricts women staff or program beneficiaries' involvement in the delivery, analysis, and improvement of programs, there is considerable scope for thinking. Some of the things that prevent women's full participation in quality program delivery and improvement are cultural, some are attitudinal, and some are organizational. For example, we know that women's effective participation requires opportunities to earn the respect of male colleagues; that men in BRAC need to understand the situation faced by both village women and women in BRAC; supervision needs to be less arbitrary so change can happen; arrangements (such as leave and having overnight guests at the area office) need to be improved so that women can better integrate their work and their family lives.

Knowledge Building: Needs Assessment Process   Diagnosis for organizational change is a collaborative attempt to aid a system to understand itself in its own terms; it uses social-science techniques to focus on the client's

perception of what needs to change and how. Working with gender compli-
cates the process, because we are not simply responding to the client's view,
but we are teaching new concepts as well. In the needs assessment we drew
on specialized knowledge and experience, and created new knowledge
through collective conceptualization with the staff and managers.

We wanted to assess the staff's understanding of gender inequality and
how it translates into assessments and action within programs. We also wanted
to develop a baseline of BRAC staff understanding of gender issues. In particular we wanted to know:

1. whether they felt there was inequality between women and men;

2. whether they felt any inequalities were inevitable or natural;

3. what they thought were the causes of any observed inequalities,

4. whether, in their view, BRAC treated women and men staff differently;

5. whether there was gender discrimination between men and women
   staff—including such informal practices as "teasing" or harassment; and

6. whether women and men experienced different positives and nega-
   tives in working at BRAC.

We insisted that the assessment ensure not only individual confidential-
ity on sensitive responses but also transparency and collective feedback. To
achieve this, we designed a series of one- and two-day workshops with more
than four hundred BRAC staff at all levels. Some sessions comprised women
and men; others were all men or all women. Most sessions were homoge-
neous in terms of participants' rank and program, but not necessarily in se-
niority. Although the initial plan had covered mainly field-based staff, we
also added sessions with middle managers and Head Office units. A detailed
description of the needs assessment can be found at the end of this case.

AFTER THE GENDER PROGRAM'S STRATEGIC PLANNING MEETING WITH BRAC SENIOR MANAGERS: JULY 1994

The temperature inside the DLO conference room was sizzling; outside
the July afternoon was hot and sticky. Most team members had slept badly, if
at all, the previous night. We had just come out of an important two-day
strategic planning workshop on the Gender Program with twenty of BRAC's
senior managers. The purpose of the meeting was to develop a vision of what

BRAC wanted to accomplish in terms of women's empowerment, and to create a strategy for accomplishing that mission based on an analysis of staff and managers' understanding of empowerment and organizational features that affect their work. However, events took quite a different turn: our data was challenged; our objectivity questioned; and the discussion we had tried to encourage around information generated through a massive needs-assessments exercise, shut down.

Some managers expressed shock at the data laid out in front of them, which challenged some of the deepest myths of the organization and named its most critical problems. The Executive Director, our strongest supporter, had not attended the meeting; but prior to it, the Team Leader had briefed him on our findings—none surprised him—and he gave us the go ahead to name the issues as we saw them. Still, we were on our own. Our BRAC team mates were worried for their careers, and the credibility of the Team in BRAC was at stake. Would our violation of what we named "the culture of silence" be our downfall? What should we do next? We decided first to carefully go over our data and findings from the needs assessment to ensure that we had not misrepresented the findings.

Here is what we found:

Needs Assessment Findings

Staff Attitudes   Staff, both male and female, at all levels and programs, believed BRAC should pursue women's empowerment, and should change men's attitudes and values as a prerequisite to this pursuit. Beyond this, however, there were uncertainties and disagreements on programming strategies, particularly regarding women's mobility, intra-household decision making and conflict, and ensuring freedom from violence. Most staff also believed that women should be promoted up the management ladder because they could do the job and do it well. However, there was a good deal of disagreement on reconciling women's family and work responsibilities, special provisions, and an accelerated career path for women. Gender relations in the workplace were often not smooth, and women faced varying levels of teasing and/or harassment. Thus, while conditions had improved for women in recent years, a great deal was left to be done.

In imagining the kind of organization they wanted to evolve, BRAC managers said they wanted to build an organization that would design a new organizational culture, structure and systems that both women and men could use and benefit from. They were not interested in separate but equal systems and rules for women and men. BRAC, they said, had always been a social pioneer; so it could learn to pioneer in this area as well.

Empowerment   Three issues stood out in BRAC staff's conceptual understanding of gender issues and in the application of this understanding to programmatic situations. First, staff's intuitive understanding of gender differences often did not translate into creative, strategic solutions regarding the core issues of empowerment. Proposed strategies and solutions tended to address symptoms rather than problems. Second, while conflict is inherent in all common conceptualizations of empowerment, staff leaned not toward confrontation but toward harmonious solutions to problems of women's subordination in the family and community. In the Bangladesh cultural and political context this was instructive and strategic, but also worrisome as it left the power imbalance and gender ideology intact. Third, BRAC staff placed inordinate emphasis on and had enormous faith in the potential of changing behavior and values through training. Thus, they tended to discount (and therefore inadequately address) the tremendous forces external to the individual—family, kinship, factions, cultural norms, gender ideology, etc.—in shaping individual behavior.

Inside BRAC   Together, staff responses painted a complex picture. BRAC was an organization in transition, from a collective to a corporation pursuing empowerment goals, in a volatile socio-economic and political environment. Externally, it was grappling with an enormous expansion in area coverage and increasing complexity and technical sophistication in program content. Internally, organizational complexity was enhanced by a series of features: a race for target achievement that left experienced supervisors with little time to nurture and guide newer entrants; newcomers, fresh out of the universities, who were moving up the corporate ladder and being handed program responsibility quickly; a management style geared to target achievement, which militates against lasting solutions to the difficult problems of women's subordination and gender-equitable change on the ground; an organizational environment in which opportunities for open discussion on personal and professional issues were becoming scarce; a brewing conflict between a nascent culture of gender equity, supported at BRAC's highest levels of policy making, and traditional patriarchal norms and behaviors; a need to forge ways for men and women to work in an organization that espouses countercultural values among people who do not necessarily believe in them; fatigue among long-standing cadres in the front-line fight; and a desire, among men and women alike, for work/family balance.

Strategic Issues   How did BRAC's dual goals—poverty alleviation and empowerment of women—play out on the ground? The evidence suggested that participation in BRAC's programs had strengthened women's economic roles and, to some extent, increased women's empowerment measured in terms of mobility, economic security, legal awareness, decision making and freedom from violence within the family.[5] However, widely acknowledged among BRAC staff was the fact that the imperatives of credit delivery were eclipsing the objectives of social change.

Moreover, the complexity intensified the closer you looked. A recent study examining women's high demand for credit and access to loans in Bangladesh found that, in close to one third of cases, BRAC women members have little or no control over their loans.[6] By virtually excluding men from credit access, is BRAC merely setting women up as conduits for credit to men and, if so, at what cost? What does BRAC do with the knowledge that many of the loans it gives to women are hijacked by men? Can it enter the conflictual household arena through program interventions and re-emerge both relatively unscathed and having achieved useful outcomes? What other responses are possible?

BRAC believed that working with men to bring about changes in the perceptions and valuations of women was essential and that men should be included in small numbers in the female village organizations. This might help counter opposition to BRAC from husbands and village elites, as men will be able to present BRAC in village fora from which women are excluded. However, it also opens up a host of complications for building women's self-reliance and solidarity. How can BRAC work to build women's capacity to pursue their strategic interests—security, and freedom from violence—which most staff believe BRAC should focus on? How can BRAC refocus its institutional-development work to build the organizational effectiveness and public-bargaining strength of women?

Integral to the answers to these questions is BRAC's assessment of its staff's ability to carry out the changes, as well as of the key supports, individual and systemic, they will need to do so. As products of a family structure dominated by a male patriarch who makes all decisions and an education system that stresses repetition over analysis, most young staff are unused to critical analysis and creative problem solving. This is exacerbated by an organizational culture that is somewhere between the societal norm and the ideal of an open, supportive environment that encourages independent thinking and local-level decision making. Staff at all levels have difficulty harnessing their intuitive understanding of social relations to generating solutions for difficult field-level problems. They recognize the need for space and opportunities for collective problem solving, but report that when they put their ideas forward, they are ignored or worse, punished for "speaking out." If empowerment goals are to be fine tuned, what skills—operating within what kind of an organizational culture and system—are needed? Answers to these key questions will chart BRAC's course and determine the purpose, audience, and shape of its gender program.

Has BRAC as an organization come to terms with its corporate nature? For the most part, its systems and standard operating procedures, including level of autonomy for decision-making among staff, once worked well—at any earlier point in the organization's history, when it was a fraction of its current size. However, these systems and procedures were being strained, with negative consequences for work quality and staff morale. BRAC's human-resource function, for example, was broken up among different line functions; it was perceived by staff to be an arcane process in which they had no voice. Moreover, current recruits came to the organization with different motivations from those who had shaped it in its early years. Livelihood issues now predominated over ideology, creating new demands from staff for favorable working conditions and career development. The changing gender mix within the organization was also challenging standard practices and cultural norms.

Between 1989 and 1993 BRAC made a series of special arrangements to accommodate women staff needs (such as giving them the option of desk work rather than field work during menstruation). However, women were reluctant to take advantage of some of these special arrangements, either because in this culture of extreme modesty it would make public what is very private, or because, as they said, they would be viewed as not good enough or somehow disabled and therefore requiring special attention. While the organization was attempting to accommodate women's needs, it was doing so incrementally, essentially leaving intact the dominant gendered organizational culture, space, and ways of working. Women, in effect, had to fit into a system made to fit men.

In the Bangladesh cultural context it is easy and acceptable for men to carry out field work at night, ride bicycles and motorbikes, and live singly in villages; for women it is not. Women who do so face harassment from villagers and from their male colleagues. If they protest, they are labeled weak and inefficient, with the strong implication that they are responsible for behaviors forced on women by patriarchal standards of what is appropriate and what is not, and for their vulnerability to physical violence. Thus, most women are faced with the difficult choice of whether to conform to countercultural values without the support of their male colleagues in a system that espouses them but practices the opposite. Those who have fought their way up the system have proven they are as good as any man; but are their struggles organizational requirements? Must women become men to succeed? Most male BRAC staff said that was not the case, but many women contested their view.

Building Ownership and Negotiating Next Steps

Convinced that our data accurately reflected what we had heard from staff and managers at all levels, and having affirmed the strength of our methodology, we resolved to meet with the Executive Director for three purposes: to brief him on what had happened at the strategic planning meeting, to let him know we stood behind our data, and to seek his advice on where to go from here. He listened to us and assured us that the issues we raised would be discussed again at the internal BRAC Strategic Planning meeting planned for the following month.

During the summer, the Team Leader held informal one-on-one meetings with senior managers to learn about their thinking on the Gender Strategic Planning meeting, and to get a sense of what they thought would be worthwhile gender work. While each had specific gender-related goals, all agreed that the gender-lens approach we proposed could illuminate aspects of organizational and programmatic quality that needed to be changed or improved in order to further BRAC's goals for women's empowerment. In October 1994, BRAC's five year strategic plan pledged, among other things, to build organizational quality that would support BRAC's programs for women's empowerment, in essence, the Gender Program. The thinking and language of the Gender Team's work had been taken by the organization and made their own. But senior managers also gave the Team specific areas to focus on: retention of women staff, improving work relations between women and men staff in the area offices, and improving program quality.

During a second round of one-on-one meetings, it became clear that senior managers, while interested in the issues, were uncertain about what exactly gender meant to organizational development in concrete terms. What would be the areas of overlap and distinctions? What would an intervention look like that aimed at creating organizational spaces for learning through doing, on issues of gender, program quality, and organizational change? What resources would it require, and at what cost?

These were legitimate questions to which there are no easy answers. In the next phase of our work, the team organized a series of work sessions with senior managers to address these questions collectively and to come to an agreement on an intervention design. While we had a conceptual basis for starting, BRAC-specific solutions had to emerge from, not precede, the intervention process itself.

An Organizational-Change Strategy

In order to translate these ideas into organizational practice, we needed to consider the questions of organizational change and quality improvement. Our change strategy was grounded in the practices and assumptions of collaborative change. It was neither a coercive strategy, which attempted to pressure or guilt managers into change, nor a rational strategy, which attempted to persuade them to change. This approach works with both the heart and the head, by supporting a learning process that accepts that there is always a psychological resistance to changing fundamental attitudes. This strategy for organizational change has the following aspects:

1. The client must "own" the change goals; the goals cannot be imposed by the change agents. The role of the change agent is to help the client achieve goals he or she has chosen;

2. The process is long-term (two to five years and beyond);

3. The process is both systemic and personal, concerning itself not only with systemic changes of culture and norms but also with the individual learning of the organization's members;

4. It is data based, informed not by universal prescriptions but by the specific requirements of that organization as demonstrated by a collaborative data collection and analysis process; and

5. The change agent does not expect to enter as an expert to prescribe the nature of the change. His or her primary role is that of facilitator or catalyst, although from time to time he or she must be prepared to give advice, particularly regarding the process, timing, and staging of the change.

This approach to change as well as considerations described in chapter two has resulted in a number of assumptions that guide our work. For example:

1. Within the scope of the intervention, managers and program personnel will define the priority problems and targets for intervention;

2. We believe in the value of action learning for bringing about individual and system change; as well, we hold that training is ineffective when it takes place anywhere other than in the setting in which the changed behavior is expected to be applied; and

3. Although we are committed to this approach, we are not committed to any particular configuration of intervention elements.

ADOPTING THE GENDER QUALITY ACTION LEARNING (GQAL) DESIGN: NOVEMBER 1994

The Team members were assembled at the DLO, ready to facilitate the second meeting in three days with the senior managers on the design of the gender program. We had planned a working dinner, and were anxious that all the directors come. During the previous week, the Team had continued its analysis of gender issues in BRAC and had begun the work of designing a gender action-learning program.

We had earlier articulated four assumptions about gender and organizational change:

1. In order to deliver quality programs that empower women, you need the perspectives of various kinds of men and women staff and of other primary stakeholders;

2. Like all organizations, BRAC is gendered. The processes for interaction and systems within which the organization's work is done were decided upon by men. Although they considered the needs of women, these considerations were filtered through men's perceptions and preferences. Therefore, working in the organization is easier for men than for women;

3. To deepen program quality, increase responsiveness to primary stakeholders, and improve impact, the organization's focus on quantitative targets must be balanced by a concern for the quality of programs and their impact on the empowerment of women; and

4. In order to improve quality, men and women front-line staff and Village Organization (VO) members must be engaged in the task of analyzing the process and the outcomes of programs so the depth and quality of the process will continually improve, along with its ability to actually empower women and transform gender relations. This analysis requires skill in gender and program analysis, the time to do it, a climate of acceptance of new ideas, and the respectful collaboration of men and women staff and members.

Working from these assumptions and from a belief in a participatory method of problem posing and solving, we took a series of steps toward developing a program design suitable to the BRAC context. We used the needs assessment findings to formulate the nature of specific gender and organizational problems in BRAC.[7] We had already had one meeting with senior managers to sharpen the program's focus and to develop a field-level intervention. They asked us to clarify the implementation phase of the program: who would be involved? How much staff time and other resources would it require? What should BRAC expect out of the program?

Our meeting was behind schedule but the Rural Development Program (RDP) Director had not yet arrived. We couldn't start without him given that RDP is seen within BRAC as the lead program, and that he is a very powerful decision-maker and opinion leader in the organization. He arrives, we start. After we make our presentation, senior managers make some comments and ask questions, but the RDP Director is noticeably silent.

Finally, he says that there is already a "training" program in RDP, which the gender program can use as a model: in the income generation program, trainers travel to the area offices where the staff are based to deliver training; this kept trainers close to programs and to program-related problem solving. This model fit the Team's requirement articulated earlier, of working with "intact teams," that is, teams of staff that normally work together in an office setting.

The RDP Director was concerned that trainers, who are already considered privileged in the BRAC system, would continue not to be connected closely to programs on the ground. If they are not connected, how can they be a useful resource for programs or adapt to program staff needs? The Team considers the proposal and quickly adopts it. Success at last! GQAL (Gender Quality Action Learning) is born!

GQAL

Our original GQAL design envisioned action-learning groups at the field, regional, and headquarters senior-management level. We were particularly concerned to engage senior managers in discussion: what did they think was important about gender? what were their mental models of women's empowerment and gender relations? We wanted to develop a common vision of their goals in this area; to describe to one another the current situation in the programs, so they could contrast it with the vision; and then to begin to set directions for change, plan action, and set into place monitoring mechanisms.

This aspect of the program was never implemented. Managers directed the Team to start work at the area office or field level, leaving it little time and resources to design and implement work simultaneously at any other level. This proved a costly strategic choice, as managers lost close contact with the Gender Program as it expanded on the ground.

In GQAL's start-up phase, beginning in May 1995, we worked with approximately 900 field level staff in twenty-eight RDP area offices (in the northwestern areas of Rajshahi, Pabna, Nawgaon, and Sirajganj) as well as in eight Health and Population Program offices in Mymensingh. In 1996, the program expanded to an additional fifteen RDP and Non-Formal Primary Education Program (NFPE) areas and two additional health program areas.

The GQAL Cycle   The GQAL cycle involves large numbers of staff in a process of defining gender-equality and organizational-change issues in one or more of three areas that they can then choose to act on: individual attitudes and behavior; programmatic outcomes; and organizational systems (see Figure 3–2). Each area office had two or three gender action-learning teams (GATs), each of which focussed on different issues.

Key to the design of GQAL is the belief in the value of action learning for bringing about individual and systemic change, and a concomitant belief in the ineffectiveness of training that takes place anywhere other than the setting in which the changed behavior is expected to be applied.

The first step in the cycle is a three-day orientation of area office staff on gender and how to make change happen. This is followed by a series of steps, carried out at regular intervals in the field: discussing and compiling issues; selecting issues; analyzing issues using a web diagram (see Figure 3–3); developing an action plan to address one or more actionable causes of the issue/ problem, developing approaches to solutions and acting on them; and, fi-

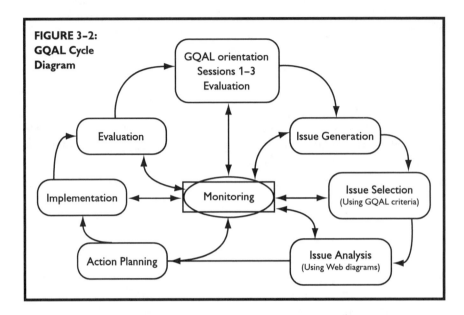

FIGURE 3-2:
GQAL Cycle
Diagram

nally, evaluating the outcomes.[8] Each of these steps is facilitated by trainer/
facilitators based at BRAC's regional training centers. (The GQAL facilitators were trained and supervised by BRAC's Gender Team. In 1995–96, the
GQAL Program had trained and worked with twenty-five to thirty facilitators.)

What Can a Gender Action Team Do?

In our design, the GAT would begin by exploring the nature of the problem in their office context. Take, for example, the issue of male resentment
of positive discrimination in favor of women with respect to promotion. From
the point of view of male managers, female staff are a "problem." It is said
that even female managers favor men. Men are considered to be more mobile, more capable of dealing with security issues and it is assumed that men
can deal with conflict better.

However, BRAC policy includes what has been termed "positive discrimination." Until recently, women were promoted faster than men (sometimes
without sufficient experience or training). Therefore, male managers felt
they had to be careful not to be too critical of female staff or in transferring
women without higher level approval. What the men saw as a limitation of
their managerial prerogatives contributed to women being "a problem" for
male managers.

Women staff may feel fully qualified to move up the ladder—even more

FIGURE 3-3: Sample Web Diagram

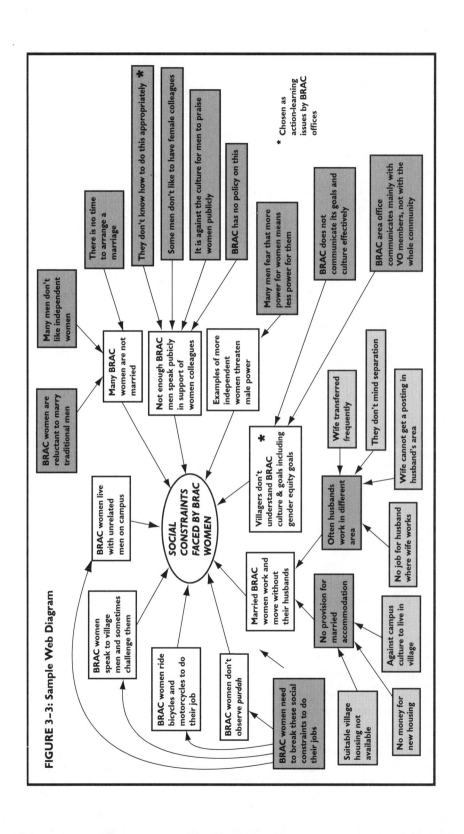

* Chosen as action-learning issues by BRAC offices

Many men don't like independent women

There is no time to arrange a marriage

They don't know how to do this appropriately *

Some men don't like to have female colleagues

It is against the culture for men to praise women publicly

BRAC has no policy on this

BRAC women are reluctant to marry traditional men

Many BRAC women are not married

Not enough BRAC men speak publicly in support of women colleagues

Examples of more independent women threaten male power

Many men fear that more power for women means less power for them

BRAC does not communicate its goals and culture effectively

BRAC area office communicates mainly with VO members, not with the whole community

BRAC women live with unrelated men on campus

SOCIAL CONSTRAINTS FACED BY BRAC WOMEN

Villagers don't understand BRAC culture & goals including gender equity goals *

Wife transferred frequently

They don't mind separation

Wife cannot get a posting in husband's area

BRAC women speak to village men and sometimes challenge them

Often husbands work in different area

No job for husband where wife works

BRAC women ride bicycles and motorcycles to do their job

Married BRAC women work and move without their husbands

No provision for married accommodation

BRAC women don't observe purdah

Against campus culture to live in village

BRAC women need to break these social constraints to do their jobs

Suitable village housing not available

No money for new housing

capable than their male colleagues. They may believe that traditional attitudes and organizational policies keeping women at lower levels should be jettisoned in favor of explicit affirmative action.

In order for staff to understand the nature of this problem in their office, the GAT would organize discussions on this issue and try to bring out facts underlying examples of presumed male resentment and female incompetence. The staff could decide on the particular aspects of discriminatory attitudes they wanted to curb, and of skills they want to upgrade; and then decide on what actions to take. For example, they might try to acknowledge and learn from each staff member's particular skills and experience, such as differing leadership styles (consensus decision making by women, for example) and program-related strengths; and build more cooperative working relationships between men and women (such as men accompanying women on evening trips to VO members and in discussions with community leaders). The staff may agree to observe one another for changes in attitude, and discuss the reasons for the change or lack of it.

We highlighted three points in our analysis:

1. These are complex and deeply rooted problems that will not be solved quickly, but it is possible to work on them;

2. The core strategy of the GAT is discussion, learning, and persuasion, which depends on the involvement and good will of the participants; and

3. The educational strategy of the GAT will need to be augmented by direct support from management.

Starting the Change Process: Training the Trainers

We decided to run a pilot program that would start at the area office level, with support from and monitoring by managers. Initially, BRAC managers wanted to reach 1,500 people through the pilot program. However, insufficient facilitators/consultants were available for such a large-scale pilot; as well, the gender team could not manage so many diverse interventions. Therefore, the pilot scheme size was reduced to about sixty area offices—three per facilitator. We began in the RDP and the HPD; leaving the NFPE until later.

Four of the Gender Team (David, Rieky, Sheepa, and Sadequr) met for five days to plan the Training-of-Trainers session. BRAC had agreed that we would work with all the staff in each selected area office: we felt that working with "intact teams" would increase the possibility that learning and change would be reinforced. Of course, this limited the time available for action-learning sessions, as it was not easy for an entire office to be shut down for very long.

We decided that each office would spend three initial three-hour sessions being introduced to the action-learning process: the first session would introduce the process; the second would engage participants in preliminary learning about gender; and the third, help participants reflect on how change takes place on both the personal and organizational levels. Then, office staff would select an issue to work on, based on their own priorities and three criteria: the degree to which the issue related to gender; the degree to which the issue would contribute to and be important to BRAC; and the capacity of the office staff to learn about and act on the chosen issue. They would analyze the issue, choose one or more causes to learn about and act on, and then develop and implement a learning/action plan. The final step would be an evaluation of the entire process and its results by the office-staff team and by the gender team. (See Figure 3–2.)

The facilitators would meet with each office each month, to lead the initial orientation sessions and, then, to facilitate the steps of the action/learning process. Facilitators would also meet monthly with the gender team and with relevant BRAC managers to share feedback, build skills, plan the next round of sessions, solve problems, ensure quality control, coordinate the program, and monitor progress. The BRAC staff on the gender team would supervise and support the facilitators.

In planning the Training of Trainers (TOT), we adopted a very simple process. We prepared lesson plans for the first three orientation sessions. We began with some group building, and then modeled each lesson; we then divided the facilitators into three small groups and worked with each group as they prepared to lead a session. We drew lots to determine which facilitator would present the session to the others in the small group.

We videotaped each presentation, after which the presenters would assess their own facilitation, the audience of peers would give feedback, as would the lead trainers (the gender-team members). Participants were given time for preparation and free time in the evenings to review the videos (a popular pastime). Each morning, we asked a small group to summarize key elements of the previous day's training, and to present a mini-lecture or training presentation that addressed an issue that had arisen on the previous day. We called this a "miniversity."

In an effort to make the program as concrete as possible we also used stories such as the ones we had used in the needs assessment process. "What Action Can We Take" is an example of a story, concerned with staff attitudes, that we constructed for use in the Training of Trainers sessions, to help trainer/facilitators engage BRAC staff in problem analysis and problem solving:

WHAT ACTION CAN WE TAKE?

The Area Office team and the facilitator were sitting in the small Program Office in Faridpur district in the middle of August 1995. It was hot, and there was much activity in the accountant's office across the campus as he was trying to complete the monthly report. Jamal, the area manager, was tired; he had been up late the previous night completing his regular paperwork so that he would be free to participate in this session.

He began the meeting by saying, "We have done good work in the last two GQAL sessions. We agreed in June that we wanted to work on the issue of respect between women and men on staff, although there were certain people here who wanted to work on profitability of women's Income Generation (IG) activities. When we discussed the problems between men and women in detail among ourselves and then talked with the VO members, NoorJahan discovered some very useful information. Can you summarize it for us?"

NoorJahan was a bit shy about talking in the staff meeting. She was a new Program Officer who had grown up in Dhaka; in her first six months in the field she had been dismayed by how hard VO members had to work. Especially troubling, she found as she talked to the women, was that some staff spoke to the women without respect and sometimes threatened them to get loan repayments. Since Program Assistants (PAs) had to cover any money not repaid out of their own pockets, it was not surprising that they pressed hard for the money. But at least, she thought, they could be respectful.

"I observed how our male staff talked to women and listened to women, both with VO members and at our meetings. They spoke much more than the women—about 75 percent of the time. They interrupted often, and did not pay attention or acknowledge the women's ideas when they did get to speak. Sometimes they teased also. I did not hear any examples of threats when I was present."

Siddiq, who had worked in the area office as PA for several years, said, "These women should be more grateful. They should not complain, after all

BRAC does for them. If they cannot work under these conditions they should leave. We treat them just the way we treat our younger sisters. Anyway, women don't work as hard as men."

Amina, the PA who did not like Siddiq's dominating attitude, took a deep breath to gather her courage and responded, "You always blame the women. I work at least as hard as you do. I always help you prepare your reports because I can do them quickly. I share information with you. And I collect my loans without bullying, so it takes me less time."

NoorJahan supported Amina's point. "When we did the detailed analysis of this issue in the July meeting, we concluded that main causes of the lack of respect were that men did not see all the work that women were doing and that they behaved differently and less respectfully when talking with women. We should keep track of all the work women and men staff are doing and we should have a fine every time someone shows the behavior NoorJahan observed in the staff meeting."

Mahmuda, the facilitator who was working with this group, tried to summarize the discussion and to help the group move forward. "Last month when we met, we thought we could improve relations between women and men. Most of us felt we should write our action-plan about these. Can we talk about what we can do between August and December to help us and to make some improvements in this area?"

"Well," said NoorJahan, "we're so overworked now we hardly have time to sit down for a five-minute rest between sunrise and late at night. For the last three evenings I missed my dinner because I was dealing with a crisis in the seri-culture groups. Because so many trees were cut down recently there are not enough leaves to feed the silkworms, and we had to organize to bring some in from another area. I don't have the energy to do any more."

"Right," said Siddiq. "I have enough trouble writing my reports now. I can't imagine keeping track of every bit of my time to compare with Amina."

Jamal said, "I agree that we do not have time to record our activities in detail. But we could perhaps do something useful in the staff meetings or talk to the Regional Manager (RM) about asking Training Division to help us talk with others more respectfully."

Mahmuda said, "If we are successful in improving our relations through our activities, we can share how we did it with other area offices in the district. Then maybe others can try it, too. Can we brainstorm possible things we might do in the next four months? Then we can begin to develop an action plan and agree on how to write our objective."

"Don't forget, we cannot go ahead until we have talked to the RM about this," said Jamal. "He must agree that we can do these things."

"Of course," said Mahmuda, "but first we must plan carefully, so he will see we can make a good plan. Let us start. Who wants to speak first?"

Discussion Questions

1. What do you think possible specific actions of the team members might be?

2. What do you think might prevent them from succeeding in their plans?

3. Do you think their ideas are realistic?

This process proved very fruitful. We were able to find a number of problems in the original lesson plans, make corrections, and re-model the sessions. All participants found this openness both stimulating and demanding. At each stage, the facilitators learned, by living the process, that making mistakes was a rich source of learning and improvement. They learned how an open-ended learning or problem-solving process is different from training that delivers pre-determined conclusions; that it "feels" different to participants and facilitators, and requires different skills and attitudes. Everyone had a chance to lead at least part of one session. Those who had two chances improved their performance markedly the second time around. (About two thirds of TOT participants were chosen to become GQAL facilitators.)

One of the challenges in designing these sessions was to keep them within the skill and experience range of the facilitators. Most were experienced trainers, but were used to top-down delivery. Most had had exposure to gender and development issues only through their participation in BRAC's six-day GAAC course. We felt that monthly sessions with the gender team would be essential to build skills as the action-learning process got underway. We also felt that we would need to continue to concentrate on a new role for the facilitators: as they were to be consultants or facilitators to the office staff teams, they might become caught between senior managers and field staff, as tensions and problems developed. An important role of the monthly meetings would be to model and reinforce constructive relationships among all the players.

GENDER ISSUES OR MANAGEMENT ISSUES? — JULY 1995

The Team had just returned from the Savar Training and Resource Center not too far from Dhaka. They had completed that month's full-day meeting with the GQAL facilitators working in the field. Most facilitators were handling a very heavy schedule and traveling long distances to get to their area offices. The training sessions in the area offices had gone well, they reported; managers were cooperative, and GAT members participated enthusiastically. "This is the first time in that we could talk about this in the area office," they were told by area office staff. Some facilitators reported that changes were already happening: managers were deciding to change the way they managed, based on feedback, new procedures in RDP, and workload changes in HPD.

The Team, however, was worried about the issues emerging from the first round. While the sessions were a big hit, most of the issues seemed management issues, not gender issues: workload, autocratic bosses, salary. Some in the Team worried that managers would not let us work on these issues; if so, that would disappoint the staff, who had trusted us to raise these issues. The Gender Program had become a magnet for staff frustration around all sorts of issues, and the program was in danger of being hijacked. Yet, regional managers in the field told us that facilitators were not adequately representing management's point of view in the sessions, and that some facilitators encouraged negative critique by the GATs in the area offices. After some discussion, both managers and facilitators identified the problem of "shifting blame" as common, and they developed ways to raise this problem with the area offices.

At the same time, there were difficult interpersonal conflicts within the core gender team. The accusations took many forms: that team members did not take responsibility for the work assigned to them; that the men were ganging up against some of the women; that the men were going over the women's heads, by talking to their old chums, the managers of regional and area offices, and by talking to facilitators about other team members' shortcomings; that the men resented being told to do things by the women; that the women were talking directly to senior managers about team members without those members being present; that men did not deal well with demands from a woman they see as their junior, and the women, in turn, were not patient with what they saw as the men's lack of understanding of the issues. A few sessions to air these differences helped somewhat, but the Team never did resolve the issues.

During the next few weeks we analyzed the issues and prepared a paper on them for senior managers. We needed to present the role of the Gender Team clearly: We had been asked to give leadership to a process to improve the quality of service to rural women and to improve gender relations within; and we believed we were doing so, through discussion, teaching, learning, and bringing gender expertise to BRAC. The gender team's role was to facilitate a problem-solving process that uses Area Office-level information, gender understanding, and management to work on issues that are important to the strategic plan, as defined in such documents as the plan for the fourth phase of the Rural Development Program. In other words, we were not advocates for particular organizational or program arrangements, such as increased participation or lower program targets. Our job was to advocate for a process that takes gender issues seriously at all levels of the organization, and to provide guidance on how the change process should work.

Are All Issues Gender Issues?

In generating issues or problems to solve, GAT members were asked to think of issues that prevented equitable gender relations or that prevented the empowerment of women in the program. The Team had developed criteria that GAT members had to use for this purpose: Is this an important issue? Is this a gender issue? Is this an issue to which Area Office teams can make a contribution? Part of the process was to make sure people took some responsibility not only for naming problems but also for solving them.

The issues that GAT members raised could be broadly grouped under the following categories:

1. Working Relationships and Staff Attitudes, such as male resentment of "positive discrimination" in favor of women, and poor working relationships among staff;

2. Management and Decision-Making, such as arbitrary and high-handed treatment by supervisors, and a climate that discourages open discussion and debate;

3. Personnel Management and HRD Issues, such as insufficient attention to staff's personal/family problems and frequent transfers; and

4. Program Issues, such as insufficient attention to area-specificity in planning and implementation, and women's lack of control over income earned through supported enterprises. We felt that all the issues gen-

erated in these categories had implications—some more direct than others—for improving gender relationships among staff and improving program quality.

Whether all issues are gender issues was particularly relevant to the categories Management and Decision-making and Personnel/HRD Issues. For example, work overload is an issue for both men and women. It is also one of the most pressing and most often mentioned. But is it a gender issue? We think it is, if the workload more likely prevents women than men from staying with BRAC because it makes the women unable to maintain family relations. It may also be a gender issue if the workload prevents staff from devoting the time to program activities that would contribute to the empowerment of poor women.

What could a GAT team do? If the team decided this was an issue they could analyze how they spent their time, logging various activities, and noting activities that wasted time and ways to save time. This information could be used to design ways of working more effectively, which could lead to experiments in working differently.

Clearly, while many issues in these two categories do not immediately appear to be gender issues, they have significant gender-related dimensions. Moreover, the strength of the links between an issue and outcomes that improved gender relationships and program quality/women's empowerment vary: some are clear and significant; others are more tenuous. It is also clear, with hindsight, that some deep-structural aspects of the culture and functioning of an organization are not obviously gender related, but inhibit the organization's gender-equity agenda.

We felt that we needed to choose issues that people care about; to find achievable goals to start; to look for small successes that can be replicated; to focus on priority goals, such as the retention of female staff, the empowerment of poor women, and improved program quality; as well as to combine voluntary and educational strategies with gentle pressure for change.

EVALUATING GQAL: JULY 1996

The large conference table in the DLO where the Team often worked was covered with bits of colored paper. We were engaged in the task of constructing a time line that highlighted the main events of the GQAL program from its inception, mapping the key turning points and their consequences. This construction of a joint understanding of the program was part of the evaluation process we designed for GQAL. Many other aspects of the evaluation had already been done: the facilitators and the GATs had been tracking achievement of the action-plan objectives; and had been analyzing the reasons for success or failure; we had held workshops with the facilitators, to assess their understanding of gender concepts and skills as change agents, using stories and simulations; we had done a similar analysis with the core members of the Gender Team. In addition, each member assessed his or her own contributions to the Team and the Gender Program.

In the weeks to follow, we planned workshops for mid-level and senior managers to assess the outcome and impact of the Gender Program as they saw them. We had just completed assessing changes at the area office level through detailed case studies done in the field. At our tea break, we discussed some of the interesting aspects of the cases.

"Remember" said Sadiqur, "in Chathar, how resistant the Area manager was to GQAL, and now he says that it builds better relationships and team spirit—values he believed we had lost and now have come back to through GQAL."

"To me" said Naheed, "the discussion in Dashghat on how building better relationships is making credit collection more efficient is very interesting . . . Now that we work more efficiently, we make the loans on time, which means that the men don't beat their wives as much, they said . . . But I wonder if we are simply channeling money through women for men's benefit? . . . Is it our role as staff to promote women's independent control over the resources we provide?"

That was a complex issue that we needed to address more systematically. Our task was helped by the positive feedback from area managers on the program as a whole. In the Health Program, for example, some of the changes made by staff far exceeded our expectations.

Many of the women program organizers at the Health Program Division's Pathar area office[9] in Mymemsingh district had close to ten years' experience—far more than the male staff. Yet, both the men and women agreed that the women participated inadequately in work-related decision making. Together the staff run a nutrition program with a feeding component for children under two and expectant mothers; a program to detect and treat TB and respiratory infections, ante-natal care, growth monitoring, immunization, a water and sanitation program, and a Vitamin A distribution program.

In their GAT, which met once a month under BRAC's new Gender Program, these men and women used web diagrams to analyze the causes of women's low profile in the office. It was true they found that the male staff were, formally, better educated; but why were women reticent to speak up in meetings? Why were their voices not heard when they did participate? Why did the manager never entrust them with the responsibility of running the weekly staff meetings? The manager was one of the few in who had taken BRAC's new Gender Awareness and Analysis course, in which issues of gender discrimination and gender equity were discussed. He was supportive of women, and wanted to change the situation. The regional manager, too, followed the program's progress closely, encouraged by his senior managers at headquarters, who clearly signaled that this program deserved attention.

When the staff, with the help of an experienced health trainer, analyzed the problem, they discovered that female staff worked with more of the health program because so much of it is related to women and children, which is more culturally suited to the women. This left the women with less time for report-writing and other leadership tasks. The men kept up with all programs because they were often asked by the women to help them write their reports. Women reportedly felt insufficiently skilled to complete the reporting formats required by headquarters. The men, however, did not need the women's help in filling out their reports; therefore, the women ended up with gaps in their information about those programs they were not directly involved in.

To address this, the area office staff decided that the women should write the men's reports and vice versa, with each group checking for accuracy. They also decided that the men and women should discuss their work in the weekly staff meeting, and that the manager should ask the women to run the weekly meetings. They did this for about four months and saw dramatic improvements: women felt more confident in their information base, and were gaining experience running meetings. In fact, they were doing it well! Now, if someone goes on leave, the reports are not held up, as all staff have up-to-date knowledge on all programs. Not only are the male and female staff working better with one another, but the Gender Program's facilitator, is also touched by this process. "I always thought that the way things were done before in the area offices was right," he said. "But now I have realized that all I am doing and society is prescribing is not all right . . . Now I have developed new eyes."

What Happened and Why?

The most commonly mentioned outcome or change achieved by the GQAL Program has been in improved working relationships and more open communication at the area office level.[10] For women, there is some indication that improved relationships with male colleagues and in the area office atmosphere have made staying in BRAC a more attractive proposition. For example, a female RDP program assistant reported to a GQAL facilitator that she changed her decision to resign after seeing such improvements in the area office. In HPD, mostly due the larger numbers of women staff, "improved relationships" have had clear gender dimensions, such as improved working relationships between men and women; women eating with male staff; and reduced gendered demarcations in work, leading to men valuing women's capabilities. In RDP, there have been small but significant gains in building more gender-equitable relations. Male staff report more respect for women staff's capabilities and, in some cases, have gone out of their way to stop community members from teasing women staff riding bicycles.

A related outcome appears to be a democratization of relations among levels of staff, specifically between the front-line workers, program organizers, and managers, and as well between area office staff and regional managers. Regional Managers report that the "commanding voices" of managers have changed to "listening voices." Some spill-over effects of this improved relationship can be seen in work efficiency, through mutual support and joint problem solving, improved time management, and work effectiveness. For example, while managers used to simply instruct staff on what to do, staff now analyze problems and try to come up with solutions jointly. This, the RMs conclude, increases staff's ownership of the work—it's no longer the manager's problem or BRAC's problem, it's theirs. In addition, staff are naming program problems early on, so, they can be dealt with before they become large. Managers report a greater willingness to listen to these problems and not to penalize staff for raising them. Another spill-over effect of improved communications at the area office has been in improved work/family balance. Managers cite a greater sensitivity to staff needs to communicate with their families, and are more willing to grant regular leave without viewing it as a lack of commitment to work. RMs have been pleasantly surprised that posting spouses in the same branch or close to home has not resulted in decreased work efficiency; in fact quite the opposite has occurred.

A clear outcome evidenced by the above is that staff members who have participated in GQAL assisted by trained facilitators, are quite familiar with

GQAL's action-learning process. They can identify and analyze an issue, develop an action plan to deal with it, and carry out a set of activities aimed at achieving their objective. This has led to increased transparency of issues and of the decisions taken to deal with them. As a result, managers who were wary of GQAL at the start have breathed a sigh of relief: they no longer believe that the process will lead to heaping of blame on their shoulders, thus jeopardizing their career prospects.

The entire process was carefully shepherded by the GQAL facilitators, many of whom have evolved from trainers to change agents and problem facilitators. Those who were experienced program personnel joined the staff as members not as outsiders, and continually engaged staff in discussion rather than in confrontation; and we saw productive outcomes. Moreover, BRAC now has a substantial—and growing—group within the organization capable of leading a gender- and organizational-change program.

Although all these outcomes seemed to us to be a strong beginning, we feel that the key accomplishment is related to capacity building. The Core Gender Team, the forty-three facilitators, and more than six thousand field staff have been trained to use action-learning to analyze and take action on gender issues. This is important, but more so is the growth in organizational capacity building, the key to longer-term change. By this we mean that the organization has learned in four key areas:

1. People;

2. Structure;

3. Managing the Inside-Outside Dialectic; and

4. Gender Justice Goal Accomplishment.

People   Central to success is attracting/finding people who have credibility in the system, and are skilled and well connected to influential field and headquarters leaders. In this case, the Core Team comprised a mixture of senior staff from both field offices and headquarters. All were skilled trainers and facilitators. Three of the four were long-time staff, well known throughout the organization. The outside consultants had a mix of gender, organization, and adult-education skills. The Team Leader, who was living in Bangladesh, had some experience with and was well-respected in the organization.

An early step in our work was to build a common understanding of what we meant by gender, and how the program would engage this issue at BRAC. What we also tried to do, in the core team, but with insufficient success, was to build a set of working methods to replace the hierarchical and patriarchal norms that team members had worked in. In their place we evolved a collegial climate that assumed accountability to the group. This may have been a contributor to a good learning environment, but it probably contributed to team difficulties we encountered later on. This team-based way of working was at odds with the larger, hierarchical structure wherein most believed that ultimate rewards resided. Team members were used to a way of working in which individuals were responsible for tasks, and advancement came from fulfilling those tasks to the satisfaction of one's supervisor and other powerful figures. For some, the team worked, and being members benefited members in career terms; but many of the group had difficulty thinking of the group as a locus of their loyalty, rather than being an individual in relation to a traditional supervisor. Thus, when conflict came, relations with various powerful people outside the group were more important to some than resolving conflict within the group.

Structure   If capacity building is to be organizational rather than individual, structures must be put in place that locate the program and the people in a particular part of the structure, tie it to organizational policy, formalize the vertical and lateral connections, and develop plans and lines of accountability. To some extent, temporary systems are necessary to enable new ways of behavior; but even temporary systems need to be tied into organizational process, not left hanging. In this case, for the first two years, the Team Leader was a consultant, not an employee, of BRAC; the Core Team took direction from her and, in turn, supervised the twenty to thirty facilitators. After the first two years, the program became established: a Team Leader, appointed from the Core Team, was responsible for supervising the Core Team members and the program. The gender program was lodged in Training Division, which enabled it to work with all programs; it was charged with implementing a plan approved by senior management, and was accountable for accomplishing goals. However, its location in Training Division caused complications: it reinforced the misperception within the organization that GQAL was a training program, not an organizational-change effort. It also caused envy on the part of other trainers, especially those based at the Training and Resource Centers (TARCs) where the GQAL facilitators were based. One reason for the friction was that GQAL facilitators were very mobile and, as a result, earned more travel money. (They were also far more stretched than other trainers; most were traveling and training in field offices more than twenty-five days a month.) As well, GQAL trainers were not bound by TARC training requirements. Senior trainers in charge of TARCs knew little about the work of the GQAL trainers, and had little control over them. This contributed to their lack of support for GQAL and, in some cases, open charges— of incompetence and slacking off—against GQAL facilitators.

Budget is also an important part of structure. In the beginning, the BRAC gender work was funded largely from outside, but BRAC's contribution came from all program divisions.

Managing the Inside-Outside Dialectic The dilemma with much organizational learning is that it requires ideas from outside, yet these ideas must make sense within the organizational context and the people that live in it. At BRAC, there was considerable infusion from the outside: three international consultants; trips overseas for the gender team to give presentations, attend short courses, and conferences; and an engagement by the gender team with other Bangladeshi NGOs learning about gender. Much trouble was taken to assess outside ideas in the light of the BRAC reality. The first month of our work as a team was devoted to understanding what gender meant in this context. The extensive needs assessment, the strategic-planning workshop, the program-planning discussions, and the monthly meetings with managers were all part of ensuring that BRAC's perspective was informing the work.

A second aspect of building capacity related to the "inside/outside" is the outside constituency that maintains pressure for change. Although we intended to work with village women in BRAC's RDP program we were unable to do this; so the most important constituency of the program is still without a voice.

Achieving Gender Justice Goals This element focusses on accomplishment, ensuring that clear goals and regular monitoring inform regular evaluation and re-focussing. The other critical aspect here is ensuring that the program not be co-opted into a show in which there is lots of activity, but nothing significant happens.

The Gender Program at BRAC developed a number of input-related monitoring mechanisms. The number of people involved, movement in the cycle, and mid-management support are discussed regularly. This is a critical discipline; however, also needed on an on-going basis is an in-depth analysis of whether things are changing at the levels that matter (both in the organization and in the work with poor women). At the moment, we cannot demonstrate a connection between the accomplishments of this program and change in key, gendered programmatic practices.

The issue of "change that matters" also focusses on the extent to which managers themselves are learning as well as supporting the program. Although we met with them often, we never engaged them in a serious analysis of the issue at their level: the GQAL work happened at the bottom of the hierarchy with periodic action from the top in response to issues raised.

These four aspects (people, structure, inside-outside and achieving gender goals) are the "what" of capacity building. We now turn to the "how."

In looking at our experience in, we see two key methods that stand out: learning by doing and political knitting.

1. Learning by doing has well-deserved credibility as a method of adult education, and was central to our work at every stage. Consultants and Gender Team preparing for a presentation would practice on one another; the needs assessment was piloted with observers who gave feedback; the Training of Trainers was all practice and feedback-based; and all members were encouraged to take responsibility for risky meetings. As consultants, we would demonstrate and get feedback before the team would accept ideas for particular meetings or training sessions.

2. "Political knitting" was a term we coined for what, at the beginning, was the work of the Team Leader, but ultimately spread as a responsibility to all members of the core team. Political knitting is the day-to-day work of staying in touch with important actors and ensuring that the program is enfolded into the organization and not seen as a temporary aberration. This largely involves gaining and maintaining the trust of managers and field personnel: ensuring that they understand what's happening, and that it meets their needs as well as those of the staff; that they are not surprised by events; and that they are part of the community of critique whose voices are heard in program re-design.

Where Does GQAL Go Next?

Currently, there is considerable demand for the GQAL program to expand to a greater number of area offices. A number of issues raised by the GATs in the first phase pertain to management and decision making, team work and relationship building. Therefore, in place of expanding GQAL to all area offices (where the GQAL process and the issues it uncovers would be limited to only that program), BRAC is considering how the analytical process inherent in GQAL can be made part and parcel of the way in which problems are raised and dealt with in BRAC's basic operating procedures. As such issues raised are also directly relevant to BRAC's standard operating principles, there is an even greater argument for addressing these issues as an integral process in functioning.

BRAC plans to explore another avenue of GQAL itself in the next phase. Because much of GQAL's impact to date has been on internal organizational issues, program-related issues took a back seat to staff concerns about living and working in BRAC. To the extent that GQAL has had programmatic effects, they appear to be related to the efficiency of standard operating procedures: such things as on-time loan disbursal and collection, and 'better discipline' of groups. Now, it is time to focus on effectiveness of programs and their impact on the lives of BRAC's primary stakeholders—poor rural and urban women members. This will mean building the capacity of staff at different levels in gender analysis of program, participative planning, and leadership for gender equality; developing a methodology for on-going analysis of gendered impacts of programs; and developing appropriate methods to consult women members in program evaluation and planning for the future. In so doing, BRAC can not only build its accountability to its members but also can set in motion a process through which its membership evolve into a vocal and empowered constituency.

Finally, in the next phase of GQAL, BRAC needs to actively enlist senior staff and managers in conversations on leadership for gender equality and social change. This should involve systematic feedback and work with middle-level managers on the outcomes of the evaluation, and in the design of new initiatives. It should also involve them and senior managers in the design of leadership-development modules to better foster gender equality and women's empowerment, both within the organization and with regard to its poor women members.

NEEDS ASSESSMENT PLAN AND TOOLS[11]

BRAC GENDER CONSULTATION/NEEDS ASSESSMENT PLAN

Purpose:

- To provide valid and compelling data for gender-related strategic planning by managers.

- To provide an orientation to gender thinking to a cross section of BRAC staff.

- To deepen the understanding of the Gender Training Team of gender issues at BRAC.

Approach:

- Approximately seventeen consultations with staff from all levels, programs and regions. Each consultation will be with approximately twenty people; n = approx. 340 people

- Each meeting to last one to two days.

- Some consultations will be for women only, others men only and others mixed. Some will be for newer staff and some for more experienced staff. They will be done in each of the four regions.

- Consultations will be led by two teams of two. Each team's involvement in this phase of the program will require thirty-five days;

- The team leader's involvement (which will include participation in the RM meetings, and discussions with the teams to conduct a preliminary analysis of the data and write it up) will total eighteen days.

- Information from the meetings will be assembled and analyzed by the Gender Training Team in preparation for the strategic planning workshop in late May.

The Questions:

I. What is the quality of BRAC staff's conceptual understanding of the empowerment of women?

II. To what extent do BRAC staff intrinsically value women's empowerment goals?

III. How should BRAC change or improve its program in order to further the empowerment of women?

IV. What support/training do BRAC staff need in order to implement these changes?

V. What aspects of the work environment and experience should be changed/improved in order to make it possible for (i) women staff to work at their best; and (ii) women and men staff to work effectively together?

In our data analysis we shall be looking for differences in responses by gender, program affiliation, and level. In terms of the organizational environment responses, we shall in addition look for differences by length of service and marital status.

The Core Consultation Design:
Activities 1 and 2 address questions I and II; additionally activity 2 addresses questions III and IV; activity 3 and 4 address question V.

Activity 1: Gender Analysis
How are poor women and men alike and different in terms of:

- Income generation, control of finances and ownership of assets

- Confidence, ability and knowledge to negotiate for rights in the family and in the community.

- Control over movement, own bodies and time.

3 small groups—each works on one of the areas.

Group output: Flip chart sheet:

- How are poor women and men alike or different on this dimension?

- Why is this the case?

Plenary discussion:

- Hear group reports, discuss the whys,

- Ask what is the most important issue to address. Each individual has two choices (mark on flip charts)

TABLE 3-1: Example of Workshop Summary Sheet for Activity 1

ISSUES	SIMILARITIES	DIFFERENCES
WORK DONE/ INCOME	• Both are able to earn and are interested in security	• Women can't work like men, women do different jobs than men • Women are dependent on men • Women earn less than men • Women work harder than men • Men work outside but women at home
NEGOTIATIONS/ RIGHTS	• Both have political rights	• Women's voices are neglected • Men have more rights over property than women • Specially women are oppressed by men • In inheritance law women have fewer rights than men • Women are not allowed to attend village shalish • Men have more access to basic needs • Men have the right to marry more than one woman
BODIES/ MOVEMENT	• Both need treatment against disease	• Women suffer from diseases more than men • Physically men are stronger than women • Women enjoy less freedom than men • Women are not allowed to go outside at night • Women cannot dress the way they want

WHY	CHANGE	ESTIMATED LEVEL OF UNDERSTANDING
• Religious prejudice and beliefs	• Increase women's literacy rate	RANGE OF ISSUES IDENTIFIED
• Ignorance and laziness	• Increase women's self-confidence	"Low"
• Lack of education		
• Poverty	• Create more income-generating opportunities for women	
• Women's dependency on men	• Remove prejudices through education	CLARITY OF PROBLEM IDENTIFIED
• Lower literacy rate of women	• Provide opportunity for women to earn money	"Low to medium"
• Early marriage	• Advocate changes in the inheritance law so that women have equal rights	
• Women don't fight for their rights		
		DEPTH OF ANALYSIS
		"Low to medium"

Activity 2: Empowerment Goal Analysis through Case Studies

Each of three groups will consider a case study related to one of the three empowerment goals in the framework.

Group output: flip chart

Plenary discussion of each case.

We prepared short stories, based on BRAC's field experience, that illustrated programming dilemmas in the three areas outlined in Activity 1. We asked participants to read these stories and define the problem as they saw it. We asked them to describe what they could do as BRAC staff, what BRAC as an organization should do, and what support would be needed to allow this to happen. Below is an example of a story we developed for this activity.

THE STORY OF ROHIM

Rohim was cycling back from the member meeting where he had collected loan payments, but his mind was not on the traffic, the rice greening in the paddy fields, or the greetings of the villagers. He was thinking about his conversation with Sakina, one of the BRAC members. She had given her loan payment, but she seemed sad. He knew Sakina quite well, so he had asked her privately if she was all right. She had told him that the repayment money had come from the village moneylender, because her husband had taken the money from the paddy husking and invested it in buying pulses (legumes) for future sale. When she protested, he said that he was responsible for making decisions in the family and had beaten her to make her behave. This sad story made Rohim worried. He knew that this happened to some of the other women in his groups, while others were able to make decisions about money with their husbands harmoniously. Some cases were even worse than Sakina's, where the husbands spent the proceeds from their wives' labor in the tea shops. He himself was so busy just collecting the money and accounting for it that he didn't feel capable of even thinking about what to do. Was this situation his responsibility? It was not easy to think of what he or BRAC could do to help Sakina and those like her. Maybe he should just shrug his shoulders and forget about it.

DISCUSSION QUESTIONS

1. What is the problem or problems in this case?

2. If you were the BRAC staff member in this case, what would you do to deal with this problem(s)?

3. What should BRAC do to deal with this problem?

4. What support or training would you need to deal with this problem?

Activity 3: The Internal Organization Conditions and Relationships

1. Introduce the four categories

   – living conditions (at BRAC)

   – nature of job (objectives and activities, skills/technology you use, schedule)

   – relationships with colleagues, supervisors and VO members; and

   – career development (training opportunities, evaluation process, promotion)

   Ask participants to write individually and anonymously on three separate pieces of paper:

   – Separate reasons (under the given categories) why they like working at BRAC.

   – Collect those papers and place them in a box marked "positive."

   Ask participants to write individually and anonymously on three separate pieces of paper:

   – three separate problems (under the given categories) they face in their work/life in BRAC.

   – Collect those papers and place them in a box marked "problems."

   On each sheet, each participant will indicate m/f, length of service in BRAC, and marital status

2. Re-distribute the Problem papers to the groups and ask them to sort them by category and put this up on the grid. Then, the groups will be

asked to identify the two most important problems in their pile and discuss them in detail. In plenary they should explain their priorities, specify why these are important, and make concrete suggestions about what can be done to solve them. Facilitators probe for specificity and examples. Facilitators then ask if participants know of any BRAC policies addressing these problems/issues.

3. While the participants are discussing the problems, the facilitators score the positive responses and put them up on the grid.

Activity 4: Organizational Gender Dynamics Discussion through Stories

Two stories will be told:

– One illustrating how women's voices were not heard in meetings

– Another one a man's comment that a woman staff member could not get married because she had worked at BRAC and was therefore impure.

Participants will be asked to think about how each of the protagonists in the story felt, why and whether these feelings are justified. They will be asked to indicate whether this kind of situation occurs in BRAC and how frequently.

Activity 5: Gender and Organizational Equality

Use the overhead of the Fox and the Crane (see Figure 3–4). Show only the first image of the fox and the crane chasing after the flat dish of food. Ask participants to describe what is happening. (Don't worry if they name the creatures "dog" or "bird"). Ask if the fox and the crane both have the opportunity to get to the food. Is the opportunity the same or different for the fox and the crane? How?

Now remove the cover over the second image. Ask participants what is happening now. How does the fox feel? How does the crane feel? Is this equal opportunity? Are both creatures gaining equal benefit? Do they think this is fair? Why or why not?

Now remove the cover over the third image. Ask participants what is happening now. How does the fox feel? How does the crane feel?

Figure 3-4: Fox and Crane

Are there any other possible happy endings to this story? (In particular, see if anyone suggests one dish that is suitable for both fox and crane).

Ask participants, if they were to transfer this fable to BRAC as an organization in terms of its treatment of women and men staff, what would be some examples of how BRAC would treat its staff differently under each of the three pictures? Which of the three pictures best represents the way participants feel BRAC should treat its women and men staff? Why?

Activity 6: Attitude Survey of BRAC Staff

The staff attitude survey was administered as part of the gender consultations and needs assessment exercises conducted by BRAC's Gender Training Team over the period March to May 1994. It consists of twenty-two questions divided into two sections aimed at gauging staff attitudes and values regarding gender dimensions of BRAC's program and organizational processes.

NOTES

1. BRAC originally stood for the Bangladesh Rural Advancement Committee. Now the organization uses the acronym as its name.

2. BRAC, *Toward Gender Equity: BRAC Gender Policy,* January (1998), 3.

3. BRAC (1998), 3.

4. Joan Acker, "Gendering Organizational Theory" in Albert Mills and Peta Tancred, eds., *Gendering Organizational Analysis* (Newbury Park: Sage, 1992).

5. Sidney Schuler and Syed M. Hashemi, "Credit Programs, Women's Empowerment, and Contraceptive Use in Rural Bangladesh," in *Studies in Family Planning* 25, no. 2 (1994), 65–76.

6. Anne Marie Goetz and Rina Sen Gupta, "Women's Leadership in Rural Credit Programmes in Bangladesh," unpublished paper (1995).

7. For an analysis of the strategic issues identified by staff and the Gender Team, see Aruna Rao and David Kelleher, "Engendering Organizational Change: The BRAC Case," in Anne Marie Goetz, ed., *Getting Institutions Right for Women in Development* (London: Zed Press, 1997).

8. For a detailed description of each step in the GQAL cycle, analytical tools, and sample outputs, see *Technical Manual: An Action Learning Approach to Gender and Organizational Change* (Dhaka: BRAC, November 1997).

9. All names have been changed in the area office vignettes.

10. An internal evaluation of the GQAL Program was conducted in August 1995. For information on the evaluation framework see the Technical Manual (1997).

11. For a full set of tools developed for the BRAC GQAL Program, see Rieky Stuart et al., *BRAC Technical Manual. An Action-Learning Approach to Gender and Organizational Change* (Dhaka: BRAC, 1997).

4

ENGENDERING ORGANIZATIONAL CHANGE:
A CASE STUDY OF STRENGTHENING GENDER-EQUITY AND ORGANIZATIONAL EFFECTIVENESS IN AN INTERNATIONAL AGRICULTURAL RESEARCH INSTITUTE[1]

Deborah Merrill-Sands, Joyce Fletcher, Anne Acosta[2]

THIS CASE DESCRIBES and analyzes an organizational-change process aimed at strengthening gender-equity and organizational effectiveness in a not-for-profit international agricultural-research organization based in Mexico. The Centro International de Mejoramiento de Maiz y Trigo (CIMMYT) [The International Center for Improvement of Maize and Wheat], has a worldwide reputation for its research into increasing sustainable production of maize and wheat, which are staple food crops in developing countries. CIMMYT was part of "The Green Revolution," having made a significant contribution to the development of high-yield varieties that helped to stave off widespread famine in developing countries in the 1960s; and it continues to improve productivity of maize and wheat systems around the world.

In order to ensure that it could retain and attract the highest-quality scientists, CIMMYT made an explicit commitment in 1995 to increasing its recruitment of women and to providing a work environment equally hospitable to and supportive of men and women.

CIMMYT contracted several consultants and a team of action researchers to help it examine its work environment from a gender perspective; and to support specific changes of policies, management systems, work practices, and work culture in order to develop a more gender-equitable work environment. This case records that process as it has unfolded over two and a half years.

The intervention has focussed on changing deeply held assumptions, norms, and values in CIMMYT that produce unintended consequences for both gender-equity and organizational performance. While the change process is far from complete, some significant achievements have been realized. Moreover, the experience is rich in insights into and lessons on the nature of the organizational change required to strengthen both gender-equity and organizational effectiveness, and on the challenges that the organization and we, as external and internal change agents, continue to face.[3]

APPROACH

Goal

Our goal has been to assist CIMMYT to create a gender-equitable work environment inclusive of both men and women; one that stimulates their fullest productivity and satisfaction in their professional and personal lives; harnesses diverse skills, perspectives, and knowledge; values different contributions and ways of working; and engages both women and men in the decision-making that shapes the work and the work environment.

Analytic Framework

We begin with two fundamental premises:

1. that organizations—their systems, practices, structures, and norms—are gendered; and

2. that effective and sustainable progress on gender-equity can occur only when the change effort integrates the goal of strengthening organizational effectiveness.

We believe that organizations, having been created largely by and for men, tend to be driven by assumptions that reflect the values and life situations of men and of idealized masculinity.[4]

This bias has had two major effects. The first is that our conceptual knowledge of organizational life is quite narrow and limited. What we regard as normal or commonplace—from appropriate workplace behavior to norms of success, commitment, and leadership—tends to value traits socially and culturally ascribed to males—independence, individuality, and rationality—while devaluing or ignoring those socially ascribed to females—support, collaboration, and connection. Thus, our understanding of the workplace and our ability to envision alternative structures and systems have been constrained by gendered norms of effectiveness and success.[5]

The second effect occurs when these norms are put into practice, creating idealized images of work, workers, and success that entrench gender segregation and inequity in the workplace.

From this perspective it is clear that creating gender-equitable workplace environments cannot be achieved simply by increasing the numbers of women within the organization, by adapting policies and procedures to women's needs, or even by providing gender-sensitivity training. These actions might relieve some of the blatant discrimination against women in the workplace, but they have little effect on the assumptions that drive behavior and create the deep structures and processes that reinforce and reproduce gender inequity. These deep structures and practices are often invisible—appearing to be merely routine, gender-neutral elements of organizational life; our approach seeks to change them in ways that will be beneficial to women, men and, very important, to the organization.

This "dual agenda" approach[6] encompasses both gender-equity and organizational effectiveness and performance. Thus, the focus is on identifying and changing those systemic issues that both reproduce gender inequity and negatively effect organizational performance. It mobilizes leadership support and commitment, connects the interests of diverse constituencies with the goals of the change process, and provides a compelling motivation to engage in and sustain long-term, systemic, organizational change.

Gender Lens

In practical terms, the gender lens shapes the inquiry in three ways. First, it focusses attention on dimensions of the organization's culture that have a differential impact on men and women. This would include, for example, the organizational culture (that is, the norms, values, core assumptions, and behaviors promoted in the organization); work processes and practices; roles and types of work; core management systems (such as performance appraisal and reward systems); decision-making and communication processes (both informal and formal); resource allocation processes; accepted leadership and management styles; and the use and management of time. (Time has a strong gender dimension, as women still have primary responsibility for the care of families and for managing private life.)[7]

Second, as most cultural diagnoses focus on "masculine" aspects of organizations, such as systems of power, influence, and individual achievement, the gender lens focusses on the more "feminine" elements of support, caring, and collaboration, shining light on, for example, work done to develop people and facilitate organizational effectiveness but often not "visible" as work or a product.[8]

Finally, as men's experience has traditionally defined "normal" the gender lens focusses on women's experience, especially those things they find problematic or constraining. Like other "learning from diversity" initiatives,[9] this approach works because women are to some extent outsiders. As such, they are often uncomfortable with the status quo. Their experience can reveal not only different ways of working and innovative practices;[10] it can also help to question aspects of the work environment rarely noticed by the mainstream. Thus are uncovered gendered core assumptions—about work, management systems, products, and organizational values—that might have unintended negative consequences, not only for women but also for men and for the organization.

Mental Models

To help CIMMYT understand how deeply rooted gendered structures and practices are, the action-research team uses the concept of mental models developed by Peter Senge. Mental models are:

> deeply ingrained images and assumptions . . . which we carry in our minds of ourselves, other people, institutions. . . . Like panes of glass, framing and subtly distorting our vision, mental models determine what we see and how we act. Because mental models are usually tacit, existing below the level of awareness, they are often untested and unexamined.[11]

Mental models are normative, identifying ideal images and modes of behavior that reveal beliefs about, for example, routes to success, exemplary behavior characteristics, organizational loyalty or commitment. They are taken for granted or tacit, rarely questioned or discussed, so apparently natural as to be unremarkable. Finally, mental models manifest themselves in the concrete practices, structures, processes and everyday routines of work life.

Surfacing mental models allows us to examine the tacit assumptions that drive behavior, structure and process. It also allows us to raise mental models that correspond to the dual agenda to the level of conscious awareness. At that point people can reflect on these systemic influences, which affect not only their personal work situations but also the organization's ability to meet its goals. Making these mental models explicit disrupts the status quo and gives both men and women new ways of looking at the systemic determinants of behavior.[12] The very "naming" of the mental models gives members of an organization a legitimate forum in which to discuss issues and values that are either tacit or taboo.

To begin to uncover the mental models, the researchers ask people to describe specific aspects of the organizational culture—written and unwritten rules of success; exemplary behavior or "ideal" workers; formal and informal work processes and decision-making schema; patterns of communication up, down, and across the hierarchy; evaluation, promotion, and reward systems; and leadership and management styles. Staff are also asked what they consider to be the most pressing challenge or problem facing their work group and the organization as a whole. The research team then analyzes the data to surface underlying assumptions that account for the behaviors, structures, beliefs, and norms that both reinforce or reproduce gender inequity and limit some aspect of organizational effectiveness or performance.

Collaborative-Action Research

The approach is both collaborative and interactive. Researchers work with members in the organization from the beginning, to set the goals, frame the inquiry and analysis, interpret the findings, and design change interventions. The researchers' role is more pronounced in the inquiry and analysis phases; the role of the organizational-change agents is stronger when designing and implementing change.

A collaborative process is critical for sustained change; it deepens the analysis and frames it in a way that can be heard and used by the organization. Equally important, it increases the knowledge and skills of change agents within the organization so that they can move the change process forward independently.

Central to the method is the belief that challenging assumptions and questioning ways of thinking require a relational context; that is, movement toward change occurs through growth-fostering interactions characterized by mutuality, reciprocity, and "fluid expertise."[13] Thus, the goal of action researchers' interactions—whether with individuals, work groups or the management team—is to model growth-fostering or generative principles.

In the interactive process, the researchers engage in mutual inquiry; that is, they attempt to understand people's experience and to offer their own understanding of the situations people describe. In doing this, they hope to unlock old ways of thinking and to create an opportunity for new possibilities and options to surface, both for the people they are interacting with and for themselves. In the spirit of fluid expertise, the researchers recognize that they have certain perspectives and ways of thinking, and they do not shy away from sharing them. But they also recognize that their expertise is limited, and that, as co-learners, they have much to gain by acknowledging and building on the expertise of their partners in the organization.

CASE-STUDY ORGANIZATION

At CIMMYT, major research areas involve conservation and distribution of genetic resources; plant breeding; plant protection and agronomic practices; biotechnology, socio-economics, and policy analysis; natural resource management; and information, documentation, and training.

CIMMYT is one of a consortium of sixteen international agricultural research centers supported and funded by the Consultative Group for International Agricultural Research (CGIAR). CGIAR comprises more than fifty governments, foundations, and international and regional organizations from developed and developing countries. The CGIAR is cosponsored by the World Bank, the Food and Agriculture Organization of the United Nations, the United Nations Development Program, and the United Nations Environmental Program. The members of the CGIAR meet semi-annually to coordinate their funding (approximately US$300 million annually), and their strategic priority-setting, monitoring, and evaluation processes. While centers are autonomous with their own Boards; they operate within a policy and funding environment shaped largely by the CGIAR. Attention to gender in both research and staffing has been part of this larger policy environment since the early 1990s, when the CGIAR Gender Program was established. The Program is designed to support the centers in their efforts to strengthen gender equity by providing technical advice, resources, information, and cutting-edge knowledge.

CIMMYT has an annual budget of approximately US$30 million from more than forty donors. After twenty years of solid support for international agricultural research, funding eroded significantly in the 1990s, as donors' priorities shifted away from agriculture and food production. The resulting decline in funding put CIMMYT under considerable stress. In the early 1990s, the center had to undertake a major downsizing in staff and a shift in funding strategy, as it was forced to rely increasingly on project funding rather than the more stable and predictable unrestricted core funding. CIMMYT also had to change its research priorities in response to growing global concerns about the environment and to donors' interest in the sustainable management of the natural resources upon which agriculture depends. CIMMYT also had to reposition itself to take advantage of the developments and op-portunities emerging from biotechnology and its potential applications to agriculture. Thus, it was within the context of significant change, both inter-nal and external, that CIMMYT embarked on its efforts to develop a more gender equitable work organization.

CIMMYT has a staff of about seven hundred, of which approximately 110 are internationally recruited scientists and professionals. The interna-tional staff comprises more than fifty nationalities, approximately one-third are based overseas. Administrative and support staff, technicians, and field staff are primarily Mexican nationals recruited locally.

In 1997, women comprised 24 percent of all staff, but only 16 percent of the internationally recruited professional and scientific staff. There are no women at the senior-management level; however, recently women have been appointed to middle-management positions, heading administrative depart-ments such as finance and human resources. On the positive side, two-thirds of internationally recruited women are employed in research, the core busi-ness of the organization. However, while 70 percent of internationally re-cruited men are "senior" or "principal" scientists, only 30 percent of women are at these levels.

The 24 percent overall representation of women in the center, and their low numbers within the professional and managerial staff indicate that women still represent a distinct minority within CIMMYT. They are, thus, vulnerable to the tokenism that influences organizational behavior towards minority groups.[14] At current levels, women tend to experience higher visibility and performance pressure and to be isolated from social and professional net-works. Moreover, they do not have the critical mass to form strong coalitions to lobby for change and influence work culture, systems, and practices.

INSTITUTIONAL CONDITIONS FOR CHANGE

Enabling Conditions

Several critical enabling forces converged to catalyze the gender-staffing initiative at CIMMYT: the presence of an emerging internal constituency of women; a genuine commitment to and interest in addressing gender issues in the workplace among some members of the senior-management team; and positive incentives from the funding community. Each of these forces had an effect on the structure of the initiative.

First, the internal constituency of women professionals interested in fostering gender-equity and a more hospitable work environment for men and women began to develop in the early 1990s. This group initially was responding to perceived gender inequities in salaries between men and women and in the job categorization of some professional women. The attention being given to gender staffing in the CGIAR provided legitimacy for their concerns and a safer environment in which to meet and speak out.

Their skills and commitment to working together on gender issues were strengthened through their participation in a CIMMYT-sponsored Women's Leadership and Management course. The influence of this group was strengthened considerably by the informal leadership provided by a member who has been a dedicated change agent throughout the process.

Second, two key members of the senior management team provided leadership of and support for CIMMYT's efforts to create a more gender-equitable work environment. The Deputy Director General attended a workshop on gender staffing organized for all CGIAR centers. His attention was captured by the experiences of another center, where linking gender staffing issues to organizational performance, using the "dual agenda" approach had resulted in benefits to both.

He immediately established a Gender Task Force (GTF), hired a consultant to examine possible gender inequities in salary and position classifications, and began discussions with the Gender Program about funding an action-research project at CIMMYT to identify aspects of the work culture that could be changed to enhance both gender-equity and organizational effectiveness.

This initiative was facilitated greatly by the new Director General. Not only did he want CIMMYT to take a leadership position in the CGIAR consortium in promoting gender-equity, but he also recognized that linking effectiveness and gender-staffing issues was in line with his vision of the changes the center needed to undertake in order to respond to new donor priorities and other external challenges.

Third, the explicit commitment of the donor community to strengthen attention to gender in research, training, and staffing provided a powerful incentive for CIMMYT to address gender staffing. The CGIAR Gender Program provided partial funding to support the work, technical assistance, and visibility and recognition for CIMMYT's efforts within the consortium. The availability of external funding made it less risky for managers to take on the initiative; and the external support and recognition helped managers and staff to sustain their efforts even when the change process was challenging.

Finally, the first consultancy on parity in salary and position classifications found anomalies and inconsistencies for both men and women. This helped to dispel the notion that work on gender was targeted only at improving conditions for women, perhaps even at the expense of men. As a result of this consultancy, some of the major discrepancies in salaries were corrected, and the center initiated a process, with strong participation from staff, for developing a more systematic and transparent system of position classifications and criteria for promotions.

The outcome was very interesting from a gender perspective. The new system resulted in 40 percent of the internationally recruited women being reclassified at higher levels compared to only 8 percent of the men.[15] This outcome helped to make the case in the center that working on gender is more than simply increasing numbers of women; it requires changes in core management systems and work practices.

Constraining Conditions

CIMMYT has had a long history of low female representation in the professional ranks, and only one woman in a senior management position. Moreover, the previous leadership was reluctant to consider gender-equity as a legitimate organizational issue; therefore, there was a legacy of resistance to such issues. Despite explicit commitment from the two most senior managers, there were initially no other champions for the work among senior management. The fact that the one female senior manager lost her job in a downsizing at the beginning of the change effort created skepticism regarding the depth of management's commitment to gender equity.

Funding pressures and downsizing also created a challenging environment for undertaking significant organizational change. Although such initiatives disrupted the status quo and opened up "organizational space" to think about new ways of working, they also made many staff feel vulnerable, overburdened with work, and hesitant to take on uncertainty.

Finally, although it was strategically advantageous that the new Director General had aligned the gender initiative with his own change agenda, it also created a situation in which many parallel change efforts were moving ahead, creating additional time and work pressures.

PROJECT DESIGN AND METHOD

The action-research team was initially composed of three members, women who represented diverse disciplines and areas of expertise.[16] It included the leader of the CGIAR Gender Program, an anthropologist who had previously worked as a researcher in another CGIAR center; a professor of organizational behavior with expertise in gender and organizational change; and a manager/consultant who had served as a Director of Finance and Administration in another CGIAR center. The team was joined, during the implementation phase, by an organizational-change specialist. The research team worked most directly with the CIMMYT senior-management team and the Gender Task Force. (Later in the process, the Change Catalyst Committee (CCC) was established to move the desired organizational changes forward.) Funding for the change effort, provided jointly by CIMMYT and the CGIAR Gender Program, is estimated at about US$160,000, excluding CIMMYT staff time.

The action-research team was based in the United States and able to visit CIMMYT only periodically (initially every two to three months). Therefore, the internal collaborators had to carry the process forward in the team's absence and to keep the team informed of important developments. (This arrangement made it more difficult to sustain momentum for change, as we discuss below.)

Several key principles shaped the approach and method of the project. First, we wanted the project to model the values the team held to be intrinsic to a gender-equitable work environment. Therefore, the project was to include diverse groups within the organization and to foster wide participation of staff in the change process; to share information widely and openly; to foster collaborative working within the team and with the organization; and to operate non-hierarchically. We believed that reinforcing the substance of our analysis and feedback with our own behavior would strengthen the initiative considerably.

Of these values, fostering a collaborative mode of working, whereby the action-researchers, as external change agents, and CIMMYT staff, as internal change agents, could interact as co-learners, was the most difficult to achieve. Perhaps because this mode of working is at odds with traditional consultancy models, in which outside experts are hired to assess the problem, generate recommendations, and oversee a predetermined implementation process, our efforts at co-creating the initiative often floundered. Interestingly, it was not only CIMMYT staff who fell back on traditional, more directive modes of working when things got tough. Often, both in our workings as a team and in our interactions with CIMMYT members, we found ourselves falling short of our own collaborative model in order to "save time" or to "make things simpler." Of course, compromising the collaborative process did neither; but the experience did help us to appreciate the complexity of enacting—rather than simply advocating—a model of fluid expertise. Despite some of these difficulties, our orientation toward collaborative principles led us to be very explicit and consistent in sharing information with our organizational partners. Each of the major phases of work was documented in terms of method and content, and a summary was shared with the senior-management team and the Gender Task Force.

The project was designed to have six phases: set-up, for negotiating and building the basis for collaboration; mutual inquiry and data collection; data analysis; feedback and brainstorming; experimentation and implementation; and monitoring and adapting. It should be noted, however, that these phases do not unfold in a linear fashion. They overlap and are iterative: for example, inquiry and data collection continue throughout the change process; observations are fed back to staff and managers on an ongoing basis.

The first four phases of the project, from entry to feedback, took approximately six months. The last two phases—experimentation and implementation, and monitoring change—have been going on for eighteen months and continue.

Phase One: Set-up

The set-up visit had two primary objectives: to work directly with people on site to finalize the project design and ensure that it was truly collaborative; and to foster a deeper understanding of our dual-agenda approach to organizational change. Organizational effectiveness and gender are not commonly linked in organizations; therefore, it is important to give people an opportunity to think about these ideas before the general interviewing begins. The leader of the action-research team gave a seminar on the approach and carried out exploratory interviews. Thereafter, a briefing note on the project was circulated to all staff and the project plan was reported in CIMMYT's weekly newsletter.

The leader also worked with the Gender Task Force and senior-management team; an interview plan and random sampling method were developed collaboratively with the GTF. The random selection of sampling of interviewees was important to ensure that a broad range of views was sought, and that findings were not perceived to be biased in favor of any particular group within the organization. As a result of these discussions, several changes to the inquiry process were made; the interview guide would be sent by electronic mail to international staff posted in other countries; a number of group interviews organized by work team would be held; and a small number of spouses would be interviewed in order to generate deeper understanding of the way the CIMMYT work environment affects and, in turn, is affected by family life.

There was considerable discussion about whether the project should focus on international staff exclusively or should include all CIMMYT staff. On one hand, it made sense to focus only on international staff, as this was the mandate of the CGIAR Gender Program and the research team did not have strong Spanish-language skills. Moreover, international and national staff are subject to different policies and conditions of work, and several human-resources initiatives were underway to address national staff issues. On the other hand, it would be difficult to understand the gendered dimensions of work culture, systems, and everyday work-practice norms without soliciting the views of all those in the workplace environment. An uneasy compromise—which led to important findings about the impossibility of separating gender from other dimensions of systemic power, such as race and class—was reached: the project would concentrate on international staff and be a pilot project; subsequently, a project using a comparable methodology, and building on findings of the pilot study would be carried out with the national staff. For the pilot project, however, a small sample of national staff working in research would be interviewed so that a more accurate picture of the current work environment and practices could emerge.

Phase Two: Inquiry

The action-research team developed an interview guide based on data from the set-up visit, our conceptual framework for understanding gendered dimensions of the workplace, and the findings of sociological research on career obstacles for women in science.[17] In line with the dual-agenda approach, questions were designed to elicit not only the respondent's view of the driving forces in the CIMMYT work culture but also a sense of the strategic issues facing the center. The open-ended questions were organized into several critical themes: the organization of work and work practices; visible and invisible work; the use and management of time, and the interface of work- and personal-life responsibilities; organizational culture (norms, values, and accepted or privileged behaviors); criteria for success, performance-appraisal systems, rewards and sanctions; decision-making processes; communications systems; internal collaboration; processes of inclusion and exclusion; leadership and management styles; and vision and strategic directions.

The team spent eight days on site for data collection. One-hour interviews were carried out with fifty-eight staff members (sixteen women and forty-two men) and seven spouses (six women and one man). In addition, five focus groups were held with work teams. The vast majority of interviewees participated actively and openly, and the interviews yielded very rich data and insights. As noted earlier, the action-research team holds these interviews to be an important intervention in the system, creating an opportunity for people to reflect on current conditions, to discuss gender as an organizational dynamic, and to envision possibilities for change. The input from spouses was very helpful for understanding tensions around work-family balance as well as the larger social context affecting CIMMYT and its workers.

Phase Three: Analysis

Preliminary Analysis   Given the collaborative nature of the project, the action-research team felt it was important, during the initial visit, to feed back to key groups within the CIMMYT community their first impressions emerging from the interviews. In doing so, the team had three objectives. They wanted to do a "reality check" to make sure that we were moving in the right direction in interpreting the data. As well, the team wanted to get the views of staff and managers on the key themes in order to enrich our understanding of the issues. And they wanted to seed some ideas as a stimulus for further reflection and, possibly, change, as they would not be returning for three months, at which time we would provide the formal feedback.

The preliminary findings were discussed with the Gender Task Force, the National Staff Committee, the ad hoc committee of internationally recruited women, and the senior management team. Their response to the emerging themes and ideas was helpful, not only in deepening the team's understanding of the organization but also in furthering the goals of the intervention. In general, they felt that the themes presented had captured critical dilemmas within the CIMMYT work culture. The discussions gave people an opportunity to find new ways of looking at old and tenacious problems, and inspired some to commit around particular themes, and to resolve to "do something" immediately.

To ensure that as many staff members as possible were informed and included in this preparation phase, a short article summarizing the data-collection process, some preliminary observations, and plans for the next phase were included in CIMMYT's weekly newsletter. These channels of feeding back preliminary findings helped prepare the ground for the subsequent feedback of the team's more in-depth analysis.

In-depth Dual-Agenda Analysis   Off-site the action-research team prepared a more in-depth and interpretative analysis of the data. It is in this indepth analysis that the salient features of this approach to gender-equity become apparent. Although the data analysis process was intensely iterative, it can be thought of as having six steps: understanding the current work environment, that is, the mental models that drive behavior, and the historical context in which these mental models have formed; identifying the organization's strategic objectives and the challenges it faces; surfacing "disconnects" between the current environment and future challenges; identifying the gender implications of these disconnects; selecting those mental models related to the disconnects with the strongest implications for gender equity and organizational effectiveness; and identifying leverage points related to the mental models that could have significant positive outcomes for both equity and effectiveness.

Once the data analysis was complete, the feedback presentation was designed in three major sections. The introduction, which we called "holding up the mirror," gave a general sense of the CIMMYT work culture. Its intention was to feed back to the organization—in its own words—themes and patterns emerging from the interviews: what it feels like to work in the organization; the norms of behavior expressed; and what challenges people feel the organization is facing.

The second section presented the dual-agenda analysis of the data. This included an overview of the concept of mental models, and a description of those CIMMYT mental models that we felt had the strongest implications for gender equity and organizational effectiveness. In order to give a balanced representation of the analysis, we highlighted the positive role these mental models were playing in the current environment as well as their unintended consequences for each element of the dual agenda. Therefore, each mental model was described behaviorally, using phrases, images, and stories that suggested its positive and less positive aspects. Then the unintended consequences of the mental model for both equity and effectiveness were described.

The final section of the presentation focussed on action, identifying possible leverage points for change and outlining the process by which the community would discuss, brainstorm, and determine next steps. A summary of the analysis is offered below as an illustration of the approach.

Summary and Analysis of Findings   *Holding up the Mirror:* A central image in the "mirror" for CIMMYT was an organization that had inspired pride, commitment, and loyalty among its staff. Reflecting on the days of the Green

Revolution, staff talked of sacrifice and selfless devotion, of the mission of the organization taking priority over everything else, including family and personal life. This legacy was an important part of CIMMYT's history and culture. Even newcomers could tell stories of notable scientists from this era—and it appeared that this history continued to exert a strong influence on the CIMMYT's work culture and values.

Somewhat at odds with this image, staff also talked of work norms and a work environment that often felt "uncoordinated," "fragmented," and "ad hoc." Staff spoke of an ever-expanding agenda: things were continuously added, but nothing was taken away, even in an environment of shrinking resources. Many also described CIMMYT as a place in which, despite an emphasis on teamwork, individuals were given considerable—and sometimes too much—autonomy and independence. In this context, people often spoke of a desire to knit people and programs more closely, to reduce competition and "kingdom building," and to create systems that would foster collaboration.

While many staff were optimistic about CIMMYT's future—particularly about the renewed sense of mission and vitality brought by the new Director General—there was also a note of anxiety: things were moving too fast. People feared that the new directions at CIMMYT would simply add to existing work rather than refocus or strategically prioritize an already overcrowded agenda.

It was clear from the interviews that the external environment affecting CIMMYT had changed dramatically in recent years: a significant decline in funding, an increase in the breadth and complexity of the research agenda of the CGIAR, and a changing model of research within the CGIAR System based on collaboration and partnering with national research organizations and advanced research institutes rather than the former model of autonomous initiatives.

Finally, a change in demographics—in terms of diversity and life situation—was affecting the pool of professionals from which CIMMYT recruited. Increased numbers of women in fields relevant to CIMMYT's research and an expanding supply of scientists from developing countries, as well as the growth in dual-career families, had led to changes in family lifestyles around the world. CIMMYT would therefore increasingly have to work with a more diverse staff with different sets of skills, values, and work styles, not to mention personal responsibilities.

The action researchers argued that these forces had converged in recent years, creating a disconnect between what CIMMYT was trying to do and how it was organized to do it. This was making it difficult for CIMMYT to respond and adapt flexibly to the challenges it was facing.

Mental Models: Building on the concept of the dual agenda and the theme of CIMMYT in transition, we identified four mental models that we believed had significant implications both for CIMMYT's ability to create a gender-equitable work environment and for its ability to reposition itself successfully in its new environment (see Table 4–1, page 123).

The first mental model—*Reliance on a Unifying and Compelling Mission*—was rooted in the legacy of CIMMYT's original mission. CIMMYT was created in response to a widely acknowledged global crisis in food production. In the early days, a powerful sense of urgency drove its work, and there was strong external validation of its importance. The problem was clear; the goal was feeding hungry people. The product—improved germ plasm—was well defined and tangible. In recent years this unifying and compelling force in the CIMMYT community had become diffuse, embracing such abstract concepts as food security and sustainable agriculture. The problems it needed to address were more complex, the urgency tempered. The outside validation was more nuanced, and the impact was, in some respects, less immediate and tangible. Yet, CIMMYT continued to operate as if its unifying mission charted its course, integrated programs, framed decision-making, and motivated staff.

The absence of this unifying mission created tensions and missed opportunities. In the past, the mission had obviated the need for strategic focus, and had provided incentives and a framework for collaboration. The more complex mission did not provide this framework; yet the mental model of a unifying mission that guided and integrated CIMMYT's work obscured the need for explicit mechanisms to determine priorities, and to support team work and collaboration.

This mental model also accounted for the way in which products were informally ranked in importance and status. While the value of germ plasm—central to the mission of the past—remained deep in CIMMYT's culture, the value of other, less visible products that are important for CIMMYT's current mission—improved methodologies, information, research support, biotechnology applications, and improved production systems—was less clear. As a result, people who worked on these products often felt undervalued.

There were several gender and organizational effectiveness implications related to this mental model. Addressing the absence of a clearly articulated strategic focus could have significant implications for research quality and efficiency. Developing explicit institutional supports to encourage and reward collaborative efforts would help encourage the teamwork recognized to be needed in complex research projects. As well, in a complex research environment in which all products were connected it was important to recognize the value of all members of the CIMMYT team.

With respect to gender equity, a clearer strategic focus would help to address time- and agenda-overload problems, and would reduce the stress felt by many staff. This had a particular bearing on staff—many women and some men—with competing responsibilities, such as families and child rearing. For these people, time was not infinitely expandable to serve an ever-growing research agenda.

Second, a more collaborative work culture, which recognized the interdependence of work and products, would bestow greater value and visibility to the work of staff who provide intermediate products, such as the output of biotechnology, economics, or pathology. This had gender implications because women tended to be clustered in these positions. In addition, many women spoke of wanting to work in a more collaborative environment, where the invisible work of providing support and enabling others would be recognized and rewarded.

The second mental model—*Belief in Individual Achievement*—had been built on beliefs about how good research is done, that fostering individual achievement was the best route to ground-breaking research. The assumption seemed to be that if CIMMYT hired the best and the brightest, gave them resources, autonomy, and latitude in defining the problems they wished to work on, and then let them alone that they would produce, and breakthroughs would happen. While some aspects of autonomy and independence were appreciated, it was a model of success that no longer fit CIMMYT's environment. While it made sense in a world that was resource rich and where the mission and product were clear and tangible; it made less sense in a resource-constrained world where problems were more complex and required diverse perspectives and collaboration.

This mental model affected the way work was done in several significant ways, and was the root of many concerns raised by staff. First, it had worked against CIMMYT, sharpening its strategic focus and setting priorities, even though staff and managers knew that it was important to do so. In this model, decisions about narrowing the agenda devolved to the individual scientist: options were kept open and new opportunities pursued because it was not clear where the breakthrough would come.

This mental model also led to a devaluation of all forms of support—as if people could be divided into those who support and those who produce. Sets of skills and forms of output not directly associated with individual achievement tended to be undervalued. Those who contributed in terms of strengthening collaborations, problem-solving, facilitating effective work processes, developing new methodologies, or managing tended to believe that their contributions were invisible. Many, at all levels, spoke of this invisibility, but those in administrative, non-scientific positions—which includes many national and female staff—felt this particularly strongly.

A third unintended consequence of this mental model is that it fostered individualized treatment and undermined efforts to create transparent policies and practices. Staff were not well informed about the distribution of benefits across levels; policies varied by program and unit. Staff at all levels perceived that everything had to be negotiated individually. While this allowed for flexibility and meeting individual needs, it also had negative consequences for the organization's diverse population: those who were less well connected or who felt outside the mainstream perceived resource decisions as ad hoc and idiosyncratic, based on favoritism rather than on systematic resource allocation that made sense for CIMMYT as a whole.

In terms of organizational performance, this mental model was affecting CIMMYT's ability to respond to its changed mission and product. The environment fostered competition and favoritism and encouraged what some called "kingdom building." Instead, what was needed was interdependence and partnership in which everyone feels important, where skills of collaboration and teamwork are rewarded, and where all contributions and products are recognized and valued.

This mental model also had implications for gender equity. Because of gender segregation in the workforce, women tended to be over-represented in formal support positions. As well, the support skills needed to collaborate, facilitate, and enable were devalued in the formal reward systems and structures, but highly valued in people's descriptions of workers they admire. Aligning the formal rewards with what was informally valued could raise the stakes on these skills. As many women felt these were the skills they brought to the workplace, revaluing these skills would have a real impact on how they felt about contributing to CIMMYT's effectiveness in this way. Finally, instituting more uniform and transparent policies, systems, and practices would help minimize bias and ensure equitable treatment of diverse staff.

The third mental model—*Default to Hierarchy*—relates to the largely unquestioned assumption, rooted in CIMMYT's past success, that hierarchy was the best way to organize. Lines of authority and decision-making were vertical, there was a strong reliance on top-down information flow, and power and influence were concentrated at the top. Core management systems—budgeting, planning, and performance reviews—were vertically organized and relied on a hierarchical cascade. Lateral lines of authority and communication were almost invisible, even though many wished they could be strengthened.

This structure apparently worked well when CIMMYT had a focussed mission and clear product. However, people had begun to recognize that top-down management was no longer working well. This played out in two ways critical for organizational performance and gender-equity—in norms about responsibility for problem-solving, and in norms about tapping local expertise.

The mental model affected beliefs about who "owns" problems and whose responsibility it is to fix them. When we asked staff for suggestions about what could be done to make CIMMYT a more effective organization, most interviewees indicated that management should take specific actions or decisions. Perhaps because they did not feel empowered or have time to make real change, staff rarely identified areas in which they could take responsibility to innovate or improve things at their own work level.

CIMMYT's vertical organizational structure also caused the frustration because of its downward information flow. This was the area in which the largest number of staff interviewed wanted to see change. Many expressed concern that management was making decisions without accessing local expertise. Scientists worried that strategic decisions on the research agenda were being made without sufficient input from the scientific community. Staff posted in other countries were frustrated that there was no way of giving input before decisions were made. Some staff characterized decision-making as ad hoc because they did not know the rationale for the decisions being made. Others felt that there was no way to give input up the hierarchy, either on strategic issues or on how the organization was run and staff managed.

The team focussed on this mental model because they believed that it had far-reaching performance and gender implications for CIMMYT. This implicit belief in "top down" as the best way to organize had created a strong sense that the people "in charge" should know more, or know better, than others. As a result, local expertise was not being accessed effectively; nor was CIMMYT taking full advantage of its staff's experience and skills.

A related concern was that because of interrupted flows of information up and down the hierarchy, decisions seemed not to be made with staff interests or concerns in mind or with a sound rationale. This had made it difficult for managers to cultivate support for critical decisions.

Moreover, hierarchical norms were breaking down outside CIMMYT, in the broader research system, where they were being replaced by skill in collaborating, partnering, and CIMMYT was bucking this trend, which caused problems in dealing with the changed external environment.

A vertical work organization had gender implications as well. Because women were less well represented at higher levels of the hierarchy, their perspectives, skills, and experience were not being accessed effectively, and their contribution to CIMMYT's overall mission was not being realized. As a result, many women felt unconnected and undervalued. However, several staff members observed that the real issue of access to influence at CIMMYT was not only one of gender but of race, class, and cultural diversity. The team believed that challenging hierarchical norms—creating ways to access the local expertise of *all* CIMMYT's workers—would enhance not only women's contribution, but that of all groups, because it would create formal opportunities for input and influence.

As the team listened to staff describe what was expected of them and what behaviors and skills were most admired at CIMMYT, a fourth mental model—that of *The Ideal CIMMYT Worker*—emerged, an image strongly rooted in CIMMYT's past. The ideal worker was instilled with missionary zeal, willing to sacrifice everything and endure hardship to get the job done. It was a model that assumed CIMMYT workers did not have competing responsibilities in private life. Another aspect of the ideal worker concerned work style. In the past, CIMMYT had prided itself on being action-oriented and hands on: good scientists spent time in the field, close to the data.

Despite some very positive aspects, this value of commitment and dedication had some unintended consequences for staff's ability to integrate work and personal life and for work structure and style.

Underlying this image of the ideal worker was the assumption that the most valuable worker is one who either has no personal life or who has someone to take care of it. From the interviews with spouses, it was clear that CIMMYT had been long subsidized by traditional families, and this situation was no longer viable. Because of demographic changes in the workforce and the increase in dual-career couples world wide, it was increasingly difficult to recruit staff with partners willing to forgo professional opportunities to take full responsibility for private life. Moreover, in many cultures, women's increasing role in the professional/public sphere was mirrored by men's increasing interest in parenting and contributing to the private sphere. Thus, it would be difficult to attract the best and brightest staff if changes were not made to allow people to integrate work and personal life more satisfactorily.

Second, this model privileged certain ways of working, and made it unlikely that new work practices would emerge. In fact, suggested changes to increase efficiency or cost effectiveness—such as delegating tasks to field personnel to reduce scientists' travel time—were met with suspicion from some members of management and research staff assuming that there was an unwillingness to make the sacrifice necessary to do things the old way.

A third issue had to do with the skills needed to succeed in the new environment of collaboration and partnership. The action researchers noted that there was evidence in the business literature that workers who focus on work *and* family—particularly caring for others—brought relational skills to the workplace[18] that were important in environments that valued collaboration, cross-functional communication, and participatory decision-making. In CIMMYT, there was a strong call for these skills and a recognition of their value. The research team argued that, in terms of organizational effectiveness, it was in CIMMYT's best interest to organize work in ways that allowed people to be involved in both work and family in order to develop these collaborative, enabling skills.

The image of the ideal worker as someone with a traditional family and stay-at-home spouse had clear gender-equity implications. First, it privileged traditional families, while women working at CIMMYT were likely to be single or in dual-earner families. Second, it is still rare to find husbands whose primary role is to care for the family. Consequently, women were at a disadvantage in this respect as well.

Leverage Points for Change: Based on the analysis, several leverage points for change were identified that could have a significant positive effect both on effectiveness and gender equity. These included initiatives that would sharpen CIMMYT's strategic focus and reduce the overcrowded agenda; foster consultation and communication, and reduce the system's reliance on overly hierarchical norms of communication and decision-making; and help people integrate work and personal life more satisfactorily.

Feedback and Identification of Change Initiatives

The feedback to the CIMMYT community was designed to encourage dialogue and broad participation by CIMMYT staff in interpreting the analysis and generating ideas for change interventions. The process was developed collaboratively with the Gender Task Force and the Director General. It had seven steps:

Consultation: Before the action-research team finalized its analysis, they consulted with the Director General and one of the Co-Chairs of the Gender Task Force about the central themes. Their input was sought on the relevance of these themes to strengthening gender-equity and organizational effectiveness to CIMMYT and its future challenges, as well as on how to present the themes to the larger CIMMYT community. This preliminary consultation helped to keep the Director General and the Gender Task Force engaged with and confident about the feedback process. Key decisions, such as having the Gender Task Force members co-facilitate the focus groups, were made together. Before the feedback visit, the Director General circulated a memo to all staff, encouraging them to participate in the week-long events and reiterating his commitment to the process.

Preview: This was followed by a preview of the analysis to the Senior Management Team and the Gender Task Force, before it was presented to the CIMMYT community. The purpose of this session was twofold. First, it gave these groups an opportunity to grapple with the analysis, ask detailed questions, and reflect on implications well before co-facilitating staff discussion groups. Second, it gave the research team an opportunity to incorporate valuable input about aspects of the analysis that were unclear or phrased in a way that would make it difficult for some to staff to appreciate the main point.

The team now sees this as a critical part of the collaborative method, and believes that no general feedback session should be held until key positional and informal leaders have had a chance to grapple with the analysis in a setting that fosters free exchange and open dialogue. In retrospect, more time should have been given to this phase of the feedback.

Plenary to feedback analysis: The following day, the team presented its analysis in a plenary session open to all staff and spouses. This, and subsequent plenary sessions, were videotaped for staff out-posted in other countries. Simultaneous Spanish translation was provided for the benefit of national staff. However, in what proved to be a telling oversight, national staff was not informed of the session until the day before the event. As a result, the session was well attended by international staff, but by only few national staff.

The Director General played an extremely important role in this session. He linked the work on gender to his larger change agenda, underscoring the strategic importance of the work. His visible support gave the work credibility and legitimacy, countered staff's concerns that nothing tangible would result from this effort, and created a safe environment, which led to open and creative discussions in the working groups that followed.

During the general discussion at the end of the presentation, an informal leader of national staff forcefully asserted his view that the analysis had missed an important mental model underlying the CIMMYT work culture—that national staff were different from and inferior to international staff and should be treated differently. There was no official response to his comment, either by management or the research team. Nonetheless, the nonverbal response of those attending the session indicated general agreement. In hindsight, the implications of this critical event were felt throughout the project.

Focus groups to discuss analysis: Small focus groups to discuss the analysis were held immediately after the plenary. These groups were organized by work units and facilitated by members of the Gender Task Force, so staff could respond to the analysis, discuss its applicability, and brainstorm possible changes that could be made at the Program or Unit level to address the issues. About eighty staff, primarily international, participated. The discussion groups were effective in getting staff to react to the mental models and think through their consequences for work practice and behaviors.

Working groups on leverage points: Working groups were held during the two days following the plenary to brainstorm pilot projects that would meet the dual agenda. They were organized thematically, by the leverage points for change identified in the analysis, and were co-facilitated by the research team and members of the Gender Task Force.

Given the issue of the different treatment of national and international staff, an additional group was created to explore this issue. The themes included: sharpening CIMMYT's strategic focus; strengthening communication and consultation within CIMMYT; enhancing recognition of CIMMYT's diverse products/outputs; strengthening collaboration; balancing responsibilities and satisfaction of work and personal life; promoting a greater sense of equity and fairness in policies and practices; reducing staff's overcrowded agendas and time pressures; and narrowing the gap between international and national staff.

A working group of spouses was also convened to explore the work/family leverage point from the family perspective. The connections between these leverage points and the mental models is summarized in Table 4–1.

The purpose of the groups was to develop ideas for concrete action steps and/or organizational experiments that affect the dual agenda. Action steps were defined as concrete changes that could be introduced quickly with limited resource implications. Organizational experiments were defined as more significant changes that would be piloted on a small scale, monitored and assessed, adapted, and then, if effective, diffused more widely.

The brainstorming unleashed tremendous energy and creativity. The underlying cynicism that nothing would change was dissipated and staff worked together to generate some very innovative proposals. The expectation was that these discussions would catalyze spontaneous innovations by individuals and work groups that would complement the more formal change efforts to be carried out at the organizational level. The working groups generated proposals for twenty-one action steps and thirty-six organizational experiments.

Plenary on leverage points: A plenary session, open to all staff and spouses, was held at which the working groups, including that of spouses, presented their proposals for changes to the CIMMYT community. Attendance and interest were strong, with about ninety staff participating, including good representation from national staff.

Brief descriptions of the experiments and action steps had been prepared and were posted by theme on the walls of the auditorium. Each person at the meeting was invited to indicate the four action steps or experiments of highest personal interest. The seven experiments that received the most staff interest also met the criteria of advancing the dual agenda.

This session, which had not been part of the original plan but had been suggested by the Gender Task Force, proved very effective. Not only did it cement staff's ownership of the ideas for change, but it also ensured that all staff shared the same information about the outcomes of the process. It also helped to distribute responsibility for implementation more broadly among staff, challenging the norm of default to hierarchy, and afforded an opportunity for natural, informal leaders to emerge.

Interested staff were then invited to volunteer for a Change Catalyst Committee that the Director General was forming to ensure that the ideas generated were moved forward and translated into real change.

Wrap up: The process was completed by a wrap-up session with the Director General, the Senior Management Team, the Gender Task Force, and the newly created Change Catalyst Committee (CCC) to review the feedback process, elicit reactions, and clarify roles and responsibilities for follow-up action. Participants were generally very positive about the process and the quality of the ideas generated. The principal concern was that the change process would be overwhelmed by other priorities, and the excitement would dissipate, leaving people discouraged.

The action-research team also met informally with women professionals to get their reactions to the analysis and the output of the working groups. The goal was to begin to build an internal constituency among the main beneficiaries of this effort, one that understood the dual agenda and would be motivated to keep the gender dimension of the initiatives in place as the action steps and experiments were implemented.

Observations　　Staff were cynical about the feedback process before it began, as many previous change efforts had not seemed to yield results. Their cynicism also related to the gender focus, the perception by some that the project had exceeded its mandate, the three months between inquiry and feedback, and the fact that many issues were old news.

However, the concept of mental models proved a powerful antidote to this frame of mind. In exploring mental models it became clear that the forces driving the old problems were deeply rooted in tacit assumptions about work, and that there was a link between many of these old problems and gender. Momentum began to build after the presentation to all staff. The tide changed with the working groups organized by programs and units, in which people talked about the implications of the findings in their own area.

By the end of the process, most staff were energized, enthusiastic, and optimistic about the possibilities for constructive change.

Experiments

During the feedback week, the Change Catalyst Committee was formed, with the responsibility of moving the ideas generated by the focus groups into action. Staff who were interested in working on implementing change were asked to volunteer to serve on the Committee. Some members of the Gender Task Force signed on to the CCC. Its initial task was to screen the proposals for action steps and experiments, develop an agenda for change, and take the steps necessary to refine the experiments and to engage groups in implementing them.

Five criteria were used to select experiments: the degree to which the experiment addressed the dual agenda and underlying mental models; the degree of interest and enthusiasm of staff as indicated by their choices in the final plenary session; the potential number of people affected; the likelihood of success, including the presence of a champion to see the experiment through; and considerations of time, money, and human resources.

The CCC eventually recommended six organizational experiments. In five of the six cases, at least forty percent of the staff members who chose these as priorities during the feedback session were female.

Experiment One: Building Staff Involvement into the Design and Implementation of the New Project Structure　　At the time of the feedback, CIMMYT was instituting a new system of mega-projects for organizing research and related program activities, as part of its new five-year plan. Mega-projects were to overlay the current system to encourage cross-program collaboration and to sharpen the organization's strategic focus. This proposed re-organization into projects was a significant departure from traditional organizing by programs.

The shift to mega-projects had come up frequently in the interviews; there were many questions and concerns about how it would work and affect research leadership, current reporting relationships, and resource allocation.

The experiment consisted of developing a new model of staff participation on the task force designing the new mega-project system and in decisions regarding both the content of the mega-projects and how they would be implemented. The experiment was designed to "tap local expertise" and challenge traditional practices based on the mental model of "default to hierarchy." The experiment ensured that not only senior managers but also diverse men and women from different levels in the organization would be involved in the task force. As well, broad consultation and staff views and input would be included throughout the process.

The process, which was supported by the CCC and implemented by the Mega-Project Task Force, did result in increased participation by women scientists on the task force and in broader involvement of staff in the design of the mega-project system set-up. In fact, the model was carried over to gather input about the staffing and leadership of the projects themselves. While this experiment was bounded in time, it modeled new ways of working and consulting within CIMMYT and was generally considered a success by staff and management. Equally important, the product of this process—CIMMYT's five-year plan based on the mega-projects—has been praised for its high quality both within CIMMYT and by an external review team of eminent scientists and research managers.[19]

Experiment Two: Strengthening Communications between the Senior Management Team and Staff   This experiment was also designed to challenge the mental model of default to hierarchy. It was intended to address limited communication up and down the hierarchy, concentration of decision-making and authority at the top, and limited use of "local expertise" on critical issues. (See Table 4–1 on page 123.)

The experiment had several components: circulating in advance the agenda for the regular meeting of the senior management team, called the Management Advisory Committee (MAC), so staff would know what topics the MAC was addressing and could bring issues or information to the attention of their supervisors before the meeting. It also reinstated the norm of

Program Directors holding regular meetings with staff to report on the outcomes of MAC meetings and to solicit feedback. In addition, the proposal added "splash back" to the standard MAC agenda. This gave managers a routine opportunity to bring staff's concerns to the attention of the senior team.

The experiment had important implications for both organizational effectiveness and gender equity. The costs of poor communication were twofold: CIMMYT was not making full use of the diversity of staff expertise and experience in problem-solving and strategic decision-making—a risky practice when managing a complex research agenda and responding to a rapidly changing environment. Second, top-down decision-making without an accompanying rationale was making it difficult for staff to support, share responsibility and act on management's decisions.

With respect to gender-equity, while many men voiced concerns about communication, the negative consequences of the hierarchical norms were greater for women, who are not well represented at the upper levels. The concentration of influence and decision-making at the top meant that women's perspectives, skills, and experience were not being tapped effectively; and their potential contribution was not being fully realized. As a result, many women felt like outsiders, which is costly for both women and an organization.[20] The experiment also had equity implications beyond gender, as many other staff, especially national staff, had expressed a similar frustration with the lack of information and inability to influence decisions.

The results of the experiment are quite dramatic. A baseline and follow-up survey one year later showed that staff perceived a significant improvement in the quality of communications. Of eleven indicators of quality of communications, staff had ranked only two average or above in the base line survey compared to five in the follow-up survey. The results were even more striking for international staff. In the baseline survey, they ranked six indicators as average or above as compared to ten in the follow-up survey. Improvements were greatest in terms of the quality and frequency of information flowing from the senior management team to staff, but feedback channels have also been strengthened.

The data suggest that this positive outcome resulted from increased efforts on the part of the senior-management team to communicate more regularly, and on the part of staff to keep informed and involved in raising issues and concerns. These changes suggest a significant decline in the extent to which communication practices are shaped by hierarchical norms.

Nonetheless, staff continue to perceive that further efforts are needed to encourage senior managers to draw systematically on staff expertise in problem-solving and decision-making. Further efforts are also needed to strengthen communications between senior management and national staff.

The survey results indicate that the introduced changes have fostered a more gender-equitable work environment. Both men and women reported significant improvements in communications, but women perceived a more dramatic change. Of the eleven indicators of quality of communications, internationally recruited women perceived a statistically significant improvement in seven; men saw a significant improvement in four. Most important, women perceive a notable and positive change in the extent to which their input is sought and the degree of comfort they feel in raising issues with their Program Leaders/Unit Heads for consideration by the senior management team.

This suggests that the experiment has served to create a more inclusive work environment and expanded opportunities for women to contribute more fully to shaping CIMMYT's research and its work environment. At the same time, the message is clear that the changes in communication practices have not benefited women alone. They have also benefited men and, arguably, CIMMYT's effectiveness as an organization.

Experiment Three: 360° Performance Appraisal Systems   Implementing a 360° or multi-source performance-appraisal system would supplement managers' input on performance with that of peers and direct reports. The goal was to interrupt the norm of default to hierarchy by giving people an opportunity to provide input on managers' and supervisors' performance. It would address the vacuum created by reliance on a unifying mission, by providing greater visibility for intermediate products and inputs. As well, by gathering input from co-workers and peers, it could address issues of individual achievement by explicitly recognizing and valuing the invisible work of support functions and collaboration. (See Table 4–1 on page 123.)

Although seemingly gender neutral, this experiment had significant potential to affect gender equity. Research indicates that multi-source performance assessment is often more gender equitable than a traditional single-source system.[21] Not only does it provide a way of lessening managerial bias against or discomfort with providing feedback to women, but it also makes visible many of the work functions that women routinely provide, both formally and informally, such as facilitation, problem prevention, support, and coordination.

While the Director General and many staff, and especially women, expressed a high level of interest in experimenting with 360° feedback both in the interviews and during the feedback meetings, it was difficult to get this experiment launched. Managers and some staff were cautious about a new approach to performance appraisal and wanted more information. More-over, the approach directly challenged deeply held assumptions and values about hierarchy and authority. To respond to these concerns, the action-research team commissioned a paper summarizing the literature on 360°,[22] gave a seminar to management and staff on the approach, and helped CIMMYT to select a method appropriate to their needs and organizational culture.

The Human Resources Management Office took over the lead in imple-menting the experiment. The CGIAR Gender Program provided matching funds so CIMMYT could hire a consultant to work with them to develop and evaluate a 360° method in four pilot units: a research unit, two program-support units (one comprising primarily Mexican staff), and the senior-man-agement team. CIMMYT's senior-management team and the action-research team felt it was important for senior managers to experience the process directly so that they could make an informed decision on how to use 360° performance assessment throughout CIMMYT.

CIMMYT elected to experiment with a 360° approach that was quantita-tive and focussed on skills and behaviors considered essential for high-qual-ity work performance. A consultant[23] provided support to the pilot groups in defining their assessment criteria and in giving and interpreting feedback. Members of the action-research team remained involved throughout to en-sure that the gender-equity aspects, such as attention to invisible work, did not get lost.

After the completion of the pilots, staff's perceptions were captured through focus groups and an assessment survey including seventy-eight re-spondents. Staff's response was very positive. Staff appreciated the objectivity of the feedback, its richness and detail, the fact that invisible work skills were highlighted, and the simplicity of the instrument. They felt it was more fair and frank than the supervisor-only approach, and that it was a more useful assessment of performance than focussing on work outputs alone. As a result of the pilot project, staff recommended that CIMMYT adopt 360° feedback as an integral part of the performance-appraisal system.

There was an interesting difference in the responses to the assessment survey of males and females who received feedback. As had been expected, women responded more favorably than men about the degree to which the objectives of 360° were met and about the quality and utility of information received.

While both groups reacted positively, women indicated more than men that they found the 360° feedback to offer a more useful assessment of performance than that provided by focussing on work outputs alone. They also agreed more strongly that 360° feedback supplements the information received from their supervisor in useful ways, and offers greater potential for fairness than the supervisor-only approach to performance appraisal. Women also agreed more strongly that the 360° feedback provided information that motivated them to improve their work performance.

Experiment Four: Strengthening Teams and Collaborative Work Practice

This experiment aimed at investing in training and coaching for several pilot-project teams to strengthen team performance and collaborative work practice. The experiment responded to staff's desire for a more explicit mechanism for team work; for more formal support for collaborative work practice; and for more recognition of team-based, rather than individual-based, models of achievement. The experiment also offered the potential to interrupt, through changes in work practice, assumptions about hierarchy. (See Table 4–1 on page 123.)

This experiment had the potential to strengthen organizational performance by providing the general skills needed to help CIMMYT move to the more collaborative mega-project system. It also had the potential to affect gender-equity by creating more explicit mechanisms to encourage team work and to recognize collaborative work practice and the products of collaboration, as well as to more effectively tap local expertise.

After a more thorough assessment of training needs, CIMMYT has undertaken a major team strengthening project. Training began with the newly appointed project leaders. The focus was on concepts and skills of leading and managing teams, and explored non-hierarchical models of leadership. Training has also been given to two pilot-project teams (one based at headquarters, one overseas). These courses focussed on skill development, but have also helped the teams to establish norms and agreements for working together as the foundation for effective team work.

The training provided to project coordinators and pilot-project teams has been very well received, and CIMMYT is exploring ways to extend it to the remaining project teams. Staff trained in pilot teams have carried their skills into interactions with other teams on which they serve, and have sparked interest in training among their colleagues. As a consequence, CIMMYT has is committed to providing team training to all members of project teams during the next year.

Experiment Five: Redefining the Division of Labor between Professional and Support Staff   This experiment was intended to challenge concepts of the ideal worker and core assumptions of work, loyalty, and commitment by redefining the roles and responsibilities of scientists and field workers to allow for more delegation. Initially, the experiment was designed to challenge norms of excessive travel: willingness to travel was seen as an informal indicator of good scientific inquiry; but it made the integration of work and personal life particularly difficult for scientists. Many, especially women with families, found the burden of travel untenable. Organizational performance would be improved by using the talents of the team more effectively, decreasing time pressure on scientists, and allowing more time for scientific reflection and writing.

However, as the experiment moved through the design phase it became loaded with many other goals, particularly that of increasing equity between international and national staff. The final objectives for the experiment were defined as improving the productivity and efficiency of CIMMYT's work teams (at one stage the experiment was referred to as the "working smarter" experiment); alleviating the overcrowded agendas of international staff; and opening opportunities for career growth for national staff.

The experiment addressed the unintended consequences of three mental models: values regarding the ideal CIMMYT worker, the belief in individual achievement, and default to hierarchy (see Table 4–1 on page 123). For the researchers, the experiment would attempt to revalue efficiency— time use and priorities (being able to give things up)—and the devaluing of long work hours and the overriding dedication to work over personal life. The change in practice could give more value to the technicians' professional contributions, recognize explicitly the value of their support role, and involve them more as partners in the work process.

The CCC was responsible for designing this experiment and identifying work groups who wanted to be involved in the pilots. Both the action-research team and the CCC invested considerable time and energy in developing the experiment and in cultivating interest among the programs. The proposal for the pilot was approved by the senior-management team and had the strong support of the Director General. Yet, after two years, the experiment has still not been implemented.

Several factors have contributed to the delay. It took several months for members of the CCC to meet with each member of the senior-management team, to explain the experiment, identify issues and concerns, and seek support for the activity. As well, two sticking points emerged related to national staff's participation in the experiment: whether they would receive a cash bonus for their extra effort, and whether participation would lead to an increase in job-category status following the experiment. (These concerns related to the mental models of not valuing support work and the gap between international and national staff.) It was finally decided that no incentive to national staff would be offered during the experiment beyond the provision of training as required, and that participants would automatically be considered for a salary-grade advance once the experiment was concluded. (This in turn affected the launch timing, as the national staff position-grading system was also being refined and had to be well along before the experiment could be started.)

A third complication arose because the team identified for the experiment was initially too busy in seasonal research activities to undertake it. When the intense period of work subsided, there was a change of Program Director, and the experiment was postponed. A further delay was due to the difficulty in finding a local consultant with not only the cross-cultural facilitation skills and ability to work within the dual-agenda framework but also the ability to liaise with the US-based action-research team. Recently, CIMMYT renewed its exploration of means to address time pressures.

It is not surprising that this experiment has been slow to implement. It has been difficult to develop a constituency for it, as it challenges some of the most deeply held assumptions about workers who are valued and work styles that lead to success. It involves changes in work practices and behaviors, rather than in management systems, depending as it does on a work group taking the initiative, rather than on the senior management team or the CCC. It addresses issues of equity in class and cultural backgrounds of international and national staff as well as gender equity. Finally, the value of the experiment in providing an opportunity to better integrate work and personal life was continually questioned. While the action-research team and the CCC have argued that addressing work-personal life balance can lead to more efficient and productive work, only a handful of staff have been willing to entertain this notion. The mental model of the ideal worker remains so powerful that it precludes the discussion of other options.

Experiment Six: Narrowing the Gap between International and National Staff   This proposal was to set up a task force of both national and international staff, to discuss gaps between the two groups, particularly differences in benefits packages. The goal was to foster greater understanding, fairness and equity. The experiment had two components: first, to develop new ways of working on potentially contentious issues by bringing together various interest groups to negotiate and develop solutions; second, to narrow the gap between the two groups.

This experiment, in its original form, also never came to fruition. A subcommittee of the CCC worked hard to design the experiment, but it became very difficult for the group to keep focussed on the process of addressing contentious issues. The strong feelings about these issues led the group to make substantive recommendations for policy changes and to press for action. In addition, differences among members of the CCC regarding the role of the committee in this area generated considerable discomfort and eventually led to a breakdown in moving the experiment forward. Once it became clear that the results were viewed as more important than experimenting with new processes, the CCC recommended that the issues be passed to the National and International Staff Committees. The work of the National Staff Committee has resulted in the implementation of several important recommendations to reduce the gap in benefits between the two groups.

Action Steps

Suggestions for twenty-three action steps were generated during the feedback session. These included creating photo boards by department, with people's names and titles labeled to make more visible those in invisible support roles; agreeing not to hold official meetings on weekends; organizing more social events for the community; and developing mechanisms to strengthen recognition of staff achievements. While no comprehensive review has taken place, many of the ideas generated have been instituted. The accomplishments of supports units, such as finance and human resources, are now recognized in the weekly newsletter, as are outstanding accomplishments of individuals from all parts of the organization. Some units have instituted new mechanisms, such as electronic white boards, to coordinate their work and improve collaboration and communications.

Role of the Change Catalyst Committee

The Change Catalyst Committee (CCC) was formed by the Director General during the feedback process. The intention was to have a group of staff to work on the change initiatives. This task was assigned to the new committee, rather than the standing Gender Task Force, in order to involve staff interested in promoting change (being "seed carriers") and to give greater

visibility to the organizational-performance aspect of the dual agenda. The
Committee was composed of people who volunteered during the feedback
week. It originally had seventeen members, representing a diverse group of
men and women and national and international staff.

The Director General appointed a senior manager to chair the Committee, providing a valuable link between the Committee and the senior-management team. Unfortunately, the senior manager, while interested in the
issue, had not been at Headquarters during the feedback week. He had not,
therefore, experienced the excitement and energy generated as staff took
on the dual agenda and began to develop proposals.

The terms of reference for the CCC were defined as:

> to support the design, implementation, evaluation, and mainstreaming of the action
> steps and experiments emerging from the Gender in the Workplace [feedback] and
> related organizational change processes. The CCC will have full autonomy to take
> decisions regarding experimentation around organizational change, and the author-
> ity to implement those decisions, except in cases where the expenditure of financial
> resources is required, in which case the consent of the [senior management team]
> will be sought.[24]

It was agreed that the CCC would: screen and prioritize the experiments,
and develop a work plan for their implementation; work with CIMMYT staff
to design and implement the experiments; support the groups doing the
experiments; act as a "learning forum" in which to reflect on the process of
organizational change, and to assess whether the experiments were bringing
about positive changes in organizational performance and creating a work
environment that fostered gender equity; monitor the experiments and rec-
ommend those experiments that should be mainstreamed; and communicate with the senior-management team and the larger CIMMYT community
regarding the organizational-change process.

The CCC began their work with a facilitated retreat to clarify their goals,
objectives, terms of reference, and modes of working together. Initially, there
was a lot of excitement and energy, as this group really felt empowered to
enact change. They met regularly in the beginning, set priorities among the
experiments, and formed sub-committees to develop plans for each proposed
experiment. The action-research team provided a set of guidelines for screen-
ing proposals to help ensure that the experiments responded to the dual agenda
and reduced the unintended negative consequences of the mental models.

The CCC had success in influencing the consultation process around the mega-projects and in getting the management-staff communications experiment up and running. The other experiments, which involved more substantive changes, proved more difficult. The scope and complexity of the proposed change raised questions, both among the members of the CCC and among other staff and managers, about the authority of the CCC and its appropriateness to lead change in areas many considered to be the domain of the management team.

As the workload became heavier and the change agenda more daunting and cumbersome, the members began to question their status as volunteers. After one year, they requested that the time invested in the CCC be formally recognized in their work plans and performance appraisals. Their proposal was not accepted by several senior managers, who argued that staff time should not be siphoned off for work that managers were paid to do. This discussion led to a re-evaluation of the role of the CCC.

Eventually, the senior-management team decided to recast the CCC as a catalytic and monitoring group, and to take on more responsibility for implementation themselves. In consultation with the action-research team, the senior-management team decided to focus on three key leverage points for advancing the dual agenda: team strengthening, 360° performance appraisal, and division of labor. Members of the management team were assigned the responsibility of implementing the first two experiments; the CCC was asked to continue to work on the third. When that experiment stalled, the CCC's role began to diminish. Eventually the CCC was disbanded; the locus for change now resides with the management team. The Co-Chair of the CCC, who was not on the senior-management team, was given explicit responsibility for keeping attention on the goal of gender-equity and for monitoring progress.

MONITORING

Monitoring the impact of the interventions has been an integral part of the dual-agenda work. To date, it has been largely qualitative, focussing on staff and managers' perceptions of impact.

Taking Stock: One Year Later

One year after the project had begun, the action-research team returned to CIMMYT to take stock of progress. The team, which included one new member, interviewed approximately thirty staff and managers, most of whom had been interviewed in the initial inquiry process. Again, interviewees were selected to reflect diversity of gender, cultural background, occupational position, and program affiliation: 80 percent of the interviewees were internationally recruited staff; 20 percent were nationally recruited staff.

In addition to their general perceptions of change, interviewees were asked whether they thought that the situation of women within CIMMYT had improved. The team synthesized the key findings and fed these back to the senior-management team and then to the Change Catalyst Committee. Subsequently, a report was circulated to all staff and a summary published in the weekly newsletter.

The action-research team concluded that solid if modest progress was being made towards advancing the dual agenda. A significant majority of the women felt that the work environment was more hospitable, making it easier for women as well as men to succeed and contribute. Equally important, men were not experiencing negative repercussions from the efforts aimed at strengthening gender equity. The team was also encouraged to learn that the broad, inclusive feedback process had catalyzed many changes in work practices and behaviors not directly related to specific organizational-change experiments.

With respect to the priorities established the previous year, progress was perceived as variable. Staff felt that significant progress had been made in communication and consultation. Information was flowing more regularly up and down the hierarchy, and staff were being consulted on most major decisions. They also indicated that good progress was being made in increasing equity and fairness, particularly with respect to the perceived gap between national and international staff: people cited several achievements of the national staff committee and the Human Resources Department. More generally, many people—particularly women and national staff—commented that the atmosphere was much more open, and that they could now raise issues without fear of retribution.

It appeared that modest progress was being made with respect to collaboration. (The team-strengthening project had not yet started.) The process of staff participation in the new mega-projects was viewed positively, as were the mega-projects themselves. People felt that staff was taking more initiative to develop collaborative activities, but that enhanced skills and more formal arrangements were still needed. Some staff observed that the focus on collaborative and non-hierarchical ways of working had stimulated CIMMYT managers and staff to work in a more equitable manner in their partnerships with national agricultural-research systems.

It was felt that modest progress had been made in recognizing diverse products/outputs. Although awareness had increased, and the concept of invisible work was now recognized, it was felt that intermediate products, such as new methods and techniques, were still not valued as highly as final products, such as germ plasm.

Least progress was perceived to have been made on issues of time. People remained concerned about issues of strategic focus and the overcrowded agenda, noting that it was still very difficult to prioritize their responsibilities.

With respect to work/personal life integration, they did not feel any progress had been made. On the contrary, there was a sense that stress and time pressures had actually increased during the past year because of CIMMYT's slower than expected financial recovery. The concept of the ideal CIMMYT worker as someone who is hands on and ready to sacrifice everything for the job was still driving expectations and behaviors.

On the whole, however, the results of the stock-taking exercise were promising. Considerable change had occurred after one year, and continuing change was expected with the launching of the projects on 360° performance assessment and team strengthening. The central concerns were the aggravated time shortage and that the need to improve work/personal life integration seemed to have fallen by the wayside.

The team's assessment was that the factors creating the time famine at CIMMYT run deep in its organizational culture and were being aggravated by the financial pressures. Staff and managers seemed to have accepted the acute time pressures as a way of life and were resistant to thinking that addressing these issues might result in creative solutions for reducing time pressures.

Taking Stock: Two Years Later

Two years after the project launch, a second stock-taking was carried out as part of a CGIAR-wide comparative analysis of progress on gender staffing. A detailed questionnaire on indicators of gender equity in the workplace was distributed to the senior-management committee, the national staff committee, all internationally recruited female staff, and selected internationally recruited male staff. Forty replies were received, representing all members of the first three focus groups. Due to short lead time, only one response was received from an internationally recruited male staff member. Focus groups were held with the first three groups to feed back the survey data and elicit further information and interpretation of the data.

The general finding was that while progress had continued, more work remained. It was clear to many respondents that as successes are achieved, expectations are raised; therefore, the organization must strive for even greater improvement. As one female scientist put it:

There has been tremendous improvement in formal systems and in leadership and management [commitment]. The corpus of CIMMYT, however, and the informal practices and knowledge base will take longer to change. This is exacerbated by the pressures we now face to do research and get money, plus try to cope with organizational change. The number of women across teams and levels is still very small.

In general, management and the international female staff felt that good progress had been made in improving the transparency and gender neutrality of formal systems of recruitment, position classification, and advancement. This feedback underscored the value to staff of a major human-resources effort to restructure and clarify formal practices. As they work under a separate position-classification structure, however, national staff were less satisfied with the fairness of the system, and were still concerned about the different treatment of international and national staff.

As suggested by the data on the staff-management communications experiment, all respondents felt that there was improved communication throughout the organization, and that management was working hard to improve the overall workplace environment. Again, however, national staff felt they had benefited less from this initiative than had international staff. It was also interesting to note that the senior-management group consistently rated higher the extent to which CIMMYT met the key indicators of gender equity than did either the internationally recruited women or the national staff committee.

The most positive feedback from the international women dealt with the good quality of interaction in the recent planning meetings of the new project teams. Several of the women, especially the more junior women, noted that these meetings had offered an opportunity for open dialogue on scientific issues with colleagues from other disciplines, programs and postings, including non-HQ staff. They observed that the new team structure, at its best, seemed to be breaking down hierarchy and favoring genuine collaboration and "tapping of local expertise." This was seen as an important cultural change.

However, several areas were identified as needing continued attention. Foremost among them were: increasing the number of women in middle- and upper-management positions, and distributing them better across functions; improving opportunities for spouse employment; and strengthening management skills through staff training in such areas as conducting recruitment interviews and performance assessments, and managing diverse staff. As in the previous year, the issue of time pressures and the ability to balance responsibilities in work and personal life remained the overriding concern.

Discussion with the senior-management team on this point during the focus group was interesting. On several previous occasions, the overcrowded agenda was brought up in senior-management meetings and dismissed as simply being "the way of life at CIMMYT," that is, it was a problem of individuals not of the system. When the survey data was mirrored back to the senior-management team, indicating the widely held view that this was a systemic problem, the tone of the discussion changed. When it was suggested that it would be useful for staff to brainstorm ideas to counter the time pressure, management seemed almost relieved—as if the default-to-hierarchy reflex had been overcome and a shared approach to problem-solving became possible. There is now new momentum and commitment in CIMMYT to tackle this tenacious problem.

REFLECTIONS AND LESSONS LEARNED

The CIMMYT initiative on gender and organizational change is still very much a work in progress. After only two and a half years, much of the change is nascent and gains are fragile. Nevertheless, it has generated a wealth of lessons and insights both in terms of how organizations are gendered and how gendered norms, structures, and process are sustained and reproduced; and in terms of approaches and methods for organizational change aimed at gender equity. Key lessons for practitioners that we, as action researchers and as an internal change agent, have drawn from this case are summarized below.

Gender in Organizations

The Dual Agenda and Holding on to Gender   Considerable emphasis was given in the CIMMYT change process to the dual agenda. A major improvement in the methodology was the explicit connections drawn between the mental models and their unintended consequences for both gender equity and organizational performance. Yet, our experience, as in similar efforts, suggests that it is very difficult for staff and managers to hold on to the connection.[25] Given their experience of these things as adversarial or zero sum, it is counter-intuitive. Thus, it is reasonable to assume that organizational-effectiveness concerns will tend to eclipse gender-equity concerns. Using the dual-agenda approach appears to be a double-edged sword. It creates a broad constituency for working on organizational change by removing gender from an equity frame, which many interpret as women gaining at the expense of men. Placing it in an effectiveness and efficiency frame legitimates it in the organization. Indeed, it is unlikely that the action-research team would have been invited to work with CIMMYT if we had not used the dual-agenda approach.

However, it also makes gender vulnerable to being overshadowed by organizational-performance objectives. We saw this happen, for example in the division-of-labor experiment. Managers were quite willing to entertain the organizational-performance hypothesis that productivity could be increased by delegating more to national staff and enriching their jobs. They were much less inclined to accept the gender-equity hypothesis that staff could find creative solutions to the time famine if work- and personal-life integration was at the center of the search for solutions. Consistently, the gender-equity dimension of this experiment were perceived as an issue for individuals, and was overshadowed by the organizational-efficiency dimension, which was seen as systemic.

We observed some of the gender dimensions getting lost during implementation of other experiments, as well. For example, while 360° performance-assessment appraisals were clearly a challenge to masculine norms of hierarchy and authority, they could be implemented in ways that could maximize or minimize the impact on gender equity. A standard 360° assessment would likely result in at least the same reduction in gender bias as has been noted in the literature.[26] However, if the criteria for evaluation included the specific areas of concern expressed by women at CIMMYT—invisible work, problem prevention, acting in ways that are best for the organization rather than for one's career—it would likely have a considerably greater effect.

The action-research team, therefore, helped to ensure that the connection between these criteria and gender equity was being held by at least some members of the work group. One of the team interviewed a number of women involved in the criteria-selection process. During the interviews, staff were reminded of their comments at the analysis stage and of why the 360° experiment had come out of the gender project. This proved quite successful, and the final instrument includes those criteria most related to gender equity.

This experience convinced us that, even with a strong internal liaison group, we must continually put time and effort into developing an internal constituency who can hold onto gender during implementation. Being able to tell the gender story is key to the long-term success and continuation of the change process.

In conclusion, we have learned that making the connection between gender equity and effectiveness is not a one-step process. Any intervention with a dual agenda can be implemented in ways that have greater or lesser effects on gender equity. Thus, an important step in the analysis is to identify those factors with the greatest potential impact and to plan how to keep them front and center. It is a mistake to think that simply designing the intervention and getting agreement on its implementation will ensure that it is implemented in a way that best achieves equity goals. Thus, in future endeavors, we will allot more resources to the implementation phase, with the specific goal of building an internal constituency to hold on to this connection.

Linking Gender and Broader Equity Issues   The focus on gender equity opened the door and gave legitimacy to talking about other dimensions of equity—race, class, and nationality. At CIMMYT these issues come together in the division between national and international staff, and run deep in the culture. In many respects the interests of the national staff commanded more attention than the call for gender equity. It might appear that this would create an alliance of interests, but it did not. In fact, although we were aware of the issue and had tried to address it during the set-up phase, we were unprepared for its effect on the project.

For example, during the feedback session, when a national-staff member declared that the gap between international and national staff was an additional mental model, it was simply added to the analysis and a group created to discuss it. However, it was not subjected to the same level of analysis as were the other mental models, and its consequences for the organization were not delineated. Thus, it did not fit the dual-agenda model of the other experiments. In fact, the constituency concerned about class equity experienced it, quite passionately, as a single-agenda, moral issue of fairness.

This created problems for our project, as the moral injustice of gender discrimination was much less salient than that of class discrimination, as manifest in the division of national and international staff; as well, class discrimination had not been an explicit part of the analysis or of any of the stated motivations for undertaking the change project.

What we learned in this project is that raising one aspect of equity naturally raises others. This does not create a natural alliance, but creates an opportunity for a planned alliance. Had we, for example, thought about the dual agenda of race and organizational effectiveness and included this in our analysis, such an alliance might have developed. Alternatively, had we been more forthright about the differences in the two approaches we might have called for a comparable analysis. Instead, the issues were conflated in ways that undermined the goals of both initiatives.

For example, issues of class discrimination came to overshadow dual-agenda concerns in both the division-of-labor and closing-the-gap experiments. In some respects, this stalled the experiments, as they became associated with one interest group. Allies willing to work on both gender- and class-equity issues, distanced themselves from the experiments that came to be seen as calling for a level of change that many staff did not feel they had the authority to take on.

We have few answers to the dilemmas this issue raised for the work at CIMMYT, but believe it is deserving of more attention. We are now undertaking work to develop frameworks and methods for better understanding and working with the intersection of race, class, and gender in organizational-change efforts.

Methodology for Organizational Change

Internal Change-Agent Groups   In designing this collaborative project, the goal was to work with an intermediary group who would support the change initiatives coming out of the gender-in-the-workplace project. Given the long-term nature of any effort to challenge underlying assumptions, internal capacity was needed to carry on the process after we left the system. Hence, we concentrated our attention on supporting the work of the CCC.

This approach had some success, most notably with system-wide change efforts. As noted above, the approach worked less well with changes in work practice, which had to be implemented at the work-group level. Moreover, as outside collaborators, the action researchers needed to work directly with the work group and the responsible managers, rather than through an intermediary group.

While we all continue to think that it is important to have an internal-change group composed of staff rather than managers, we believe that it should be composed of "seed carriers"—staff involved actively in change experiments. Such a group could then become a locus for learning and sharing experiences. We also learned that is important for such a committee to be given a clear mandate, to have the strong and visible support of management, to have mechanisms of accountability to staff and management, and to have its membership formally recognized. We believe that the volunteer status of the CCC undermined its legitimacy and led both managers and members to see committee work as something to be done on members' own time, even though the issues being addressed were a high priority for CIMMYT.

Collaboration with Managers   A central lesson that we are taking away from this experience concerns the action researchers' connection with senior managers. By working with an intermediary staff group and seeking to model non-hierarchical ways of working, the research team lost contact with the senior managers critical to initiating and supporting dual-agenda change efforts. This arrangement also likely aggravated tensions with regard to power and authority between the CCC and the senior-management team. While the Director General gave the CCC authority to act to catalyze change, the CCC felt uncomfortable taking up that new authority and the other members of the senior-management team felt uncomfortable relinquishing authority. As the work of the CCC progressed, the tensions between the CCC and the senior-management team increased, largely because of the ambiguities regarding the locus of power and authority. Eventually, in our view, these tensions reduced opportunities for launching experiments because the Directors felt outside the change process.

These tensions culminated in two critical instances of the senior managers curtailing the work of the CCC. They withdrew support for the CCC as a learning forum for organizational change, saying that this was management's role; and, they denied the CCC's request that committee time be formally recognized in members' work plans and performance appraisals. Their action was based, in part, on what the managers' saw as a lack of CCC results.

These decisions precipitated the discussions between the research team and the Director General that led to the "take-stock" exercise. An important outcome of this exercise was agreement among the team, the senior-management team, and the CCC that senior managers should have more responsibility for implementing the change experiments; and that a closer working relationship needed to be developed between the research team and the senior-management team. This has had positive results, in that two managers are now clearly responsible for the 360° and team-strengthening experiments, and they are pushing these forward. However, the research team has not been able to build a strong connection and collaboration with the senior-management team and we fear that the learning function and explicit connections to gender-equity may get lost.

The change also disempowered the CCC, which struggled to find a useful role in the on-going change process and was eventually disbanded. This raises concerns as to whether the shift in structure of the collaborative relationship has unintentionally reinforced the mental model of default to hierarchy with negative consequences for gender equity. Clearly, more attention needs to be given to defining appropriate roles for change-agent groups, managers, and action-researchers in this type of collaborative action-research project.

Developing and Sustaining an Internal Constituency   An important lesson emerging from the CIMMYT experience is the importance of having an internal constituency committed to fostering gender equity. The nascent group of professional women concerned about inequity was a critical facilitator of the change process. Many were strong supporters of the initial work and contributed actively to designing change experiments. Many understood, and could articulate the mental models and their implications for gender equity.

They also appreciated the dual-agenda approach in that it provided a legitimate frame in which to raise issues connected to gender equity. It also took the spotlight off them as a source of criticism and discontent by identifying the issues as systemic, rather than individual. However, their active role in promoting change diminished once the CCC was given the formal mandate to move change forward, and the research teams' contact with them lessened.

We have learned that it is critical for an action-research team to keep direct contact with this internal constituency throughout the change process. When the team reconnected with this group during the take-stock exercise and subsequently in the launching of the 360° experiment, it became clear how important this group was to carrying the change forward. They do not want to see gender disappear; they can articulate the connections between the mental models and gender equity, and they can keep these issues alive in the everyday discourse of the organization.

Recognizing and Communicating "Small Wins"   The CIMMYT experience has underscored for us the importance of recognizing, valuing, and building on "small wins" in the long-term and complex change process.[27] It is important to set milestones, to recognize when they have been reached, and to communicate this progress widely.

At CIMMYT such communications took several forms: articles reporting progress and achievements were placed periodically in the center's weekly newsletter and in the newsletter for CGIAR-supported centers. The CGIAR Gender Program provided several opportunities for the Director General and staff to report on the gender and organizational-change initiative and its achievements to donors and to senior managers from the other centers. A special presentation was also prepared for the external review panel that reviews the center's performance and management every five years. Such activities have helped to demonstrate momentum, to keep people energized, and to sustain commitment.

Scaling Up and Diffusing Learnings and Innovations   One of the main challenges that has emerged in previous gender and organizational-change efforts focussed on changing work practices relates diffusing the learning and innovations in such a way as to have broad impact in the organization.[28] The CIMMYT action-research project was designed to lay the foundation for diffusion from the beginning, but at a price. The extensive interviewing and the broad participatory approach used in the feedback session—in which staff experienced the process together—laid a strong foundation for shared understanding and broad impact. A large number of people in the organization were exposed to the analysis, worked with and developed it, and participated in generating ideas for action steps and change experiments. The mental models provided handles with which staff could keep assumptions explicit and sustain awareness and discourse on how the mental models are affecting decisions, behaviors, and values. This clearly had an impact on individuals' daily work practices, behaviors, and interactions.

However, we have learned that this approach is most supportive of introducing and sustaining changes in systems and practices at the organization level, such as strengthening communications between senior management and staff or developing more consultative processes for strategic decision-making. It has been less successful in stimulating experiments at the level of the work unit and work practices.

At CIMMYT, this is most evident in the division-of-labor experiment, which challenges deeply held assumptions about "good" work and workers. These assumptions and values run deep, and factors within CIMMYT and its environment continue to aggravate the time pressures. (If significant change is to occur, staff need to experience the benefits and energy that can come from using time more efficiently and freeing time for personal life responsibilities and interests.) This implies that the team should have spent more time on the implementation phase, both in talking with work groups in order to identify a group interested in experimenting with alternative work practices, and in supporting that experiment.

Conclusions

Our belief is that there are two fundamental ways to challenge mental models that shape gender equity and organizational effectiveness. The first is by interrupting the discourse and developing new ways of understanding and talking about gender equity, norms, and work practices in the organization. (This is what some colleagues have called "generating narratives.")[29]

At CIMMYT this was done very successfully through the use of mental models and the broad participation of staff in the feedback session. Many of the ideas and concepts generated through the inquiry and analysis are now an active part of the language of CIMMYT.

The second is by interrupting work practices that derive from and reinforce the mental models. This was the intent of the organizational experiments and is only partially completed at CIMMYT. The interruption of practice can be done only through experiencing new ways of working. Just as staff and managers at CIMMYT have experienced new ways of communicating—and this has challenged assumptions about the benefits of hierarchy—it is important that CIMMYT continue to experiment with new ways of doing work, if the mental models of the ideal worker and individual achievement are to be challenged successfully.

To catalyze energy and help the organization refocus on such remaining opportunities for change, a second, more bounded round of inquiry, analysis, feedback, and experimentation may be required. This underscores the iterative nature of the change process and the recognition that organizations have varied states of readiness to take on various issues. After successfully instituting changes at the systems level and seeing the impact, CIMMYT may now be ready to experiment with potentially more fundamental changes at the level of work practice and work groups.

Table 4-1: Summary of Mental Models, Their Unintended Consequences, and Organizational Experiments

Mental Model	Unintended Consequences for...	Experiments
1. Reliance on a Unifying and Compelling Mission	• Developing strategic focus • Invisibility of some products • Mechanisms for collaboration	• Strengthening staff input into mega-project design • 360° performance appraisal • Strengthening teams and collaborative work practice
2. Belief in Individual Achievement	• Overcrowded agenda • Devaluing of collaboration and support • Individualized treatment	• Division of labor • 360° performance appraisal/Strengthening teams and collaborative work practice/Division of labor • Closing the gap between national and international staff
3. Default to Hierarchy	• Norms about problem solving • Failure to tap local expertise	• Strengthening management-staff communications/360° performance appraisal • Strengthening management-staff communications/ • Strengthening teams and collaborative work practice/Division of labor
4. Ideal CIMMYT Worker	• Balancing work and personal life responsibilities • Work style and structure	• Division of labor • Division of labor
5. Differentiating International and National Research Staff		• Narrowing the gap between national and international staff/360° performance appraisal

NOTES

1. This action-research and learning project was carried out under the auspices of the CGIAR Gender Staffing Program and The Centro International de Mejoramiento de Maiz y Trigo [The International Centre for Improvement of Maize and Wheat] (CIMMYT). The authors express their deep gratitude to CIMMYT's Director General, Timothy Reeves, its managers, and staff for providing the opportunity to carry out this initiative. CIMMYT opened the doors to the action-research team and provided full support for and active participation in the work. As was the intent of this project, both the action-research team and CIMMYT staff have learned a great deal about gender and organizational change in the process. We also gratefully acknowledge financial support from both CIMMYT and the CGIAR Gender Program. The CGIAR Gender Program is funded by several members of the CGIAR, including The Australian Council for International Agricultural Research, The Ford Foundation (USA), The International Development and Research Center (Canada), The Netherlands Ministry of Foreign Affairs, and the Swiss Development Corporation.

2. Deborah Merrill-Sands is the Associate Director of the Center for Gender in Organizations at the Simmons Graduate School of Management, Boston. Joyce Fletcher is a Professor of Management at the Center for Gender in Organizations at the Simmons Graduate School of Management, Boston. Anne Acosta is Donor Relations Officer and Gender Staffing Focal Point at the The Centro International de Mejoramiento de Maiz y Trigo [The International Centre for Improvement of Maize and Wheat] (CIMMYT) in El Batan, Mexico. She was Co-Chair of the Gender Task Force and the Change Catalyst Committee during the project.

3. A working paper with more information on the methodology and specific outcomes is available from the Center for Gender in Organizations, Simmons Graduate School of Management, 409 Commonwealth Ave., Boston, Mass., 02215 USA, cgo@simmons.edu.

4. Kathy Ferguson, *The Feminist Case Against Bureaucracy* (Philadelphia: Temple University Press, 1984). J. Acker, "Hierarchies, Jobs, Bodies: A Theory of Gendered Organizations," *Gender and Society* 4 (1990), 139–58. A. Mills and P. Tancred, Gendering Organizational Analysis (Newbury Park: Sage, 1992).

5. Joyce Fletcher, "Relational Practice: A Feminist Reconstruction of Work" *Journal of Management Inquiry* 7 (1998), 163–86. Joyce Fletcher, *Relational Practice at Work: Gender, Power and the "New" Organization* (Boston: MIT Press, 1999).

6. Lotte Bailyn, Joyce Fletcher and Deborah Kolb, "Unexpected Connections: Considering Employees' Personal Lives Can Revitalize Your Business," *Sloan Management Review* 38, no. 4 (1997), 11–19. Deborah Kolb, Joyce Fletcher, Debra Meyerson, Deborah Merrill-Sands and Robin Ely, "Making Change: A Framework for Promoting Gender-Equity," *CGO Insights* no. 1, The Center for Gender

in Organizations, Simmons Graduate School of Management, Boston, Mass., October 1998.

7. Arlie Hochschild, *The Second Shift* (New York: Avon Books, 1989).

8. Fletcher (1998, 1999).

9. David Thomas and Robin Ely, "Making Differences Matter: A New Paradigm for Managing Diversity," *Harvard Business Review*, September–October 1996 (1997), 79–90.

10. Thomas and Ely, 1997; Patricia Martin, *Men, Masculinities, and Working: From (Some) Women's Standpoint.* Paper presented at Case Conference, Simmons Institute for Leadership and Change, April 14, 1998.

11. Peter Senge, Art Kleiner, Charlotte Roberts, Richard Ross and Bryan Smith, *The Fifth Discipline Fieldbook: Strategies and Tools for Building a Learning Organization* (New York: Doubleday, 1994), 235–36.

12. Joyce Fletcher, "A Radical Perspective on Power," *Association of Women in Development Trialogue* 2, no. 2 (1997).

13. Fletcher (1998).

14. Robin Ely, "The Effects of Organizational Demographics and Social Identity on Relationships Among Professional Women" *Administrative Science Quarterly* 39 (1996), 203–38. Rosabeth Moss Kanter, *Men and Women of the Corporation* (Boston: Basic Books, 1997). J. Yoder, "Rethinking Tokenism: Looking Beyond the Numbers," *Gender and Society* 5, no. 2, (1991), 178–92.

15. C. Cafati, K. Baldini, K. Hoadly and J. Joshi, "Achieving Parity in Employment Status," *CG Gender Lens.* A newsletter of the CGIAR Gender Program (Boston, Mass.: The Center for Gender in Organizations, Simmons Graduate School of Management, 1997).

16. The original action-research team was composed of Deborah Merrill-Sands, Leader of the CGIAR Gender Program and team leader for the CIMMYT work; Joyce Fletcher, who joined the team as a specialist in organizational behavior and feminist theory; and Nancy Andrews, an independent management consultant who had served as a senior manager in another CGIAR-supported center. The team was subsequently joined by Maureen Harvey, an organizational-change specialist with extensive experience in gender and organizational-change projects in the private sector. Linda Spink, a management consultant and trainer from TRG, Inc. worked closely with the team as the consultant supporting the experiments on 360° feedback and team strengthening. She also did consulting with the senior-management team at CIMMYT. Each member brought valuable perspectives and experiences to the team and their contributions are gratefully acknowledged.

On the CIMMYT side, the individuals most directly involved in the initiative were Anne Acosta, Co-Chair of the Gender Task Force and CGIAR Gender Staffing Focal Point; Krista Baldini, Human Resources Manager; Kathy Hart, Director of Finance and member of the Gender Task Force; Larry Harrington, Chair of the Change Catalyst Committee; Roger Rowe, Deputy Director General for Research; and Timothy Reeves, Director General. The broader set of partners included the members of the Gender Task Force, the members of the Change Catalyst Committee, and the members of the senior management team. We also wish to acknowledge the time, energy, and critical ideas provided by CIMMYT staff and managers who participated actively in this process. Although this has been an intensive collaboration, the authors accept full responsibility for any errors or omissions in the presentation of the case study.

17. M. Fox, "Gender, Environmental Milieu, and Productivity in Science" in H. Zuckerman, J. Cole and J. Bruer, eds., *The Outer Circle: Women in the Scientific Community* (New York: W.W. Norton Company, 1991). Bridget Sheridan, "Strangers in a Strange Land: A Literature Review of Women in Science," CGIAR Gender Program, Working Paper, No. 17, Simmons Institute for Leadership and Change, Simmons College, Boston, 1998. G. Sonnert and G. Holton, "Career Patterns of Women and Men in Science," *American Scientist* 84, no. 1 (1996), 63–71.

18. Bailyn et al., 1997; Fletcher, 1998; U. Johansson, "Constructing the Responsible Worker: Changing Structures, Changing Selves." Paper presented at the Academy of Management Meeting, Vancouver, British Columbia, Canada, August 1995.

19. CGIAR, *Fourth External Review of CIMMYT* (Washington: CGIAR Secretariat, The World Bank, April 1998).

20. Fox, 1991; Sheridan, 1997; Sonnert and Holten, 1995.

21. M. Edwards and A. Ewen, *360° Feedback: The Powerful New Model for Employee Assessment and Performance Improvement* (New York: American Management Association, 1996). M. Edwards, A. Ewen and W. Verdini, "Fair Performance Management and Pay Practices for Diverse Work Forces," *ACA Journal* 4, no. 2 (1995).

22. W. Gormley and Linda Spink, *Exploring Multi-Source Feedback and Assessment Systems,* Organizational Change Briefing Note, no. 4, Simmons Institute for Leadership and Change, Simmons College, Boston, 1997.

23. Linda Spink from TRG, Inc.

24. CIMMYT, *CIMMYT in 1995–96,* Annual Report, El Batan, Mexico: International Maize and Wheat Improvement Center CIMMYT, 1996. "Terms of reference for the Change Catalyst Committee." Internal memorandum, July 25, 1996.

25. Robin Ely and Debra Meyerson, "Advancing Gender Equity in Organizations: The Challenge and Importance of Maintaining a Gender Narrative," *Organization* (forthcoming).

26. Edwards et al., 1995; Edwards and Ewen, 1996; Gormley and Spink, 1997.

27. Karl Weick, "Small Wins: Reflecting the Scale of Social Problems," *American Psychologist,* January (1984), 40–49.

28. David Kelleher and Kirsten Moore, *Marginal to Mainstream: Scaling Up Gender and Organizational Change Interventions,* Report of a Case Conference Sponsored

by the Simmons Institute for Leadership and Change, June 1997. Boston, The Center for Gender in Organizations, Simmons Graduate School of Management. Conference Report, No. 1, 1998.

29. Ely and Meyerson, forthcoming.

5

KEEPING GENDER IN THE PLOT: A CASE STUDY OF THE BODY SHOP

Deborah M. Kolb and Debra Meyerson

THE COLLABORATIVE ACTION research project with The Body Shop began in early 1996. Its purpose was to build on other action-research projects that used a "gender lens" to experiment with ways that an organization could strengthen its performance while eradicating gender inequities. The goals of The Body Shop project extended this work in two ways: the development of a cadre of internal change agents who could use a gender lens to foster ongoing inquiry and change in the organization; and the development of a pedagogy for disseminating the approach externally.

Our work on previous projects[1] suggested that it was valuable to locate the gender analysis around key business problems. We had seen that a business concern, such as absenteeism or delays in new-product introduction, can be illuminated in terms of understanding the cultural underpinnings of work through the gender lens.

Like these earlier projects, this one would take a "dual agenda" approach to change, that is, it would connect business issues with a gender analysis. However, despite successful interventions, there were problems diffusing this knowledge beyond the sites in which experiments were conducted.

In this project our goal was to identify a small group of collaborators inside an organization who would share our commitment to making organizational changes that would both benefit the firm and promote gender equity. We originally proposed a project that involved teaching and consultation with internal change agents through off-site training and development:

The proposed project will apply a "gender lens" in the context of an educational and intervention experiment. The intent of this work will be to develop a collaborative pedagogy and template program that involves working with participants to apply the lens of gender to understand, critique and revise assumptions, practices and policies in the particular organizational contexts in which they work. The collaborative pedagogy will include methods for working with participants on how to precipitate change in their particular contexts.

This chapter reports on our experiences in developing internal change agents in this case-in-progress and on a process of experimentation and learning. In it we explore four elements of the process:

1. Our experience in locating the project within the organization in order to identify change agents who would collaborate with us. At this point we discuss the difficulties in trying to translate theoretical approaches to gender into pragmatic approaches that internal change agents can use.

2. Our development of a framework and pedagogy to help potential change agents understand our approach to gender and change. Our intent was to develop an intervention process both critical and generative: analysis suggested by a gender lens would probe deeply into underlying assumptions, values, and practices; yet these very questions could pry open possibilities for alternative transformational ends. In this section we present the framework we developed and how we used it as a pedagogy in two change-agent workshops.

3. Our experience with an experimental intervention in a plant. It became clear early on that our dual agenda approach—connecting business issues with a gender analysis—was hard for people to understand in the absence of concrete, relevant examples. We therefore moved quickly into a collaborative project on the shop floor in the Colour Division. We hoped that this project would demonstrate the value of the gender lens and dual-agenda approach. We learned most concretely about the problems in keeping the dual agenda in balance. Based on this experience, we refined our methodology by incorporating narrative as a central feature.

4. A final project that was carried out in collaboration with some of the change agents in the Marketing Liaison Group in the hope of transferring knowledge by working together. However, it became difficult to

sustain our collaborators' attention when the project was not connected directly to their "real" work or immediate function. We realized that, if we wanted to help people learn about the dual-agenda approach, we would have to relate it directly to their everyday work. Our current project in collaboration with the corporation's Learning and Development Group to work with the senior team of the organization is an effort to link all the elements together.[2]

In each of these interventions, we have been challenged, not only to develop collaborative working relationships, but also with "holding onto gender." The final section briefly summarizes this challenge and what we have learned about it.

Background

We (Kolb and Meyerson) conceived of the project. Although we had similar intellectual and political objectives, we brought distinct resources to the collaboration: Kolb had relevant experience with an earlier Ford Foundation-supported action-research project on linking work and personal-life issues with strategic business concerns; Meyerson had developed a strong relationship with Anita Roddick, the founder and Chief Executive of The Body Shop, and had run a successful training workshop for senior women managers in the firm.

We wrote the initial proposal and became the project's principal investigators. Rhona Rapoport, a consultant to other Ford Foundation projects and a pioneer in the area of work and family, became consultant to our project. A few months after we were funded, Gill Coleman, Curriculum Director of the New Academy of Business in the UK, joined our team. Gill saw our work as a vehicle to develop some innovative curriculum material on gender and organizational change for the academic program she was building. Robin Ely became an important part of our team prior to our first on site workshop. Robin's interest in applying feminist theories, and learning about the boundaries of relevance, was similar to our own. For a short time, Pam Ballo helped collect data on site. Ann Rippin, a UK-based researcher, is now the principal person on site. Ann joined the team during our first formal experiment and has played a crucial role ever since. Most recently, Maureen Harvey has been moving into a principal role on the team to take the project into its next phase.

Our purpose was to apply a gender lens to existing feminist theories, which mounted critical analyses of organizational processes, structures, and knowledge, and to translate the results into an approach that change agents could use. As we stated in our funding proposal, "The perspective of gender brings into focus the processes by which certain forms of work, types of practices and values, and groups of people acquire legitimacy and privilege. A gender lens also points to the underlying dynamics of power which hold in place entrenched assumptions, values, and practices."

A gender lens suggests a set of critical questions that probes deeply into underlying assumptions, values, and practices. These include:

1. How do dominant structures, practices, and values such as hierarchy, rationality, competition, and control reflect assumptions and values rooted in gender relations? How do these deeply entrenched assumptions and values close out the possibilities of alternative arrangements and relationships and so resist fundamental change in existing organizational cultures and practices? How can these alternatives be recovered and translated into practice? For example, what assumptions and beliefs sustain the mandate of heroic corporate growth, and how does this mandate legitimate certain forms of organizational practice and de-legitimate others? What does a heroic-growth mandate imply for the relationship between work and family? How does the relationship between work and family shift when we relax this mandate?

2. What forms of activity count as work? What forms of activity are systematically valued and devalued, and how do these patterns relate to gender? How does the valuing and devaluing of different styles and forms of work shape the distribution of opportunities and rewards? How can existing reward systems, both formal and informal, be revised to credit different forms of work? For example, how do certain forms of work, such as informal, behind the scenes mediation, get excluded from systems that account for and assess work? How can we reformulate these systems so that they acknowledge and reward "invisible" work?

3. What is the relationship between the sphere of work and the sphere of home and parenting? How do deeply held assumptions about gender and gender roles hold in place and privilege one sphere of activity over the other? How do these assumptions play out in the more obvious and popular solutions to "work-family conflicts"? How do these solutions co-opt fundamental change and so enable the sphere of work to dominate and spill into the sphere of family? How can the bound-

ary of work and family be blended at the individual and organizational levels to produce gender equity at work and at home? How can we transform work and how we think about work so that it more fluidly accommodates and supports home and family life? What roles can organizations and education play in making this happen?

4. How is the ideology of individualism and competition sustained within the organization, despite efforts to increase teamwork and collaboration? How do gender relations help to maintain this ideology, and how does this ideology and the practices it upholds undermine certain forms of collaboration? How does this ideology systematically undermine the "feminine" values of caring and compassion? How do individualist practices undermine efforts to integrate work and family spheres? How can work be transformed to resist the ideology of individualism?

In order to translate our theory into practice, we needed a leader of an organization who was willing to work with us in this uncharted endeavor. We found one in Anita Roddick, the chief executive of The Body Shop International (TBS). This is a publicly held corporation based in southern England, with US headquarters in Wake Forest, North Carolina. We believed The Body Shop to be a uniquely suited laboratory for several reasons. Anita Roddick founded The Body Shop in 1976 and is, to this day, the soul of the organization.[3] She is deeply committed to the advancement of women throughout the world and wants her organization—and the New Academy of Business, which her organization has sponsored, to provide opportunities, hope, and skills for women.

She and other senior managers are concerned that the daily practices within The Body Shop live up to, and reinforce, the values of caring, compassion, and social responsibility for which the company is known. Yet Roddick and others see a seemingly unbridgeable gap between her idealized organization—valuing family and encouraging the integration of masculine and feminine values, practices, and styles—and the everyday reality of a high-growth, public, multinational business. At all levels of the organization, the "values" problem is viewed as an organizational priority; unlike in most corporations, values and "the business" are seen as inextricably intertwined.

The Body Shop has more than 1,650 shops around the world (as of July 1997) and trades in twenty-four languages in forty-seven markets. It employs more than 3,900 people. Through its community trade program, it trades with twenty-three suppliers in thirteen countries; 87.3 million customers made transactions in 1996 on over four hundred different products. In 1997, the company registered close to one billion dollars in retail, including franchisee, sales. The manufacturing plant at Watersmead, its corporate base, produced 8,300 tons of bulk product. The Colour Division plant produced almost 2,300 tons. The filling room in Watersmead filled forty-eight million bottles. In its facilities in the US, Canada, and Australia the company filled an additional 19.7 million bottles. In 1996, the company successfully sponsored the largest petition ever, generating four million signatures against animal testing in the cosmetic industry.

The Body Shop takes a very public stance on gender equity. Women play significant roles at all levels in the retail shops, and are well represented at the middle management ranks; however, as in other multinational firms, there are few at the most senior levels. In its local community of Littlehampton, TBS is known for providing excellent child-care benefits. Indeed, its child-care center attracts both unskilled and skilled labor to the company. It offers flexible work schedules, although these are not widely used, especially by middle management.

At the time of writing, we have focussed our efforts on select divisions within the corporate headquarters, in large part as a result of our experiences in trying to develop working relationships with internal change agents.

LOCATING THE PROJECT AND BUILDING A COLLABORATION WITH CHANGE AGENTS

According to our design, the initial phase involved identifying internal change agents and beginning to develop a working relationship with them. However, first we needed the approval of key gatekeepers, including the company's Executive Committee. We also wanted to identify possible collaborators who could help us develop a strategy for building a cadre of change agents inside the company. Most people with whom we met on our early visits had read our proposal and greeted the project with great enthusiasm.

To get the project off the ground, we described our dual-agenda approach, and tried to show how using a gender lens could contribute to organizational changes that enhanced both the business and gender-equity goals. We told success stories from other projects—how our work had led to reductions in absenteeism and shortened product development cycles. In the meetings with executives, we emphasized how our approach could help them bring their work practices in line with their espoused values, which would enable them to work more productively and cohesively.

In our presentations, people likely heard what they were most interested in hearing: that we could help them solve their business problems. At our initial meeting many executives wanted to collaborate with us on projects that would address business problems in their departments; few were directly concerned with gender. However, our aim was to work on projects that would address both gender issues and business concerns. Regardless of whether the message about the role of gender in the project came across clearly, we received the go-ahead for the work.

Looking back, this was the first incident in which gender got lost, or at least subordinated. In the stories we told about other projects, we emphasized our success in solving business problems, implicitly minimizing the degree to which gender equity would be affected in our work. Our promise was that gender as a lens, as a critique, would lead to insight; but we made no claims about how gender relations or equity would be affected. From the start, we pushed gender to the background of the dual agenda; that others failed to bring it forward is not surprising.

In addition to our presentation and follow-up meetings with the executives, we met with a group of potential internal collaborators, assigned to us by the Chief Executive and her liaison. This group would form the core of what we would expand to a larger cadre of internal change agents. These were women in various staff functions, whose work clearly was in line with what we envisioned, including the director of the learning and development group, the person charged with maintaining the "corporate culture," and the new director of organizational development. The CEO affirmed her commitment to the project, and assigned a manager reporting directly to her to be our liaison.

Working with this group of collaborators, we experienced our first explicit brush with the problem of translating the gender lens and the dual agenda into practice. This problem took several forms.

First, people had a hard time understanding what we were talking about, as the way we were defining gender was complicated. They understood gender to mean women. We were trying to expand this notion, but didn't have a clear alternative to offer them that could transform their understanding from gender as biological sex to a more systemic concept.

Second, what we were proposing was an ambiguous, ill-defined critique and generative process. We thought that, if we provided the theory and analytic approach, they would provide the experience and context: together we would create a way of applying our approach, in a particular context, that would have concrete business benefits and specific improvements in gender equity. This was too amorphous for them to embrace in any practical way.

They kept asking for outcomes, deliverables, metrics, timetables, and mea-surements—all reasonable requests when being asked to collaborate on a significant action-research intervention. However, we could not yet provide them with anything that concrete.

Third, while we could provide theory, and concrete examples from other sites, such examples were either not seen to be directly relevant, or if they seemed relevant, our collaborators did not understand why we could not simply adopt the solutions developed in other projects, thereby sidestepping the ambiguous and time-consuming process we were proposing. However, we insisted on working through "the process" with them because, from previ-ous experience, we knew that looking at work practices through a gender lens was essential to developing contextually relevant solutions.

Finally, our collaborators were worried about being associated with our project should it fail. This concern was particularly dangerous as we described the project in emergent and organic terms, which meant our process might become attached to any business concern. We might be seen as the "white knight," galloping in to solve the business problems of various parts of the organization. Their experience suggested caution, given the organization's tendency to pin its hopes on employees and consultants who promised quick solutions.

For all these reasons, those assigned to act as our internal partners were not ready to collaborate with us. They did not understand our approach well enough, and they were not willing to risk entering into the open-ended pro-cess we were proposing. However, they had to go forward with us, given the commitment we had secured from the senior team, particularly the Chief Executive. So we jointly struggled for a direction.

Developing a Framework and Pedagogy

We decided that two things had to happen in order for us to go forward. First, we needed a specific site in which to ground our theory in a demonstra-tion of the potential of our approach. Therefore, our first task together was to identify a local project. Our partners quickly focussed on the Colour Divi-sion as the perfect site for our work.

We also needed a pedagogy to help potential collaborators understand gender in a more complex and critical way. We also needed a forum in which to teach our approach to these potential partners. We determined that at this forum we would bring together examples we were collecting in the Colour Division and our theories of gender and organizational change. Such trans-lation was critical if we wanted our collaborators to be enthusiastic about how our approach might work in The Body Shop.

However, we still needed a useful framework within which we could engage our collaborators. Existing feminist theory about organizations that had informed our thinking about the project was not very user friendly. In order for potential change agents to work with us, they needed to be comfortable with the theoretical tenets of our thinking. To make them so, we needed a way to take their understanding from "gender equals women" to the more complex sense of the ways that organizations are gendered.

The framework we developed (and have continued to refine) accomplished two purposes. First, it translated various theoretical feminist perspectives with distinct definitions of "gender" into recognizable approaches to intervention. Second, identifying different formulations of the "gender-equity problem," suggested the criteria by which changes that promoted gender equity could be assessed.

First, we will describe the framework; then we will describe how we used it in a workshop with change agents.

Frame 1: "Fix the Woman" or Liberal Individualism   The first, and probably most common approach to understanding gender equity and change rests on a liberal, pluralistic vision of society and organizations. Gender, from this perspective, equals biological sex. In this view, men and women are assumed to have equal access to opportunities, and they rise and fall on their own merit. Women's lack of achievement relative to men's is attributed to women's deficits in important skills or attributes that keep women from competing under the presumed assumption of context of equal access.

The goal of this "Fix the Woman" approach—and thus its vision of gender equity—is to minimize the differences between women and men so women can compete as equals. (Development programs targeted at women are the hallmark of this approach.) While it might be shown that a woman has the technical skills for a job, she needs to become political, assertive, and strategic if she is to succeed in the way men have. The problem—and solutions—rests squarely with the individual woman. Our collaborators were familiar with such programs; and some had participated in the one that Meyerson ran the previous year.

Important benefits of these programs can accrue to individuals: as a result of such efforts, some women had been promoted into middle-management positions. "Fix the Women" programs can also produce role models, for those who follow. However, as important as these programs are, they leave in place the structures and systemic forces that create an uneven playing field for women.

Frame 2: Create Equal Opportunity or Liberal Structuralism   The second frame in which to look at ways to achieve gender equity relates to structural barriers. Gender is still defined in terms of differences between women and men; but the deficiencies of individual women are not viewed as the source of the problem. Rather, the problem is seen to be rooted in the structures of organizations, what Rosabeth Kanter calls "differential structures of opportunity"[4] that create a sloped playing field. In this frame, the focus is on the gender segregation of occupations and workplaces and on the degree to which women are discriminated against in hiring, evaluation, and promotion processes, in part due to the biases that come into play when women are an extreme minority. From this perspective, gender equity is achieved when structural and procedural barriers fall, so women can compete with men on a level field.

Interventions in this frame include affirmative-action policies and procedures to bring more women into previously "male" jobs; more seemingly objective and transparent policies for job postings, evaluation, and pay systems; mentoring programs; alternative career paths such as "Mommy tracks"; and the provision of work and family benefits, such as child care and flexible work schedules. The latter recognize that a significant structural barrier for women has been their caretaking responsibilities outside of work. Interventions of this sort have been formulated in terms of making accommodations or adjustments for biases.

These structural and programmatic interventions have contributed to the hiring and advancement of women: numbers do matter. However, they have not substantially changed many of the conditions that create and sustain gender inequities. For example, even though flexible work benefits are available, using them creates negative career consequences and serves to reinforce gender roles. As well, efforts to recruit and promote women, and programs that provide parents with special benefits create backlash, which can undercut the goals of these programs. In the absence of cultural change in an organization, structures and policies cannot, on their own, create equity.

Frame 3: Value the Feminine or Women's Standpoint/Advantage   The third frame shifts the focus from eliminating difference to valuing difference. This perspective is rooted in the writings of feminist-standpoint theorists who conceptualize gender in terms of socialized differences between men and women, embodied in masculine and feminine styles or "ways of being." Masculine and feminine identities, from this perspective, are shaped by different life experiences and social roles.

Gender equity would be an acknowledgment and valuing of the feminine dimensions of public and private life—in other words, recognizing and celebrating differences.

The gender-equity problem is conceptualized in terms of the feminine voice having been silenced. Women are disadvantaged because the attributes and skills associated with women and femininity (such as, nurturing, listening, emoting, relating) are devalued relative to attributes and skills associated with men and masculinity (such as, directing, talking, thinking, doing). Framing the problem of gender inequity in this way gives rise to corrective measures that focus on acknowledging differences and valuing them. Intervention strategies to value the feminine attempt to raise awareness of relevant differences between men and women, and to demonstrate how traditionally feminine devalued activities or styles—listening, collaborating, and behind-the-scenes peacemaking—are beneficial to everybody in the organization. If the first two frames seek to minimize or control diversity, interventions in the third frame set out to value diversity.

Interventions to value the feminine have raised awareness about the partiality of a male standard. However, from the perspective of gender equity, recognizing differences does not lead to change. Any difference based on masculinity and femininity must also recognize the power dimensions of such oppositions. The masculine standard is the "neutral" one against which the feminine and other differences are measured. Those who enact a feminine style, even when its contributions are recognized, find their efforts (and often themselves) valued only marginally. Thus, the biggest barrier to achieving gender equity in this context is that it does not challenge the mechanisms that produce and reproduce the differential and hierarchical valuing of difference between the masculine and the feminine.

Frame 4: Resisting and Re-visioning the Dominant Discourse or "Post Equity"[5]   In the fourth frame a more complex and comprehensive perspective on gender is posited. Gender is an axis of power, an organizing category that shapes social structure, identities, and knowledge. To say that organizations are gendered means that advantages and disadvantages, exploitation and control, action and emotion, meaning and identities are patterned through and in terms of distinctions between what is constructed as male and female, masculine and feminine.[6] We can identify a number of microprocesses that produces gendered knowledge, practices, relations, and identities in organizations. While the specific nature of these processes depends on context, the types of processes that lead to gendered organizations seem to be generalizable.

Acker identifies five overlapping processes by which organizations are gendered, which we have adapted in developing our framework.[7]

The first includes the formal benefits and procedures, such as job evaluations and the provision of work and family benefits, that appear neutral, yet have different impacts on men and women. At the plant, for example, a universal provision for sick leave was not used by young women too embarrassed to ask their supervisor for the leave when they had menstrual cramps. Thus, "sick leave," the legitimate benefit, was taken by men; women "missed work," thereby becoming part of the "absenteeism problem." That women had fewer opportunities and responsibilities than men was seen as a normal and reasonable outcome of their high rate of absenteeism.

The second mechanism of gendering includes informal work practices that appear neutral, yet have different impacts on men and women. These include norms about when meetings are held, systems of reward and recognition that determine behaviors, and processes that determine which forms of work are valued (and seen). For instance, Fletcher has shown how seemingly benign organizing processes designate some forms of activity "real work" and other forms of activity—such as employees helping one another, planning, and building commitment—virtually invisible and therefore unvalued.[8]

The third set of gendering processes includes the symbols and images that express, legitimize, and reinforce gendered divisions. These symbolic mechanisms, often imported from the culture at large, create and sustain images of masculinity and femininity within particular contexts that can vary by class and race. For instance, when time at work is viewed as a symbol of commitment, individuals who have responsibilities outside of work are systematically disadvantaged. In general, these symbolic processes and images penalize women who carry a disproportionate share of dependent-care responsibilities.

The fourth set of gendering processes includes the patterns and values associated with dominance and submission between men and women of various races and classes. Research in a variety of fields has documented the ways in which these interactions reinforce gendered divisions and support images of men as actors and women as supporters. How this plays out can vary by context, class, race, but patterns can be recognized. In The Body Shop, new managers who wanted to gain the authority to do their job found themselves fighting turf battles with other managers because their roles and authority were ill defined and in flux. This skirmishing also affected men and women differently, as attributions about men who compete for turf are dramatically different than attributions about women who act in a similar manner. If a woman acts competitively, she will experience a marked decline in her allies; if she does not, she will experience an undermining of her authority.

The fifth set of processes follows from the others and concerns the ways people internalize gender identities and reinforce them through their behavior, including what it means to look, act, and talk like a man or woman. Again, the gender identities that get played out vary by race and class. In the plant, for example, women (almost all white and working class) held that the gendered division of labor—women worked the line, men supervised—was appropriate and consistent with what it meant to them to be women and men. It was, they claimed, "unmanly and emasculating for men to work the line. That was woman's work." Men were better suited to supervise this work.

The gendering of organizations is enacted in such mundane interactions, routine processes, and the substructures they produce; and, of course, these five processes overlap and reinforce one another. In organizations (and in communities and families), they are the concrete manifestations of the "gender equity problem," which interventions are intended to address.

In our workshop with change agents, we used this framework of gender equity to provide our collaborators with an understanding of the perception of gender and gender equity in the fourth frame. The data we collected in the plant (described below) provided examples that enabled us to make our theory more concrete. For instance, we used the job of supervisor, one held exclusively by men in the plant, to engage our partners in a critique using the five processes. A job description for the position of first-line supervisors made it easy for our partners to see that the attributes required for that position—discipline, authority, and constant availability—would draw men to the position but discourage women, who would question whether they had the requisite skills. As our partners looked more closely at what supervisors actually do (as opposed to their job description), they clearly saw the gendering in the job description. Supervisors' actual work involved motivating workers on the line, dealing with conflicts and crises, and acting as liaison. The skills required for these activities were certainly ones that women have; yet the terms in which the ideal supervisor was defined in the job description created gender barriers to jobs women might be able to perform admirably.

What the change agents came to see (and got quite angry about) was that the formal description of attributes and symbolic and cultural "masculine" definitions of the "ideal supervisor" could partially account for the total absence of women in supervisory positions. Moreover, they could see how the women in the plant could internalize these definitions and come to believe that they—and other women—did not have what it took to be supervisors. However, given the work that supervisors did day to day, it was not at all clear that the attributes for which they screened—and therefore the kinds of people they promoted into supervisory positions (heavy on discipline and exercise of authority)—were best suited for the job.

These discussions helped our collaborators see the interconnections among formal, informal, symbolic, and interactive processes that led to gendering in the plant. They could recognize how these processes would lead to the conclusion that most women were unfit for supervisory positions and then how those perceptions might cause the women to identify themselves as people who could not hold management positions. Thus, they could see that the five processes of gender worked together as an exercise of power to perpetuate oppressive gender relations in the plant.

During the workshop, we used the example of the supervisory job as a way to talk through the implications for change that would be suggested by each of the approaches in our framework. It was easy for our partners to identify intervention strategies from the first three frames to deal with the problems identified in the job. They agreed that the first frame would suggest training programs to help women develop the discipline and assertiveness required by the cultural definition of the ideal supervisor. The second frame would suggest changing parts of the job description (such as constant availability for work), so that it did not automatically screen out women. The third frame would suggest that plant officials look for ways to recognize and reward the more traditionally feminine skills that women on the line were thought to possess (such as listening, helping, and caring for one another). They could also that these approaches alone would be inadequate to change gender relations in the plant.

Intervention approaches were less concrete from the fourth frame. They could see that we would need to enlist people from the plant to collaborate on working through a critical analysis of the five sets of processes set out above, analyzing the ways they result in gender inequities and ineffective outcomes for the business. Experimentation would involve disrupting these processes by reforming formal procedures and benefits, and by explicitly challenging and changing norms, informal work practices, and cultural images of supervisors. Such practical steps would focus directly on the work itself, changing it as a means of resisting and revising the dominant discourses in the plant. As well, we would work experientially with the work group to create new narratives that support the dual agenda embedded in changing work practices.

Some of our partners at this workshop understood the fourth-frame approach conceptually, seeing the many ways in which their organization was gendered and the variety of processes that collude in maintaining the gendered order. However, the workshop was merely a first step to using the frame in ongoing, real-time projects. We engaged partners in two distinct projects: working with us in the Colour Division and structuring a project with Market Liaison.

Contextualizing the Approach in Colour Division[9]

The work with Colour Division, a manufacturing operation that produces the cosmetics line, began as a means of developing a site within The Body Shop that could be used for learning. A number of reasons made it a good place for us to demonstrate our approach. The plant was very old-fashioned and sex-segregated by job and level. The line workers and line leaders were predominantly women; virtually all supervisors and holders of most other jobs that led to management positions were men. A recent survey of employees had found morale in this division to be extremely low, and that people had little hope for their prospects within the firm.

In addition, the plant manager was open to experimenting with different approaches. He had recently entered into an ongoing training program with the Director of Learning and Development, one of our collaborators; and he was actively looking for methods to humanize and revitalize his plant. He had inherited an old-fashioned and highly regulated production facility, run along very traditional lines. He felt that output and quality standards were much lower than need be, and that people were not treated with respect. Shift patterns were often changed on short notice; there were slack periods, when people had little to do and feared for their jobs, and very busy periods, when demand could be met only by taking on large numbers of temporary staff. Above all, the manager felt that those doing the production jobs would have ideas for how their work could be better organized. He would like to hear them, but the culture of the plant did not encourage people to take initiative or speak out. He expressed a view that both line workers and middle managers needed to change the way they worked. Given these factors, there appeared to be considerable potential for demonstrating the value of the gender-lens and dual-agenda approach.

In consultation with the plant manager, we assembled a "work" group of women and men who represented a wide range of ages, jobs, and levels within the Division. This group consisted of people who rarely had an opportunity to be listened to by plant management, and they were quite interested in getting involved.

In retrospect, it is interesting that neither our invitation to the work group (drafted by us but sent out by their manager), nor the letter sent to a larger number of interviewees proposed by the work group, mentions gender. However, during our first meeting with the work group, we did explicitly describe both elements of the dual agenda.

The group called itself the Silent Working Amendment (SWAT) Team, and we worked with it to gather information about gender relations and the organization of work within the plant. Data collection involved both working on the line and interviewing twenty-eight people representing a cross-section of people in the plant. We used a semi-structured interview format, which included questions about gender. Prior to the June 1996 workshop with change agents, members of the intervention team conducted the interviews; after the workshop, several partners from our internal change-agent group joined us in the interviewing.

Analysis of the data revealed several themes. There was rampant gender stereotyping of both people and work roles, embedded in a strong culture of control on the shop floor. The gendering of roles affected women's opportunities for advancement and the relative valuing and devaluing of various activities and roles. Women were routinely harassed and intimidated by supervisors, especially regarding sickness and absenteeism. People were rewarded and promoted for working overtime and weekends; this disqualified a disproportionate share of the female labor force, who had primary responsibilities at home. Employees who wanted to be considered for promotion and opportunities had to be willing to show the flexibility to work extra hours, but little flexibility was provided in return. Our analysis suggested that only men and traditionally masculine work were recognized, valued, and rewarded, although women and traditionally feminine/"invisible" work might be equally important to the Division's efficiency and effectiveness. The work environment was also clearly causing problems to the manager, in the form of high staff turnover, quality problems on the production line leading to large numbers of "re-works," and high levels of absenteeism and sickness.

We held a feedback meeting with the SWAT team, at which we described the picture we had gathered from the interviews. We did so tentatively, because we were giving them our construct analysis of their experience. The collaborative element of this intervention was the way they either agreed with our analysis or substituted their own. In fact, at this meeting our partners engaged in developing new descriptions of their experience using a gender perspective.

As we talked this through with the work group, women in the group embellished what we were saying with anecdotes and instances that supported the gendered interpretation. They also talked about the ways the women on the line supported one another and covered for one another when one person was sick, or had to leave early because her child was sick, ensuring that the work was done. They articulated some of the many forms of invisible work that went unrecorded and unrewarded in the work environment.

A fragile space for discussing gender was opened. For a brief time people in the group tried out meanings and interpretations of events that challenged those they had long accepted; they began to describe their own experience in new ways. The meeting ended with us asking the SWAT team to think about what, if any, changes they wanted to make to the work environment as a result of the stories they had told and heard, how they would communicate what they were doing to their colleagues in the plant, and how they would get senior managers to support any suggestions they developed.

In a second meeting, the SWAT team designed a work experiment that involved converting two lines on the shop floor to self-managed teams (SMTs). For about six months after that meeting, the group met weekly and spent several days on off-site retreats, planning and designing the implementation of the experiment. To gain support within the plant, the team developed and delivered (multiple times) an elaborate presentation on the history and logic of their proposed experiment. The SWAT team also helped select and train the workers for the SMTs.

One of our change-agent collaborators helped the SWAT team develop its strategy and process. However, when, because of increased work load and concern with higher-priority projects, she handed the project over to her assistant, the gender aspect of the dual agenda was subordinated to more practical concerns. Although the assistant understood the gender orientation of the project, it was secondary to the teamwork training, which was a major innovation for this group. Moreover, when the SWAT team, proud of its planning, promoting, and implementing of an SMT, handed off the experiment to the SMTs, the stories of gender and the history of the project were lost in getting the new teams up and running.

The lines moved to "self managed" in April 1997. The division manager asked the SWAT team to help manage this effort, and we were involved in team building and conflict resolution, devising means of measuring, maintaining the involvement and support of senior management, and developing broader internal "ownership" of the experiment.

Although the idea for and justification of the experiment developed out of a "gender lens" analysis, those involved did not consistently appreciate how gender remains implicated in this intervention. However, we remain convinced that this intervention could challenge the culture in ways that would allow more women to rise into supervisory jobs; question the nature of supervision by recognizing and rewarding "invisible" yet essential, work; and allow both men and women to achieve a more satisfactory integration of work and family. If these changes occurred, they would challenge the gendered order of the plant. But it was also possible that this experiment could also "work" in a narrow sense merely by changing behaviors of supervisors and people on the line.

In working with the Colour Division, we came to appreciate another reason why holding on to gender can be so difficult. The "gender" part of the dual agenda was our primary concern; but the business part was of prime interest to those we were working with—and they brought detailed knowledge of their work to the relationship. As a result, we continually had to assess how far we could push the gender aspects of the work without either appearing to sideline the business issues or incurring resistance that might damage the collaborative relationship. The people in the plant, from the manager to those working on the line, needed to see the potential benefit to them. At the outset, at least, that benefit needed to be something more tangible than abstract notions of "gender equity."

Talking in terms of "creating a more gender-equitable work environment" or even a "work environment in which men and women are more equally valued" had little immediate meaning for people. But talking in terms of building a "work environment in which everyone's contribution is valued and there is more flexibility" seemed to be of sufficient interest for our potential collaborators to build on. As our discussions became more concrete—decision-making, job-descriptions, and promotion procedures, among other issues, were raised—people were able to connect with their own experience and develop commitment to the project. However, the issue then seemed to be work, not gender.

We learned that experiments do not, on their own, change the gendered order. The connections between the experiments and gender need to be collaboratively articulated to be seen and appreciated. Thus, we came to see the importance of narrative as central to our methodology. Our challenge, therefore, was to help our collaborators build new gendered narratives into the vision of the experiment. We therefore continued to meet intermittently with members of the SWAT and of the two line teams to keep the gender narrative in the forefront of their thinking.

As these narrative interventions give meaning to the changes in the workplace, they have the potential to challenge and change the gender stereotypes within and beyond the plant.

We also worked with the division manager to help him understand and give importance to the dual objectives of the intervention. In addition, we met with some members of the SWAT team, outside the workplace, to learn about their perceptions and feelings about gender roles and relations inside and outside the workplace, and how these feelings and thoughts have been affected by their involvement in the SWAT team.

Work with Colour Division has inspired learning in a number of dimensions. First, to work with internal change agents one needs a site that provides a contextual grounding for concepts. Our experience in Colour Division enabled us to develop a meaningful pedagogy through which change agents could recognize how gendered processes play out in context. Second, we recognized how easy it is to lose the gender part of the dual agenda in the work. This has led us to consider the importance of narrative in keeping gender in the agenda. From this work, we have been able to clarify the major elements of the methodology.

Our approach to change involves three conceptually distinct forms of intervention that, in practice, overlap: critique, experimentation, and narrative generation. Critique involves revealing the specific ways in which the five gendering processes of the fourth frame contribute simultaneously, in that context, to the reproduction of gender inequities and to the instrumental concerns of the business. The critique is driven by the dual agenda to identify potential levers for experimentation.

The second element, experimentation, follows from the first. The critique provides a space in which people can reflect on the connections between gender and work practices. In this space, people could talk about gender and discover the systemic ways it operates in the plant. Experiments can change the way people work by interrupting the processes that lead to gender inequities and business ineffectiveness. (It is important to label these changes "experiments," in order to call attention to the ways in which these interventions resist and reconstruct what is "normal.")

The third component of change is narrative generation, that is, building deliberate meaning around the behavioral experiments. (This became very clear as a result of the experimentation in Colour Division.) Narrative is about stories; and part of the project involves collaboratively creating new stories that people can continue to tell, stories that keep fourth-frame understandings of gender in the plot line.

Incorporating narrative in the method involves naming the power/gender connections in the critique, so that people can appreciate that gender is not about individuals but is cultural and systemic. In our work with senior management, for example, it has involved developing a narrative that moves beyond individual idiosyncrasies to systemic roots as an explanation of why senior women leave the firm. When people reflect on their experience, they can see how they are implicated in and affected by gendering processes.

To explicitly link gender and business issues to the experiment, narratives need to be constructed that create visions of what would change in both parts of the dual agenda if the experiment were to succeed. Indicators need to be developed that can be incorporated into the story line as the experiment unfolds. Finally, a story-telling constituency—such as the members of the SWAT team—needs to be created, whose stories retell how gender is implicated in and equity enhanced by the experimental intervention. Collaborative construction of narratives is a form of critical intervention essential to keeping gender equity in the dual agenda.

DEVELOPING A COLLABORATIVE PROJECT
IN MARKETING LIAISON

In the June 1996 workshop for change agents, a collaborative project in Marketing Liaison was planned. The goal was to identify change agents in a particular site who would, with our consultation, identify and be responsible for a project. At the end of the workshop, some participants assigned themselves to the Colour Division project; others helped formulate a new one in Marketing Liaison.

Marketing Liaison was an appealing site for several reasons. We learned, from a member of that department at the workshop, that time-management and inefficiency problems plagued the department and obstructed employees' achievement of a desirable work-life balance. Second, the site provided a possible entry into the larger Marketing department, which seemed primed for an intervention. Third, unlike the Colour Division, Marketing Liaison is small and well-bounded. Fourth, this project could diffuse to other sites as the group functioned as a liaison to retail units around the world. Fifth, it was a microcosm of the organization as a global enterprise. Finally, the dynamics of the Marketing Liaison group appeared to reflect a larger, seemingly gender-neutral cultural norm at The Body Shop: a focus on the "here and now," which rewards heroics and devalues planning, anticipation, learning from the past, relationship-building, and a work-life balance.

In collaboration with two internal change agents, we completed data collection, analysis, and preliminary feedback to the group. Analysis involved several rounds of conversation among research-team members, partners from the change-agent group, and a member of Marketing Liaison. The analysis led us to insights into factors that contribute to and inhibit effective collaboration and cooperation, within and outside the department; work- and personal-life integration; constructive balance between proactive and reactive (that is, "here and now") approaches; and appreciation of both less visible and heroic activities that contribute to the vitality of TBS. After analyzing the data, the research team and members of the change-agent group met with members of the department to reflect on what had been learned from the interviews.

At the second session, the group devised experiments involving flex time; e-mail channeling; and covering one another's calls. It was our hope that the experiment would enable members of the department to be more efficient in prioritizing and controlling their work flow and their time, both at and outside work, and would assist them in thinking about ways to work more effectively as a team. More important, we had hoped that the experiments would challenge those norms that support heroics and individualism, as they undermine effective work practices and the less valued, less visible, feminine "work" of information sharing, cooperation, and nurturing. Also, insofar as they enabled more effective use of time, we expected that the experiments would help build a culture that supported work- and personal-life integration.

The preliminary stages of this project accomplished several objectives. Most notably, the research team and the internal change agents worked together during each stage of the data collection and analysis; this was a constructive test of our collaboration, as team members were able to use the framework in collaboration with us. However, the experiment had mixed results at best, as our assumptions about the role of internal change agents were problematic. We had intended that a few internal change agents, who had worked with us but who were not part of the Market Liaison function, would carry out the work, helping with the implementation of the behavioral experiments, and, more important, helping the group to understand and to build new narratives around the deeper, gendered implications of these experiments.

Personnel changes and restructuring in Marketing made our project a low priority for members of Marketing Liaison and for our change-agent partners, so our expectations were not realized. In addition, the group seemed satisfied to change only some minor elements of their work, and showed little desire to reflect on their practice and the deeper implications of relatively superficial behavioral adjustments.

The Marketing Liaison project was instructive in several ways. First, because it involved some members of the change-agent group, we saw how understandably easy it was for them to put a project aside to concentrate on their pressing *real work*. That led us to rethink who change-agent partners should be. As we have learned more about the issues, we have brought the project closer to people's—and the company's—"real work."

This repositioning has several components. First, we have redefined the criteria for internal partners to people whose "real work" is linked to ours. That work might be an organization-development, learning, and/or change function, such as Learning and Development at The Body Shop. Or it might be senior managers working on issues in which gender is prominent. Second, we have tried to reframe projects to give our partners a different (and more critical) perspective on the work they are already trying to accomplish. Third, we have been raising the profile and the strategic significance of our work, by working closely with senior managers and by tying our analysis to central strategic issues of the company.

Most of our work with change agents is now located in the Learning and Development Group. From the onset, we had been working informally with the Director of Learning and Development (L&D) and some of the senior staff. When we reviewed possible groups that might benefit from our approach to their work, L&D was an obvious candidate because it interfaces with most parts of the organization on training and other change initiatives. L&D is a self-contained group with a supportive manager; the group is aware and observant of how it works (and doesn't) as a team, and seems to be open to reflecting on how it is shaped by, and helps shape, The Body Shop culture. Finally, and most important, it has recently become more involved in senior-management development processes.

In collaboration with the Manager of Diversity and the then Director of Learning and Development, we connected our project to an incipient diversity initiative. The Diversity Manager was charged with developing a plan to increase diversity at all levels of the company. Although there were ways to improve recruitment and promotion, she believed that real change would come only from the kinds of cultural changes we were advocating with our dual-agenda approach.

Collaboratively, we presented our analysis to the corporate Board of Directors plus the Executive Committee at a special meeting. The Manager of Diversity gave her presentation, and then we gave ours. The focus of our dual-agenda analysis was competence and the inability of The Body Shop to make use of the skills of its employees. We showed three main ways that new-comers respond to the lack of clearly defined roles, ambiguous authority, and unbounded time: the heroic role, solving problems visibly; the building role, in which the incumbent stays out of the limelight, building a team to do the work; and the reactive role, responding to what comes along as it happens. We had seen that these roles are not only gendered, but were enacted and reacted to differently when played by men and women. Moreover, only the heroic role-player would succeed—the others had authority and responsibility gradually taken from them, which made it difficult to do their jobs.

In this presentation, there was a tight coupling of competency issues with gender; for each point we made, we showed both the business and the gender significance. Support from the Diversity Manager and the Manager of Learning and Development was important, and each was able to provide personal stories about the connections between gender and competency.

CONCLUSION: HOLDING ONTO GENDER

The Body Shop project had as its goal the cultivation and development of internal change agents who could carry out the critical and generative work the dual-agenda perspective suggested. Our goal was to identify a small group of inside collaborators who would share our commitment to making changes in organizations that would both benefit the firm and promote gender equity. While we have not achieved that goal, we have learned a great deal about how to cultivate and develop change agents.

Specifically, we have developed a methodology for teaching about gender, which we have used with other groups of change agents; they have come to see the potential in working in the fourth frame. As well, we have added to the elements of critique (analysis) and experimentation that of narrative as essential to holding both gender and business in the dual agenda. The understanding of the importance of narrative arises from our learning, in this and other projects, how easy it is to lose gender in such interventions. In addition, we have identified the likely leverage points for such change: we must connect our work to the "real work" of people in the organization.

Despite what we have learned from our experiences, it is clear that holding onto gender is a challenge that requires continual attention. We have seen how easy it is to lose the gender plot line given the pressure to build collaboration and gain support for the project. We offered the gender lens, not as an intervention, but as a means of getting at organizational problems; but we now clearly see that the critique is, in itself, a potentially powerful form of intervention. The members of the change-agent workshops who could apply the fourth frame to their work became powerful allies who could keep the gender part of the dual agenda in the foreground.

Second, we recognize the forces that conspire to lose gender in the dual agenda. When we position our work in terms of a business problem, the business problem understandably overwhelms gender concerns, which seem a lower priority. Thus we need to make the connections to gender continually. We saw how this can work in our presentation to the Board: not only did people see the connections, but some also shifted their understanding from individualized, idiosyncratic explanations of why senior women left the firm to recognizing systemic factors.

Losing gender is exacerbated when we connect our projects to the "real" work of internal change agents: the definition of the problem shifts from being explicitly gender based to being seemingly unrelated to gender. Merely dealing with the problem will not, in itself, make any changes in gender relations. Changing how decisions get made, and clarifying roles and responsibilities might have an impact on people's ability to do their jobs competently; but it will not affect the gender inequities inherent in the kinds of work that is valued. Even a commitment to eschew individual heroics, which might create a more hospitable place for diverse ways of working, does not guarantee that gender relations would change.

What we learned from our experience in Colour Division is the need for people to be able to reflect on the connections before they quickly move to solutions. (For example, in our meetings with the Executive Committee after the Board presentation, we spent several hours reflecting on these connections; and, for the first time, most of the group came to appreciate the connections and wanted to work on them.) After that reflection, we need to work collaboratively to figure out how we will recognize changes in gender relations and, thereafter, to maintain an ongoing narrative about the connections.

Finally, we recognize that talking about and working with gender is not easy. Collaborators are likely to resist the gender critique when their interests are threatened by the analysis. True, their interests can be threatened merely by being associated with "gender" issues; but the threat often runs deeper. To talk about gender is to talk about the distribution of power and opportunity. These issues are not easy to discuss: people can become defensive. As some have vested interest in the status quo, there will be conscious and unconscious resistance to the project. (This is a natural part of trying to work on the deep assumptions about work and gender in an organization.) Working with critical people, giving them the opportunity to tell their stories is helpful. On a number of occasions this process led to new experiences, to people recognizing the part they play in keeping existing practices in place.

As we move forward, these insights into the challenges of holding onto gender are critical. Gender is now in the foreground of our work. We are collecting narratives about gender in the organization that can serve as a benchmark for future analysis. All future collaborations will be based on a mutual articulation of gender issues as well as business concerns. In our analyses, we now trace the different impacts of actions for men and for women. We try to give these issues meaning by creating experiences whereby individuals can recognize both how they are complicit and the consequences—for themselves as men and women, and for the organization. Throughout the process, we are developing stories that keep gender as part of the plot line of the dual agenda. The results of our experimentation with narrative are still to be told.

NOTES

1. Lotte Bailyn, Rhona Rapoport, Deborah Kolb and Joyce Fletcher, *Relinking Life and Work: Toward a Better Future*, Report to the Ford Foundation, based on a collaborative research project with three corporations (New York: Ford Foundation, 1996); Lotte Bailyn, Joyce Fletcher and Deborah Kolb, "Unexpected Connections: Considering Employees' Personal Lives Can Revitalize Your Business," *Sloan Management Review*, Summer (1997), 11–19.

    This project is currently on hold. A new CEO took over on July 15, 1998. We will be meeting with him to determine his interest in continuing with this phase of the project. Another potential project with the Manager of UK Retail is also under discussion. This, too, would be based on collaborating with internal change agents working on their own business issues using the dual agenda approach.

3. In July 1998, Anita Roddick stepped down as CEO and became Co-Chair of the Board.

4. Rosabeth Moss Kanter, *Men and Women of the Corporation* (New York: Basic Books, 1977).

5. We settle on the label for this frame tentatively, after much debate within our team. Unlike the other frames, no endpoint or vision can be articulated with the language and constructs of the dominant discourse. And we cannot speak from outside of the discourse. Thus, this frame asserts an ongoing collaborative process of critique and generation, and goes beyond traditional notions of gender and end-state notions of gender equity.

6. Joan Acker, "Hierarchies, Jobs, Bodies: A Theory of Gendered Organizations," *Gender and Society* 4, (1990), 139–58.

7. Debra Meyerson, Deborah Kolb and Robin Ely, "A Framework of Gender Equity and Organizational Change," Invited talk at Lucy Cavendish College, Cambridge University, Cambridge, England, February (1998).

8. Joyce Fletcher, "Relational Practice: A Feminist Reconstruction of Work," *Journal of Management Inquiry* 7 (1998), 163–86.

9. Many of the ideas in this section come from Gill Coleman and Ann Rippin, "Losing Gender in Collaboration," *Organizations* (forthcoming).

6

WOMEN, GENDER, "RACE" AND ORGANIZATIONAL CHANGE IN THE CONTEXT OF A NATIONAL TRANSITION:
THE NATIONAL LAND COMMITTEE — A CASE STUDY FROM SOUTH AFRICA[1]

Michelle Friedman

Giving women special attention will divert
us from our main purpose. . . .

LYDIA KOMPE WAS a fieldworker with the Transvaal Rural Action Committee (TRAC), an affiliate of the National Land Committee (NLC). In 1986, she called a meeting of rural women, from about ten communities, with whom she had been working. All were victims of gross human-rights violations stemming from apartheid-inspired population relocation policies; all were facing a serious land crisis.

Eight years later, Lydia explained to other NLC fieldworkers how gender relations became salient to the struggle at the community level. "We were lucky because when we started there was a crisis. The men . . . saw we [men and women] have to jointly fight this crisis."[2]

I started organizing women and trying to put confidence in them that they also have to be part of the decision-making body of the community. The . . . women are the ones that are affected by all these threats of forced removal. When the government officials arrive in their community, the first people to be approached are the women at their homes where they are looking after the children and their homes while their husbands are maybe in the veld looking after their cattle or even in town as migrant workers.[3]

In those early days, Lydia did not get much support for working specifically with women from the white female TRAC researcher with whom she was working.[4] But because she saw the need and was committed to it, she did this work in her free time. Much later, once the Rural Women's Movement (RWM), which grew out of that initial meeting, had a formal identity and was stronger, TRAC gave Lydia's work direct support. Lydia's courage and tenacity to stand with the rural women with whom she identified in the face of resistance from both community men and her workplace were central to changing work practice in TRAC and, later, in the NLC.

How did Lydia's impetus move through the network, and what has been its impact?

INTRODUCTION

This case studies a process within a national network of NGOs during the political transition in South Africa. Its central theme is that a growing consciousness within a constituency can shape gender work within an organization. It shows how context—in this case, the national situation—creates opportunities for gender work, and how change agents and constituencies together can shape agendas and processes, and can result in organizational responses and outcomes. It is primarily about context, change agents, and constituencies pushing and pulling an organization.

It also reflects on some of the dynamics and dilemmas of different understandings of gender relations and their consequences: the shaping of priorities; latent and emergent conflicts; and the inextricable connections between gender relations and other social relations.

I[5] worked with the NLC, first as a consultant and later as their national gender coordinator, from mid-1991 to the end of 1994. I accepted the post with excitement and trepidation. I was excited by the potential in working with a regionally diverse and nationally coordinated organization working with grassroots land-claiming communities. Moreover, I would have resources and organizational support for my work. My trepidation stemmed from my uncertainty as to what the day-to-day practical work of a gender coordinator entailed. With no other instructions, my brief was to make sure that all aspects of the network's work were "gender sensitive."[6]

CONTEXT

International Context

During the past two decades, a vibrant debate, ideological and experimental, has been waged over the effect of the development process on the lives of women. We have explorations and approaches to women in development (WID), women and development (WAD), gender and development (GAD), integrating gender into development, empowering women, and so on.[7] It is a confusing terrain, especially in South Africa, where apartheid isolation resulted in many of the UN Decade for Women (1975–85) givens not becoming part of popular discourse.

Some development and NGO activists first encountered the concept of "gender" from funders keen to see an increased "gender profile" in their project partners. It is unsurprising, then, to hear the accusation that "gender is donor-driven" or that it is "an imperialist import being imposed upon us by funders." In our case, while there was some interest in the issue, such external support (or pressure) and resources certainly contributed to the process.

Historical and National Context

This story was contemporaneous with South Africa's transition from national-liberation struggle to protracted negotiations and finally, in April 1994, to our first national democratic election. Anti-apartheid activists were shifting gears from challenging oppressive state practices to developing new state policies. The impetus for the gender-specific work in NLC was also a political struggle, which shaped the work from a number of perspectives.

One of the most heinous historical inequities resulting from colonialism and apartheid is South Africa's race-biased land policy: black Africans (85 percent of the population) were relegated to 13 percent of the land, much of it confined to "Bantustans" or "homelands."[8] Land laws and a repressive migrant-labor system have resulted in virtually no functioning peasantry, but high levels of rural poverty, land degradation, and landlessness among African women and men living in rural areas: "The black rural areas remain dependent on incomes earned in the urban centers and/or on welfare remittances, such as state pensions, and the income strategies of most households revolve around these opportunities rather than farming."[9]

It is no wonder, then, that "cyclical rural-urban migration has become a way of life in South Africa—where the majority of rural households are better viewed as members of dislocated urban communities."[10]

Moreover, rural women are deprived and disadvantaged compared to rural men with respect to access and control over limited land and other resources, including income-generating opportunities, labor, employment, training, and decision-making structures.[11]

The apartheid era (1948–94) exacerbated the skewed land laws and dispossession of colonial days. Earlier land laws gave black people owner-ship rights to small pockets of land within the so-called "white" areas. The apartheid era instituted "forced removals": either people were relocated or their land was incorporated into the Bantustans, in which they would have less access to resources. "It has been estimated that between 1960 and 1980 alone some 3.5 million people were dispossessed of their land and relo-cated, to give spatial shape to apartheid and to shore up white minority rule."[12]

In response, the NLC's precursor, The National Committee Against Re-movals (NCAR) was formed in 1984, as a network of affiliated land-activist service organizations to ensure that regional anti-removals work could be coordinated and located nationally: The NCAR was not mobilizing a gener-alized land struggle against historical dispossession, but was monitoring hu-man-rights abuses associated with apartheid-generated land dispossession.

The political context also saw the need for socially, economically, and politically oppressed people to organize against unjust material conditions. The NCAR like the later NLC, supported empowerment approaches to de-velopment that insist on beneficiaries' agency. The affiliates were not con-stituency-based organizations, such as industrial trade unions; however, com-munities struggling to reclaim land (often represented by committees of eld-erly men), interacted with and were integrated into the NCAR network.

By the time the NCAR became the National Land Committee (NLC) in 1989, it was clear that the key liberation movements would soon be unbanned. The country would finally negotiate the demise of the last white government in Africa. The NCAR, therefore, had to move from crisis management to a proactive land strategy, from oppositional politics to developing policy and negotiating with the state.

Although there is a long history of women's resistance in South Africa,[13] the political mobilization and organization of women specifically to oppose patriarchal oppression deepened during this period. Since the unbanning of the liberation movements in 1990, we have witnessed massive growth of overtly articulated gender consciousness, and of women fighting for women's rights and challenging patriarchal assumptions.[14] Much of this latter activity took the form of influencing the negotiations process rather than organiza-tion building. However, one significant exception was The Rural Women's Movement (RWM), founded to further the material and political interests of rural women as women.[15]

It was in this climate that the NLC initiated its gender sensitization and "integration" process. By early 1994, the interim national constitution, a crucial policy-enabling macro environment, had been negotiated. It included two key clauses relevant to NLC constituencies: the restoration of land to those dispossessed by apartheid, and a gender-equity provision.

The latter was the result of an intense struggle regarding the constitutional relationship between gender equality and custom, traditional law, and culture, aspects of which are inherently patriarchal and significant in determining women's access to land. Traditional leaders favored constitutional recognition of custom and traditional law, in all its gender inequality. Organized women's groups insisted that gender equality supersede customary law and culture.[16] The women's lobby, strongly supported by the RWM, won the day and, thereby, the possibility of women gaining independent access to land, unmediated by their relationships to male kin.

Organizational Context and Culture

In the period under review, "anti-removals" communities were a large part of the NLC constituency base, and their work had a great influence on NLC work practices.

Whole "communities"—whether freehold title holders or tenants, women or men—were mobilized against a common, external enemy. The priority was resisting the removal, not the interests of different sections of the community. However, Lydia Kompe, working with the Transvaal affiliate, and two other black women organizers working with the Western Cape affiliate were instrumental in organizing local women in squatter communities.[17]

The anti-removals focus's need to carefully document people's histories led research to be conceptualized as action research, integrated and directly related to individual community issues, struggles and legal negotiations. As the early work was voluntary and required research skills, many of the early land-activist staff in the NCAR were white, political-activist men and women, and a handful of black males.[18] An "activist" work culture developed that assumed one had "no other life."

In the early 1990s, in response to the changing national climate, the focus of the NLC affiliates expanded beyond "forced-removal" communities. In a 1991 mission statement women were identified as a particular target group: The NLC works with those communities which have been dispossessed or denied real access and rights to and control over land—these include victims of forced removals, farmworkers, and labor tenants, the residents of informal settlements and women in particular.

By 1992, when the "gender intervention" began, fieldworkers' ability to

facilitate negotiation among diverse community interests and to develop local institutional capacity was becoming fundamental to the work.

Staffing

Like many other service organizations in South Africa, the affiliates began small. Over the years, however, affiliates and the national office have
developed into fully fledged NGOs with paid staff.[19] The network was un-
usual in its fairly high proportion of white women playing leading roles.[20]

Over time, however, an increasing number of black activists have been
employed, most of whom were not in "management" positions in 1992.[21] The
later development of black leadership resulted from early capacity-building
processes focussed on developing staff through action and experience.

Fieldwork and Research

Although the distinctions between fieldworker and researcher were some-
what blurred, whites tended to be researcher/writers and blacks researcher/
fieldworker/organizers. Early on, action research was directly related to individual community issues and struggles. As land activists dealt with lawyers
and paralegal issues, an important aspect was research and writing.[22] Over
time, the writing element was detached from fieldwork and linked to research,
particularly for policy purposes.

The network initiated a national research program to contribute to a
national land-reform policy agenda.[23] Policy research, by definition, is more
concerned with setting in place overall mechanisms than with implementing
ongoing community-level programs. However, because of the staff's lack of
experience in policy research, their approach tried to sustain the links between policy work and community-level organizational and developmental
fieldwork. Attempts to shift NLC's research focus, between late 1991 and
early 1994, floundered in part due to the lack of an alternative style of policy
formulation.[24] Rural conditions have made it difficult to build a coherent
constituency; consequently, policy content has been based on "research."

The Network as Organizational Form

By 1989, the loose network of autonomous affiliates with no tight national structure became increasingly problematic and fiercely debated. Affiliates wanted to retain regional autonomy, and to participate loosely in na-

tional processes; yet national political processes were demanding coherence. Moreover, the national office staff was growing, and the relation of the office, the NLC executive, and the affiliates less defined.[25] (The executive was made up of formal representation from the affiliates; the director of the national office was accountable to this body.)

It was into this broad and shifting context that the NLC "gender" process was "inserted." The network, while innovative and strategically capable of responding to changes in the external environment, inadequately addressed its internal structuring: "Instead of tackling and restructuring current NLC structures, new structures were established to implement NLC's work."[26] Eight task forces,[27] set up in 1992 to unite affiliates on issues of common concern, became the key mechanism for developing the three-year plan; yet the link between the task forces and the three main content programs—Advocacy and Development on Land Claims; Research and Organization Development—remained unclear.

The initial blocks to organizational learning were the state of flux of the organization, tensions between the national and affiliate levels, high staff turnover, and unconsolidated new organizational structures. The struggle to reorient to a new macro context, and pressures to be politically strategic and to get things done "out there" eclipsed reflection on organizational and work practices. The view by some that "gender" was irrelevant or driven by funders did not help to create a learning environment.

The network built its gender strategy on constituency-based pressure groups such as the RWM—a rural African women's organization—and Lydia Kompe's status within the network. Lydia summed up her expectations at the first formal NLC workshop on gender issues:

My interest is to look into and change the situation of rural women . . . I wanted to discuss this situation with other affiliates to see if we could work nationally within the NLC . . . Even the progressive organizations, the service and political organizations don't adequately cover rural areas. Maybe NLC's involvement will highlight rural women to challenge political organizations.[28]

A black woman born in a rural area, with little formal education but vast political experience organizing in the urban trade unions, Lydia was strongly motivated by her identification with rural people and their problems: "I have got my own rural home in a rural area, here I am working as a migrant. At the end of the day my life will be spent in my village where my house is, not where I rent."[29]

In addition to this organic grassroots pressure, the network had a white woman director—born in an urban area, with a middle-class, academically trained, and anti-apartheid activist background—determined to ensure that future land-reform policy would be "gender sensitive." From the beginning, therefore, the gender work in the NLC involved both separate organizing to empower women and build leadership, and integrating[30] gender into policy frameworks. A number of members at affiliate level were also supportive.

KEY MOMENTS IN THE PROCESS

Four phases, from mid-1991 to early 1995, mark the early years of the "gender intervention" in NLC.

The first discussion, which I facilitated, on how "gender" could be pursued at a national level occurred at a 1991 meeting of the national research team. Five representatives at that meeting committed their affiliates to pursuing the issue. The most experienced person in the network in land and gender research was nominated to coordinate this process. However, by early 1992, affiliates were still unable to undertake what their representatives had committed them to. In response, the national office hired me, again as an external consultant, to run a series of workshops with interested affiliates to assist them to "integrate" gender issues into all aspects of their research.

In these initial workshops affiliates began to define what gender meant in their organizational and work contexts.[31] The workshops also became a needs-assessment/feasibility study, culminating in an evaluation attended by representatives of the seven participating affiliates. The group at the evaluation decided that they should employ a full-time national gender coordinator for two years. She or he would not be based in any department, but would be accountable to the director formally and informally to a gender task group (GTG).[32] All interested affiliates would have representation on the GTG.[33] The commitment of the NLC executive and affiliate directors remained unclear.[34]

The first phase (June 1991–June 1992) laid the groundwork for a longer-term process. Emphasis was placed on gaining support for and creating a formal, structured and resourced space for coordinating and strategizing the gender work. All activities were directed to building internal capacity and developing a plan.

The second phase (Aug. 1992–Nov. 1993) comprised sharing experiences and enhancing the network's structural capacity to respond to the many needs raised in the feasibility study. Financial resources were obtained, I was hired

FIGURE 6–1: Key Activities in NLC Gender Process 1991–95

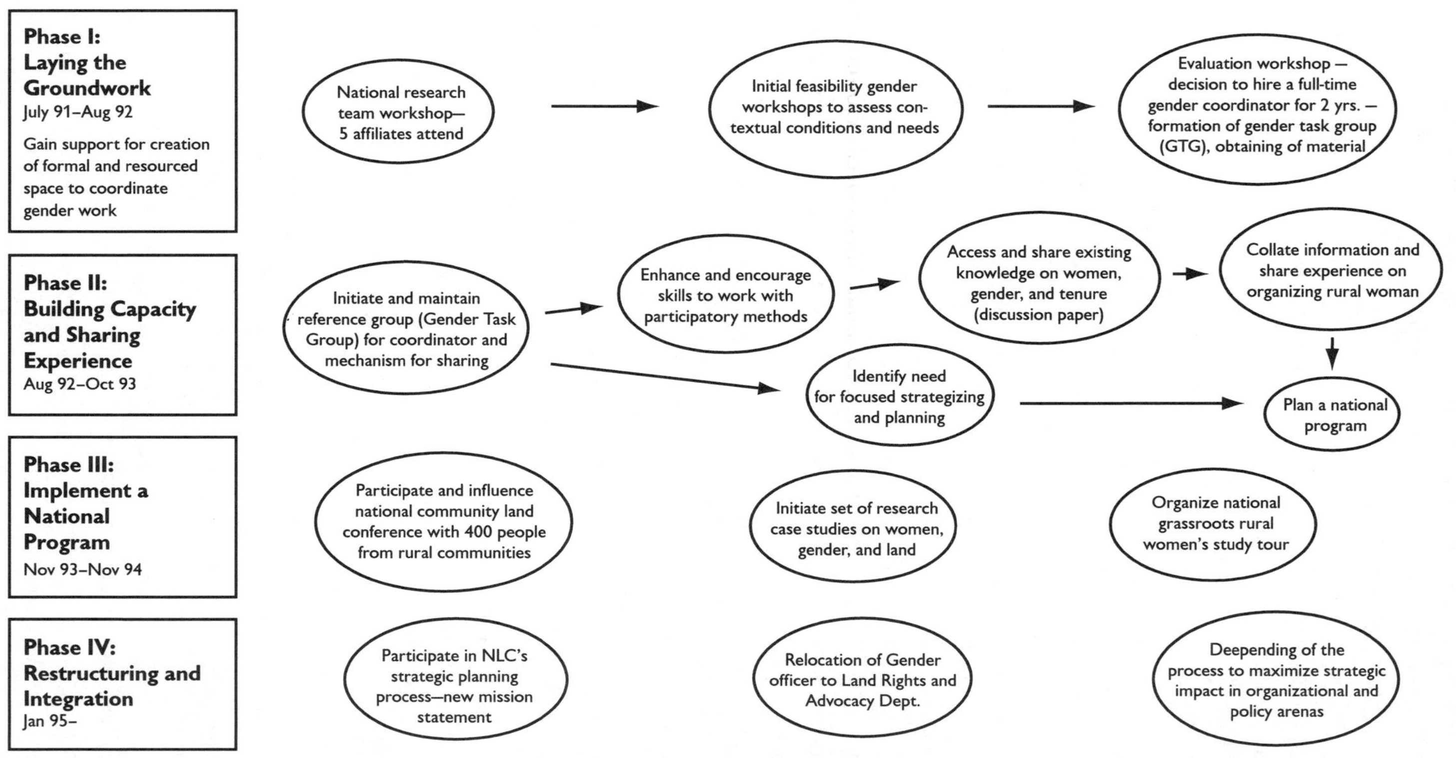

**Phase I:
Laying the
Groundwork**
July 91–Aug 92

Gain support for creation
of formal and resourced
space to coordinate
gender work

**Phase II:
Building Capacity
and Sharing
Experience**
Aug 92–Oct 93

**Phase III:
Implement a
National
Program**
Nov 93–Nov 94

**Phase IV:
Restructuring and
Integration**
Jan 95–

National research
team workshop—
5 affiliates attend

Initial feasibility gender
workshops to assess con-
textual conditions and needs

Evaluation workshop —
decision to hire a full-time
gender coordinator for 2 yrs. —
formation of gender task group
(GTG), obtaining of material

Initiate and maintain
reference group (Gender Task
Group) for coordinator and
mechanism for sharing

Enhance and encourage
skills to work with
participatory methods

Identify need
for focused strategizing
and planning

Access and share existing
knowledge on women,
gender, and tenure
(discussion paper)

Collate information and
share experience on
organizing rural woman

Plan a national
program

Participate and influence
national community land
conference with 400 people
from rural communities

Initiate set of research
case studies on women,
gender, and land

Organize national
grassroots rural
women's study tour

Participate in NLC's
strategic planning
process—new mission
statement

Relocation of Gender
officer to Land Rights and
Advocacy Dept.

Deepending of the
process to maximize strategic
impact in organizational and
policy arenas

as the full-time coordinator, and the GTG became functional. The triannual GTG meetings were used to share experiences, build skills and confidence, plan, strategize, and evaluate.

At its first meeting in late 1992, the GTG defined three objectives. The first addressed the many constraints facing women in NLC affiliates' constituencies. "Seeing women at the grassroots level empowered" was informed by the TRAC/RWM experience and the assumption that empowerment is enhanced through organizing. Without social organization, unequal power relations cannot be transformed. The second objective, to ensure that non-oppressive meanings of gender be integrated into all aspects of NLC work, was informed by a gender and development "integrationist" approach. This objective could be acted upon by both women and men and could include social relationships within the organization and in the communities. The third objective, to influence the broader policy and development environment, was influenced by "mainstreaming" approaches.

Strategies had to keep these three goals in mind, and activities organized by the GTG straddled these different areas. At this and follow-up meetings indicators were developed to help GTG members clarify their goals, when changing access to resources and transforming power relations at personal, group, and social levels.[35] At this stage there was no conscious intention to change internal NLC culture or existing organizational power relations.

In response to the feasibility study, the GTG emphasized developing a methodology for accessing information and experience from "elders" in the network. It also focussed on strategizing and planning, with regard to NLC organizational processes and national objectives, including a national gender program. Key activities included a national participatory-methods training workshop for fieldworkers,[36] the development of a strategy for influencing a large community land conference, and a structured debate on organizing rural women. Gendered analyses of all areas of NLC work were done, and existing knowledge on gender relations and tenurial forms was consolidated into a discussion document.[37]

The implementation of a national program marked the third phase (Nov. 1993–Dec. 1994) of the change process. A huge, successful Community Land Conference was held in early 1994, at which women delegates from rural communities were extremely vocal about their needs and issues. A national study tour[38] for fifty grassroots women was organized. Nine research case studies were implemented, to provide more nuanced information and analysis on the gendered nature of key land questions. An attempt was made to ensure that the entire NLC vision document was gender sensitive.

By the end of the third phase, internal changes were becoming visible: more women were employed in the field, and efforts were made to influence all organizational programs. Increasingly, men were being challenged to take responsibility with women for transforming unequal gender relations. Within the communities, women's voices were increasingly heard through specific research projects and more appropriate methodologies. The need for separate organizing space to develop confidence, leadership, and lobbying power among women came to be more widely recognized. Finally, consolidating the findings in regionally specific case studies allowed the network to identify relevant national-policy issues.

Through rotating representation to GTG meetings, GTG-organized activities and ongoing NLC work helped issues to emerge from within communities, and increased support. National gender struggles, the elections, and the policy context added external pressure.

Training for insiders was facilitated through a national participatory-methods workshop; sharing of experiences and structured debate; drawing on "elders" experiences, insights, strategies and joint development of research designs. GTG meetings were used for training; outside resource people participated in particular themed sessions, and discussion papers on relevant issues were circulated. At the affiliate level, consultants were hired to pursue deeper issues or developed gender programs. Some individuals attended externally organized training courses.

I left the network at the beginning of the fourth phase. During 1994, the whole network participated in a lengthy strategic-planning process. For the first time the network's strategic objectives now specified that it was working with groupings of marginalized women and men. Differences within communities were more overtly recognized, and the GTG's separate structure was questioned. Calls were made for greater structural integration, while recognizing the ongoing need for a focussed "gender space." It was no longer clear whether the GTG could accommodate the newly articulated needs:

1. Fieldworkers working with women needed ongoing support;

2. Women fieldworkers needed strengthening;

3. Space was needed to develop and critique field-methodology and organizational practices from an anti-sexist point of view, as well as to identify focus issues for lobbying purposes; and

4. Space was necessary to develop strategies for implementation at policy, organizational and national levels.[39]

The GTG agreed to transform the position of gender coordinator into a gender officer, housed in the Land Rights and Advocacy Department, as part of the general restructuring; but it has battled to reformulate the separate space. There was increasing recognition of the need to transform power relations within the network; and it was evident that the growing tasks and responsibilities were too large for the GTG and national coordinator alone.

In brief, most strategies were consciously oriented to and guided by work activities "out there." All changes necessary for implementation—building support within the network and the GTG, hiring more women fieldworkers, developing new work practices, and reconstructing vision and mission statements at national and affiliate levels—happened by the way, as part of the process. Only after some years were the necessary changes to internal organizational practices specifically articulated. After I left, a sexual-harassment and anti-discrimination policy document was developed; more recently, proactive measures have been suggested to engage directly with the institutional culture.

This summary makes what felt like chaos sound so smooth, so planned, so organized. What really happened? What were the key sites of conflict? An exploration of a few key themes follows.

THE ROLE OF CHANGE AGENTS IN SHAPING THE AGENDA AND PROCESSES OF GENDER WORK

I have noted the motivations and influence of the director and the fieldworker organizer with regard to the introduction of a national "gender process." As national coordinator I, too, played a role, informed by my white, middle-class, urban background. I had academic experience with gender analysis, political experience in both the violence-against-women movement and anti-apartheid community-based women's organizations, as well as professional experience with gender and rural development.

I assumed that, as for most oppressed groups, identifying our needs, breaking silence, being heard, articulating, and fighting for our needs are the first critical steps. Conflicts between dominant and subordinate groups can be prevented from erupting when wants, needs and preferences are shaped so that:

both accept their role in the existing order "either because they can see or imagine no alternative to it, or because they value it as divinely ordained and beneficial." Power relations may appear so secure and well-established that both subordinate and

dominant groups are unaware of their oppressive implications or incapable of imagining alternative ways of being and doing.[40]

I assumed that the best way to learn is by doing, experimenting, reflecting on the experience, and then re-thinking what to do: ideas must be continuously tested in "reality." Sharing experiences, comparing and evaluating
with others working in similar contexts, and finding new information from
sources beyond ourselves also contribute. Listening to others with similar
problems or issues moves issues from the personal level. A key assumption
was that learning and lasting change does not occur through coercion but by
being "organic" and linked to people's realities. Although one of my initial
tasks was to focus on the research aspects of affiliates' work, participants'
expressed expectations made it clear that such a limited focus was inappropriate: the brief would have to include "fieldwork" and accommodate regional affiliate variations.

The initial design of the process thus acknowledged that meanings and
understandings of "gender," and of gender relationships as lived relations of
power—between men and women, between women and women, and between
men and men—are contested and must be given space:

It must be recognized that all affiliates are at different stages in the process and that
it is therefore difficult if not impossible to construct a uniform way forward . . . The
national office needs to be sensitive to where the affiliates are at in their own process.
. . . Affiliates need to decide what they want to do—how far they want to take the
process and what it will mean for their work. In terms of this they must decide what
kinds of input they need.[41]

As affiliates had autonomous powers, they were able to choose whether
to attend GTG meetings, and whether they would designate specific representatives. Some individuals came regularly and constituted a core group.
Others initially came because of personal interest and commitment, not because their affiliates fully supported them. This created a dilemma: I did not
want to force regular participation or limit membership to particular representatives. Core GTG members were all change agents in their own contexts, and we wanted as many people as were interested to be exposed to
GTG methods, processes, internal training, and strategizing. However, the
group also wanted to develop its members and new strategies, and to move
toward developing a coherent national program. The need to initiate new
members at virtually every meeting hampered continuity and potential deepening. Nevertheless, the GTG succeeded in holding space for individuals to

gain confidence to raise issues and to challenge their own affiliates on returning home.

As national coordinator of the gender program and GTG, I had primary responsibility for ensuring that the national objectives were met. I played an important role in linking processes and in managing tensions between "leading" the task group and "following" issues raised from affiliates very different in commitment and style.

In my efforts to respect affiliate autonomy, to facilitate space for sharing experience, and to build the national program from field concerns, I used my leadership to allow space for contested meanings. One white, female ex-executive member complained that I "did not take more leadership."[42] Yet a young, black, woman fieldworker said that "GTG should move from being a 'Michelle thing' to a group thing."[43]

I might have been a facilitative coordinator, but I was nevertheless one of the white people in senior positions. I was thus a member of both a dominant group with structural privilege, that is, white, and of a non-dominant group, that is, a woman. I might have had a structural leadership role, but Lydia Kompe had a de facto leadership role, especially with "newer" women fieldworkers and researchers. Her political acumen and experience were widely respected as a source of wisdom.

Despite the structural constraints, I assumed that responsibility for the process—especially at the affiliate level—needed to be shared. I decided on an approach that challenged hierarchical norms and ways of working to maximize the potential sharing of experience among affiliates and to strengthen the relationship between those responsible for "research" and those responsible for "fieldwork." Conscious attempts were made to maximize participation in meetings, GTG planning, and decision-making in order to facilitate both business and personal development. Many evaluation meetings noted the difference between the GTG meetings and other national processes: "Coming from a male-dominated organization this empowers me as a woman."[44] "Methods used in GTG meetings make the process productive and less tedious."[45] "These meetings are structured in a way that helps us to deal with class, education, and language problems...The methods used here help to prevent the differences from interfering with participation too much."[46]

DYNAMICS AND DILEMMAS OF GENDER WORK
AS THEY WERE PLAYED OUT IN THE NLC

Different Understandings of Why NLC Should Focus on Gender

Given the politically sensitive context, and the socially constructed nature of gender relations, I assumed on entering the network that not all women and men would have the same experience or understanding of "gender," and that gender therefore needed to be jointly explored. From the first formal NLC workshop to focus on gender issues, important differences emerged. Resistance to the workshop process itself was expressed as "gender" being imposed by outsiders or as not relevant to the NLC context. A view, mostly that of black men, held it to be part of an imperialist agenda, paid and pushed for by NLC. ("This is not something we want or need, rather it is imperialist, donor driven.") Another view, mostly held by white men, was one of uncertainty and curiosity as to its relevance ("I had addressed it academically and then forgotten about it"; "I don't know how gender impacts in rural areas"; "giving women this special attention would divert us from our main purpose").[47]

There was also curiosity about the topic. "Others (black and white men and women) who had also not asked for it, expressed their unfamiliarity and inexperience with the topic, and welcomed it as an opportunity to face up to the issue in some substantive discussion."[48]

Some expression of strong interest and a desire for more knowledge:

came from those people (mostly women, black and white, some men) who are committed and interested in the issues and who also see gender as a national issue. ("If we don't address it, we'll be left behind"; "It is a critical issue especially in a period of transition.") . . . Some wanted to learn how to "integrate gender" into the research work. Others wanted to explore tactics and techniques that could help in organizing work or in encouraging already strong women to be more part of leadership and decision making. ("We need to ensure that gender does not become the monopoly of the middle class.") Some men wanted to explore what their role as men is or should be and some women wanted "men to understand the hardships that women feel and not just see the women as cooks." There was also recognition by some that "we need to be clear in our own minds before we can work with male-dominated communities sensitively." . . . Finally some people realized that "leadership's views do not necessarily reflect the views or interests of the broader community and we need to address this."[49]

These four points of view had to be acknowledged and worked with in the national process; yet strategies developed by the GTG bedeviled efforts to obtain national coherence. At times, different perspectives erupted into heated conflict in which "gender" became a catalyst for surfacing other organizational tensions and conflicts.

Emergent Conflicts and Strategies for Working with Difference

From the beginning of my consulting work with NLC, it was clear that what "gender" means and what to do about it were contested. It was also obvious that network staff tended to reflect existing apartheid hierarchies. Even though Lydia Kompe's work with the RWM was instrumental in the initiative, it was my body—white, female, and middle class—that arrived at all the affiliates during the initial feasibility workshops. As national coordinator, I was seen to be holding the gender priority.

Those who resisted the gender perspective were able to argue cultural irrelevance by associating "gender" with "white woman." The workshops did not overtly focus on feminism or on sexuality and sexual orientation; yet implementation of gender-training workshops and the design of strategies for gender work were carried out mainly by white woman development workers. As one affiliate put it: "Some participants saw gender issues and feminism as one and the same, and associated them with white, lesbian women." For many, "the issues represented by the term "gender" were experienced as an assault on their race and cultural identity."[50]

Two structural attempts to acknowledge and address existing hierarchies were implemented by the GTG. First, at the needs-assessment evaluation it was agreed that affiliates would be encouraged to send one "researcher" (likely to be white) and one "fieldworker" (likely to be black) to the GTG meetings.[51] This was to prevent "gender" being perceived as a white, research issue; and a way of bridging the research-fieldwork divide, while valuing the organizing experience of the Transvaal affiliate. Second, efforts were made to maximize participation in GTG. Lydia suggested that "this group is the only one in the NLC where we are managing to incorporate all of us."[52] English was the language of these meetings, although those for whom English was not their first language were welcome to express themselves in their mother tongue.

Although the initial feasibility workshops were designed to "hear" and, perhaps, to recognize different perspectives, there was seldom time to explore resistance or overt conflict in depth. In response, I decided that the first national GTG initiative should focus on practical-skills development, as it seemed most concrete. At the first formal GTG meeting, I and two white women proposed that the GTG organize a workshop focussing on skills development in participatory methodologies. (One woman was a colleague responsible for training and education in an affiliate; the other was a consultant in methodology.)

Although we knew that such methods would get beyond "the rational," we were unable to anticipate the variety of conflictual issues that emerged during the training week: perceptions of being forced to attend the workshop; ignorance of what the workshop was about; mistrust of the GTG; denial of the importance of gender as an issue; men's suspicion of a possible takeover of the GTG by women; and the "race" dynamics constellated by three white facilitators.[53] The process raised race/power relations and structural problems within NLC, which were later pursued in other processes. In hindsight, it seems obvious that with a minority white government still in power, and an organizational culture that focussed all its energy outward, in the first publicly created space race tensions would emerge. Other issues of conflict—gender relations, age and experience, political positions, and tensions between black researchers and fieldworkers—were underplayed so the group could solidify around the identity of "black."

The experience highlighted the need to recognize the complicated intersections of gender relations and other hierarchical relations, and that processes that undermine rational control elicit powerful emotions. The generated conflict is a necessary part of the change process.[54]

Subsequently, GTG members recognized that while there were structural problems within the network, negative consequences of unequal differences between members could not be assumed. Evident inequalities on the basis of "race," educational levels, and ability to speak English were sometimes challenged by the self-confidence and/or experience of less structurally privileged members. Therefore, the flexibility to accommodate competing and multiple identities was necessary.

Women and/or Gender? Implications for Strategy

Throughout my stay in the NLC there was ongoing debate (and, at times, confusion) about the concepts "women" and "gender." Transforming oppressive social relations, including those of gender, is extremely complex. People enter the debate/struggle with different life experiences and political assumptions. Moreover, talking about who we are as women or men, as it can question our core identity as individuals, can be painful as well as difficult. We should not be surprised therefore when "gender" is interpreted in multiple ways or when "gender work" generates strong feelings, whether positive or resistant.

Organizing "Women" Separately

Like many others in the NLC I assumed that an organized constituency and consciousness is necessary to transform oppressive social relationships. This assumption informed NLC's work with land-reclaiming communities, and stimulated debates within the network about its role in organizing rural social movements.

Lydia Kompe's work in building the RWM as a constituency typified this approach with respect to "women." Her strategy rested on the assumption that women are likely to be more structurally disadvantaged than men in their race and class groupings; hence women need to organize separately to challenge isolation, build support, assist in struggling with internalized oppression, and strengthen "voice." Once sufficient strength has been built, it becomes more possible to confront oppressive structures, develop strategies, and form alliances. Lydia's strategy was contentious[55]: not everyone in the network agreed that it was NLC's role to treat women in land-claiming communities as a separate category or that doing so was the most strategic approach.

Some doubted whether these women wanted such change: NLC was in the business of struggling for land rights and access to land, not of the empowerment of women. Others asked whether it shouldn't be the "role of another organization such as the African National Congress women's league (ANCWL) to organize women? If the ANCWL exists in our area are we not competing with them?"[56] Even those who accepted working separately with women had critical questions: If women in communities are organized into separate women's structures, how do they become effective in more general decision-making structures? If they aren't, how do women who get elected to general structures develop the confidence and skills necessary to operate effectively, and to argue for and defend gender-specific interests? What is the necessary relationship between elected representatives and a constituency base?

Furthermore, how would such a strategy be translated into practice? Would affiliates need designated women to do this work or should everyone carry the responsibility for making sure that women in communities were organized? How does an affiliate get to this point? When I started, there were very few women employed by NLC in the communities. An important starting point was to get more women committed to the work who could not be identified as "white western imports" employed in the network. At the last GTG meeting I coordinated, an evaluative comment suggested that:

Women's presence is needed in the network to apply pressure—because if the problem doesn't affect you, you won't be interested. Without pressure to make people change, they won't change . . . As women, we have to learn how to deal with sexism in ourselves and in our colleagues . . . We have to be conscious of these things and committed to challenging them . . . in the affiliates.[57]

With experience, more questions were raised about separatist strategies. For instance, strategies that fixed women in one identity, rather than in their multiple identities, are likely to flounder.

Questions were also raised as to the limits of what women fieldworkers could effect. As a researcher working in an area serviced by one of the affiliates put it:

[Most of] the people that were working on those lands were . . . either farmworkers, domestic workers . . . or labor tenants on some of the black spot farms . . . If one followed a kind of legal claim system, they would have no access to land . . . I'm not sure that a woman fieldworker would be able necessarily to unpack that because of the interlocking of the men in power with the men who have historical claim to land.[58]

Moreover, people found it difficult to understand that building women's independent strength was only one strategy for challenging oppressive gender relations. If we understand that all social relations are gendered, then it is easier to see that focussing on women specifically is not the only available strategy.

Working with Men and Changing Policy Frameworks

Working with men to change their behaviors and practices is another strategy. Focussing on changing policy frameworks, institutional rules, procedures, and field methodologies can also alter power imbalances. Affiliates initially most resistant to "gender work" tended to be dominated by black men, especially in the field; so a dual strategy was needed. An affiliate that had always worked specifically with women reported how they "have learnt how important it is to develop strategies but also to not think that gender work is only working with women."[59]

One year earlier, Lydia had talked about her discovery of the strategic importance of involving men:

It is important for a gender group like us, when we feel we are strong enough, we should start slowly moving to involve men . . . particularly young men who see things differently from our old husbands who click on tradition and culture. It is not easy because they see themselves as men and they see themselves as superior to us. But slowly if we work on them so that they take what we discuss here and use this to make other men see that change is necessary—this is another way to broaden our scope for change.[60]

Lydia also recognized that different contextual conditions required different strategic responses. When communities were resisting forced removals:

We had a joint focus on one enemy—and men were convinced from that basis. We said there is no way that we (i.e., women) can win this struggle in isolation . . . If these men idle around and do nothing and have nobody to give them something to do—to keep busy, to empower themselves—yet women are doing something, then you have a problem . . . Men and young men who are idling around are going to feel threatened, feel jealous, and . . . sabotage our [work].[61]

The research strategy aimed at influencing policy formulation provided another opportunity for affiliates to grapple with their approaches to and understanding of gender issues. Interested affiliates were commissioned to produce case studies that provided information useful to the formulation of national land-reform policy. Ideally, researchers would have applied a sophisticated framework to their analysis of how land relationships were gendered. Some effort was made to develop common guidelines for the research, but the variety of affiliate contexts and researchers' experience prevented such coherence. In consequence, some of the case studies focus specifically on different women's experience. The more complex studies develop analyses of different groupings of both women's and men's perceptions, and of the relationship between the two at household and institutional levels.

In some cases, affiliates chose a directly organizational approach to the case-study research. In the initially more "resistant" affiliates, the research case study acted as a precursor to and opened space for later organizational work or gender programs. It also helped foster the recognition that unless more women were in the field and able to access women in the communities, the chances of women's voices, needs, priorities, and perspectives being heard and acted upon were minimal. Without accessing women's experiences it was also impossible to understand the complex nature of the relationships between women and men in different positions, or how gendered realities impact on land use, access and control. Policies without organization are unlikely to be implemented; and organizations without enabling policy frameworks can't effect transformative change.

Structural Solutions to Challenging Existing Gender Relations

For the first few years, we assumed that individuals attending GTG meetings, through their awareness and by their presence, would be able to influence other task groups and broader affiliate work. Six months before I left the network, an evaluation concluded:

GTG has been most successful when we have done something as GTG or when we have strategized and intervened in an already existing process. We have been less successful when we expected individuals from the GTG to carry responsibilities for gender work in other situations such as task groups . . . [because] . . . GTG representatives do not always have a practical grounding to talk from . . . We need to have positions in affiliates with a specific task to work on gender issues. We also need a position/structure in NLC that focusses on gender issues (a form of GTG), i.e., without separation we will not achieve integration. In addition to this, we also need ways of working/methodologies in our work on the ground to ensure not only "incorporation" but a thoroughly gender-sensitive approach (i.e., this could include how field teams are constructed). One of our main weaknesses is that men say they don't feel comfortable here.

We also need to make sure that we don't only respond to "existing" issues (in whatever form) but we also need to introduce initiatives of our own . . . to include gender questions from the beginning.[62]

As a structure, the GTG succeeded in keeping gender relations on the agenda of affiliate programs. It was less effective in institutionalizing organizational learning (especially given high levels of staff turnover), and did not affect all NLC activities and campaigns. Nor did it achieve the desired "integration" with other task groups or develop sufficiently proactive strategies at executive level.

Gender Gets Lost

As in other contexts, when gender issues are combined with other needs, either all needs are satisfactorily met through the process, or some get lost. Gender concerns often end up as the casualty. At a national evaluation meeting in October 1993, GTG members reflected: "It is a problem getting gender onto staffing meetings' agendas—there are always too many issues." Yet, "if gender work is separated from other affiliate work, then it is even more difficult to synthesize the two."[63]

By November 1994, efforts were being made in a number of affiliates to build a gender component into the job descriptions of field staff, and to ensure that all staff, not only those working with women in the communities, are responsible for ensuring gender sensitivity.

Gender issues are only part of the internal cultural dynamics; often they compete with "mainstream" organizational-development issues. Getting to the point at which power dynamics (including those of gender) of organizational issues are automatically present in all organizational development processes and interventions will be long, slow, and arduous.

LEARNING

For most of the time I worked as gender coordinator, I felt that I was involved in a chaotic process. The urge for quick results was in constant tension with the inevitably slow and difficult nature of the work. Learning how to hold this tension while valuing the work was one of my hardest challenges. It is only with hindsight that I can see the problematic assumptions as well as the coherence and strategy that emerged during the process.

I was given an impossible task: two years to change an organization that was primarily about land and men into one that looked at land, women and men, and their interrelations. Such changes require: new staff (women fieldworkers); different methods (that can access the silences); different organizational processes (more reflection and evaluation); better integration between fieldwork and policy work; additional research skills (ones that can "see" a double-gendered reality); new job descriptions for general staff; and new organizational structures. Such mammoth changes inevitably unleash resistance, from both men and women; sophisticated strategies are needed to use the space won by a separate gender officer in the most usefully interventionist way possible.

Structure and Responsibility

With hindsight it is easy to see that work to be coordinated by the GTG was qualitatively different from that of the other task groups, which was apparently field/content or campaign driven. The decision to structure the formally constituted "gender work" as a "task group" was made without much critical reflection. Nor were the differences between the nature of this work and other tasks—and their impact on output—analyzed. For one thing, "gender work" did not have discrete boundaries, as did the other issues being coordinated via task groups; it had to influence all levels and all aspects of NLC work.

Drawing on assumptions that valued anti-hierarchical organizing and the need to build a constituency, the GTG recognized the importance of the director's support,[64] yet emphasized building support from below. In consequence building active support and responsibility among the key network leadership layers was neglected. We were unable to see the problems inherent in assuming that individuals with commitment, interest or experience in working with gender relations could be conflated with a "structure" or with ultimate responsibility.

Although the NLC director was an important catalyst for the initiation of the work, neither the NLC executive nor affiliate directors had to take any responsibility for it. That was left with the national gender coordinator. Having full responsibility is different from coordinating and acting as a resource person who can monitor activities or help strategize. We should have ensured that other task-group coordinators, affiliate directors, and the NLC executive as a whole had responsibility for ensuring "integration"; the gender coordinator's role would more appropriately be that of a resource person. This view is now clear, but at the time I am not sure it would have been possible to do things differently.

I therefore agree with the most recent coordinator that placing responsibility for all gender-related activities in one structure is both difficult and inappropriate. Rather, there needs to be a division of this work, both conceptually and in terms of practical responsibility:

1. the strategic and policy analysis work should be tied to *all* content areas of NLC programs, including work-practice issues and the nature of the "product." Responsibility should lie with national program coordinators;

2. the organizing and field work focussing on the empowerment of rural women within existing community structures; and

3. the need to address the racism and sexism faced by network staff as issues of internal organizational culture. These affect staff's ability to perform, and should be addressed through all formal human-resources and organizational-development processes in the network. The need for separate fora for women and men is still being debated.[65]

Process

I retain my initial belief that, for the NLC "gender work" to have meaning and longer-term impact, it would have to be part of a broader institutional change/organizational-development process and social-change strategy. The process did not focus on a single layer of the organization: it was
responsive to context; able to accommodate multiple meanings; and attempted to link with existing organizational opportunities. Thus, it laid a
broad foundation to be built upon. As the process deepened and people
gained experience, some of the strategic issues around content could become more focussed, as the complexity and multi-leveled nature of the issues
expanded to include internal dynamics. The early emphasis on developing
skills in participatory methodologies created space in the network for the
recognition that gender relations are an important social power relation that
is always contextually situated. I learnt quickly that processes identified with
"gender work" are a magnet for all manner of sensitive and conflictual issues,
and that this should be prepared for.

I also learnt that a commitment to participatory methods and a challenge to automatic assumptions of control are necessary, but not sufficient to
transform the status quo. Participatory methods can create spaces, can help
build confidence and self-esteem; but on their own they cannot transform
power relations.

Power relations cannot shift until responsibility is shifted. Unless
(marginalized/oppressed/disadvantaged) people take (or are given) responsibility, no amount of training, participatory methods, or process will shift
power. This is especially true in non-hierarchical situations, such as collectively run organizations, where the power involved in decision-making processes tends to be obscured. Without formal responsibility and access to decision-making power, not much will change.

Conceptualization: Integration versus Transformation

Conceptualizing the challenge in terms of integrating gender into existing processes creates a problem, as the very definition is limited. The language can imply that "gender" does not already exist in these processes, even
though it does, albeit in a form that we might not want. Moreover, "integration" implies an inclusion into the existing structure; yet, if "gender work" is
done well, it is likely to substantially alter the way everything is done. Hence
the perception early in the process: "giving women special attention will divert us from our main purpose." Such all-pervasive changes are slow, and can

be experienced as extremely threatening. It is important to keep flexible and able to respond to conditions as they move.

Six years into the change process, the network is now probably in a position to tackle some of the deeper issues: how work is organized; and the impact of the activist work culture that assumes, among other things, that one has no "other life." "Gender" has been institutionalized in the system to the extent that it is an issue that will not go away; resources are committed to coordinating and organizing the work. There are a considerable number of women and men in the network committed to transforming gender relations both "in here" and "out there" in communities. It is perhaps more possible now to shift final responsibility from the gender coordinator and the GTG to all program coordinators, affiliate directors, and the executive; and to start seriously addressing issues of deep structure.[66]

Working from a transformational perspective rather than an integrative one would recognize the centrality of transformed gender relations to the organization's core mission. It would examine how power is exercised in daily work practices and in the structure of the working day, and how the organization of work-time affects workers' ability to perform effectively. Experiences of a diverse work force would shape organizational culture rather than the demand that workers fit in to what exists. However, one must be continually mindful that the external context will limit the extent to which any organization can transform social realities. For instance, the current South African state has opted for market-based land reform; as such, the likelihood of transforming access to and control over land resources for poor rural women is slight.

Conclusion

This study sets out aspects of one of many stories that explain how the NLC began to reorient its mission and practice to be more inclusive of different women's concerns, and more complex in its engagement with gender relations. It has emphasized the significant role that an organized constituency—part of the NGO's client group, together with supportive workers within the NGO—can play in a changing organization. It has demonstrated the value of a separate structure that can be resourced to facilitate and prioritize ongoing work to transform oppressive gender power relations; it also pointed out some of its limitations, particularly if key organizational leaders do not take responsibility for the transformation process. The case highlights how impossible it is to engage with gender relations in a vacuum or with a preconceived blueprint. Meanings of gender relationships are continuously inter-woven with other social relations, including those of race, class, age, space, and time, and require flexible responsiveness.

Efforts to institutionalize integrating alternative views of gender relations into the organization's culture stress a processual approach that resisted quick-fix technical solutions and recognized that any achievable endpoint is transi-tory: the goal posts will always keep moving. A multi-faceted strategy built an internal group of supporters and challenged existing structures and prac-tices. This strategy operated at multiple levels, including those of the com-munity/client group; the staff members of the NGO; general organizational strategies; and processes, research, and organizing.

Since I left, the staff turnover has been massive—hardly anyone I worked with is still with the organization. The current culture in the national office has been described by an NLC evaluator.[67] as masculine and youthful. Per-haps we should heed the slogan of a local NGO working specifically with women farmworkers: "development is about becoming—never arriving."

Postscript

In 1997, Penny Plowman, an independent consultant, was commissioned to do an evaluation of the NLC gender program. Her report praises the in-crease in levels of awareness about gender issues at personal, organizational and field levels; the existence of gender programs in nearly all affiliates and the positive role of the work of the GTG in raising broader organizational development issues. She did however call for a more coherent gender strat-egy at a national level and for greater attention to be paid to ongoing gender awareness training.

NOTES

1. I would like to thank the National Land Committee (NLC) both for the experience I gained while working with them as their gender coordinator and for supporting the initial writing of the original case upon which this chapter has drawn extensively (Michelle Friedman, "Breaking the Silence—Women, Gender and Organizational Development: A Case Study of the National Land Committee, Gender Strategy—in Transition," unpublished paper, 1995a). I acknowledge all readers of earlier drafts, in particular Tessa Cousins, Colleen Crawford Cousins, Bronwyn James, Shamim Meer, Melanie Samson, and Penny Plowman, as well as the extensive comments gained during the book writing workshop in Ottawa in April 1998, and editorial support from Aruna Rao.

2. NLC Gender Task Group (GTG) Minutes, October (1993). All NLC Minutes are held in the NLC offices in Johannesburg.

3. Lydia Kompe, Janet Small and Beauty Mkhize, *The Rural Women's Movement. Holding the Knife on the Sharp Edge* (Johannesburg: Transvaal Rural Action Committee, 1994).

4. GTG Minutes, March (1994).

5. Elsewhere in this book, Tripp explores the power dynamics involved in the writing of a case study. As in Tripp's case, many actors participated in the events depicted in this story. Probably each of us would write it differently. During the change process, many workshops and meetings were minuted in great detail. While I rely heavily on these "records," and have considered the views of colleagues who commented on various versions of this text, the story recounted here is inevitably told from the perspective of my raced, sexed, classed, gendered and abled body. Consequently, my assumptions and biases, conscious and unconscious, are woven throughout the case.

6. An important part of the NLC process included developing indicators of "gender sensitivity" in an attempt to give this politically neutral term a contextually relevant meaning.

7. See Shamim Meer, "Gender and a Land Reform Vision" in NLC Land Reform Vision document (1995) for an assessment of where NLC stands in relation to this debate.

8. For a more detailed gendered analysis of land dispossession and the consequences of migrant labor see Meer (1995).

9. Cheryl Walker, "Land Reform and Gender in Post-apartheid South Africa" (paper presented to Gender, Poverty and Well-Being: Indicators and Strategies—An International Workshop, Trivandrum, Kerala, November 1997).

10. Masiphula Mbongwa, Rogier van den Brink and Johan van Zyl, "Evolution of the Agrarian Structure in South Africa" in van Zyl et al., *Agricultural Land Reform in South Africa* (Cape Town: Oxford University Press, 1996), 59. Cited in Walker (1997), 2.

11. Michelle Friedman, "The Rural Challenge: Women and Land," in *Southern Af-*

rica Report January (1994); Shamim Meer, ed., *Women, Land and Authority in Rural South Africa* (Cape Town: David Phillip, 1997); Walker (1997).

12. Walker (1997), 10.

13. See for example, Helen Bradford, "'We Are Now the Men': Women's Beer Protests in the Natal Countryside, 1929," Seminar Paper delivered to the History Department, University of Witwatersrand (1984); Frene Ginwala, "Women and the African National Congress, 1912–1943," *Agenda*, no. 8 (1990); Cheryl Walker, *Women and Resistance in South Africa* (London: Onyx Press, 1982).

14. Amanda Kemp, Noziwe Madlala, Asha Moodley, and Elaine Salo, "The Dawn of a New Day: South African Feminisms," *The Challenge of Local Feminism* (Boulder: Westview Press, 1995).

15. Kompe, Small and Mkhize (1994).

16. Friedman (1994).

17. Josette Cole, personal communication (Cape Town, 1996).

18. In the 1980s, black activists tended to become politically active in the liberation movements rather in the "struggle NGOs"; moreover, given the history of education in apartheid South Africa, research skills were relatively undeveloped among black Africans.

19. By the end of 1991 the nine affiliates had a combined staff of more than seventy people; Josette Cole, "Internal Background Discussion Document on NCAR/ NLC for the Period 1984–1993," prepared for NLC strategic planning process (1994).

20. Many of the white women who started off as fieldworkers in the NCAR network are today active in senior government positions (Land Affairs) as advisors or policy makers/influencers.

21. Since the gender program was initiated in mid-1992, a concern with race power relations surfaced strongly and a concerted attempt at instituting an affirmative-action program in this regard was commenced. A number of changes have been implemented. See Colleen Crawford Cousins, Tessa Cousins, and Michelle Friedman, "Holding the Space: Explorations of Power and Control in Training and Development." Avocado Paper Series 06/94, (Durban: OLIVE Information Services, 1994).

22. Walker (1994), Personal Communication, Pietermaritzburg.

23. It should be noted that this research program was launched prior to the existence of the Land and Agriculture Policy Centre's (LAPC) national and overarching research program into land and agrarian reform and rural-development policy.

24. The network also lacked the human capacity to coordinate, manage, and prioritize the national research program.

25. Cole (1994).

26. Cole (1994), 6.

27. Task groups were identified as: Restoration and land claims; labor tenancy;

farmworkers; research; gender; urbanization; rural local government; development and planning.

28. Minutes of the first formal NLC gender workshop, held as an NLC research workshop in Pietermaritzburg, July 1991. Minutes held in the NLC office in Johannesburg.

29. Lydia Kompe, interviewed in "A Driving Force," *Land Update* no. 17, Sep./Oct. 1992, 6.

30. Thanks are owed to Jane Bennett for pointing out that the term "integrate gender" is confusing because it implies that specific meanings of gender do not already exist. Use of "integrate" is therefore in quotation marks to alert the reader to this slippage. In fact, gender activists commonly mean integrate alternative or less oppressive meanings of gender relations.

31. Of ten affiliates, entire organizational workshops were held with five, and workshops with smaller subgroups within an affiliate were held with two. One affiliate did not express any interest. The ninth affiliate was very new and had its organizational workshop only seven months after the feasibility-study evaluation. (See Michelle Friedman, "Report to the National Land Committee" on the series of gender workshops held with affiliates, 1992.) The tenth affiliate was formed about a year after the process had begun.

32. Concurrent with the initiation of the GTG, a number of other task groups were being formed to coordinate and plan other aspects of network activities (Cole, 1994). The group at the evaluation meeting accepted existing network structures as the appropriate mechanism for pursuing national gender processes.

33. Minutes of the NLC Gender and Research Workshop, Pietermaritzburg, 21–23 June, 1992. Minutes are held in the NLC offices in Johannesburg.

34. At a GTG meeting some time later, one of the executive committee members expressed the view that the gender coordinator "position in NLC was imposed. The executive was not properly consulted." Cole, GTG Minutes March, 1993, 17.

35. Friedman (1995a).

36. Colleen Crawford Cousins, Tessa Cousins and Michelle Friedman, "Participatory Methods," Report from the workshop held for National Land Committee affiliates at Kwazamokuhle, Natal, Feb. 8–14, 1993.

37. Catherine Cross and Michelle Friedman, "Women in Tenure: Marginality and the Left Hand Power," Discussion paper for NLC affiliates on tenure issues and gender questions (1993).

38. Michelle Friedman, "Learning from Doing: Rural Women's Study Tour," *Agenda* 24, (1995b); Janet Small, "A Lesson for Life—The NLC Women's Study Tour," *Speak* no. 66, Johannesburg, 1994a ; Janet Small, "Women Arming Themselves for the Future. The NLC Women's Study Tour," *Land Update* no. 34, October 1994, 1994b.

39. GTG Minutes, July 1994.

40. Naila Kabeer, *Reversed Realities—Gender Hierarchies in Development Thought* (London: Verso, 1994).

41. Friedman (1992), 5.

42. Cole, personal communication, 1997.

43. GTG Minutes, July 1994.

44. GTG Minutes, March 1994.

45. GTG Minutes, November, 1993.

46. GTG Minutes, October 1994

47. Friedman (1992).

48. Friedman (1992).

49. Friedman (1992), 6.

50. Bydawell (1997), 44–45

51. Although men were never barred from attending GTG meetings (and in fact sometimes men would attend), in practice, it was usually women who were the most committed participants.

52. GTG Minutes, November 1994.

53. See Crawford-Cousins et al. (1994) for an analysis of the conflicts and dynamics during this week.

54. Arnold Mindell, *The Year I. Global Process Work* (Britain: Arkana, 1989); Arnold Mindell, *The Leader as Martial Artist. An Introduction to Deep Democracy* (New York: HarperCollins, 1993).

55. I understand that, more recently, a number of the affiliates that initially strongly resisted separate organizing of women have learnt that it is one of the crucially important strategies necessary to confront patriarchal gender relations and maximize women's participation in land-reform processes.

56. GTG Minutes, October 1993.

57. GTG Minutes, November 1994.

58. Anne Mager, GTG Minutes, October 1993, 5.

59. Daphne Mashile, "Reflections from the Transvaal Rural Action Committee's Perceptions on Gender Integration at Local Affiliate Level." Report for the GTG Meeting, November, 1994.

60. GTG Minutes, October 1993. [Note: I'm omitting the Lydia Kompe allusion because it is implicit from the text, EB]

61. GTG Minutes, October 1993.

62. GTG Minutes, July 1994.

63. GTG Minutes, October 1993.

64. This is not to deny the support from a number of affiliate directors; however, support and responsibility are two different matters.

65. Melanie Samson, Proposed Process for developing a National Gender Strategy (Discussion document, August 1997).

66. For discussions on the "deep structure" of an organization see Anne-Marie Goetz, "Managing Organizational Change: The 'Gendered' Organization of Space and

Time," *Gender and Development* 5, no. 1 (1997); and Aruna Rao and Rieky Stuart, "Rethinking Organizations: A Feminist Perspective," *Gender and Development* 5, no. 1 (1997).

67. Lynnette Maart, personal communication, Cape Town, February, 1998.

68. Penny Plowman, "Review of the NLC Gender Programme." Final Report to the NLC, unpublished paper, Johannesburg (1997).

7

TANK GIRLS, TROUBLE, AND THE EMPIRE STRIKES BACK: A CASE STUDY

Rebecca Tripp

ON JULY 10, 1997, the general manager of a large, low-income, public-housing organization in a Canadian city was fired. The organization's new board had declined to meet with senior staff, appeared unwilling to learn about the organization or to articulate new strategic directions; board members held frequent in-camera meetings and were rude to staff at open meetings. The board was clearly shifting toward privatization despite the general manager's opposition both to the sale of public-housing stock and private-sector management.

Her termination discussion with the new chair lasted four minutes. He offered to maintain her e-mail on-line until she could send a farewell to staff, with whom she had worked for more than four years. He then asked her to leave the building and rescinded his offer. She did, leaving behind the organization and twenty five years of public-service work.

Those of us committed to constructing different organizational possibilities, and involved in the change process she had begun, immediately felt the reverberations—for the residents, for staff, and for public-sector organizations.

This is not the story about one individual or one lost job, but about an organization trying to change its service-delivery practices to become more humane, caring, and respectful, by altering organizational and individual conduct and ways of thinking. And it is about organizational change as a discursive activity, marked by power, and imbued with possibilities and limitations that affect what an organization, and the people associated with it, can do.

INTRODUCTION

Change Work and Questions of Power

My intention in writing this case study as a problematic narrative is to reflect the complexities, the unevenness, and untidiness of organizational-development consulting and organizational-change work. First, however, I want to underline the unreliability of words. They are important sense-making tools, but inadequately represent the "change work" we undertake, while shaping what we can think, say, and do. Words have the power to order our perceptions and, therefore, our thoughts about those perceptions.

The concept of deep structure, offered elsewhere in this text, is a way to make sense of what lies underneath the surface of everyday organizational experience. The plays of power that affect the deep structures and mental models in organizations also affect us as change agents: we contend with "structures" that we often cannot "see," but must infer. Power is continually at play through these troubling interchanges.

I use the term "trouble" frequently in this text: the trouble of the bureaucracy, the trouble bodies underwent, the trouble of thinking differently. Thus, writing can be a means to trouble theory, to question thinking, to interrogate practice. It is also a provocation, to enliven our practice and to remind us of the play of power circulating through us as languaging subjects shaped by language.

My intention in the writing then is:

1. to tell a story about a change intervention;

2. to use and trouble taken-for-granted notions of organizational consulting and change work; and

3. to grapple with the problem of change work as meaning-making and therefore as a problem of power.

UH—An Initial Description

UH is a pseudonym for a large, urban public-housing organization in Canada, established in the early 1950s to address the desperate need of low-income families for affordable housing. Thousands of families now wait for publicly assisted housing. Almost no construction dollars are being allocated to public housing; the provincial government is determined to divest itself of its responsibility for public housing, and to privatize it as much as possible.

UH has had, and continues to have, a reputation as an appalling landlord with entrenched organizational difficulties.

In an attempt to improve its service delivery, internal effectiveness, and reputation, the new general manager articulated a commitment to humane and equitable treatment of residents. In 1993, she initiated the Equity Project, focussing on employment equity. In 1996, she undertook the Business Planning Process, which sought to integrate equity into strategic planning. I will refer briefly to the former but concentrate on the change work of the latter during its eighteen-month existence, until the general manager was fired.

Description and the Problem of Belatedness

Having spent almost three years at UH, I see and describe the troubled complexity of the organization differently now than when I began.

What can be "seen" and "known"—and when—is a function of power relations in play; these shape what can be known, who holds which functions of influence in what structures (and what can be put into words to legitimize which functions of influence). These functions, structures, and discourses are difficult to perceive, interrogate, and unmask without troubling them. And, like those already at play, the power relations set in motion by our change work frequently became inaccessible to questioning or unmasking. For power conceals its tracks, implicating everybody in its concealments.

For example, at the outset, those of us working to "change" UH talked about it in the neutralized rhetoric of organization behavior: middle-class manners, professional ethicality, a hopeful attitude. UH was "troubled" or "difficult," not "violent" or "impossible." If one of us did speak more intensely or negatively, others tended to disengage from or refocus the conversation, thereby disinclining us to grapple with the depth of the difficulties.

Given the belatedness of "knowing," I remain troubled, in writing about UH and the consulting intervention, by the tendency of terms to simplify, homogenize, and stabilize meaning, when what is being described is complex, various and unstable. I trouble myself, as well, with my descriptions of the many others who are represented in this story, but whose own lived experience remains outside it. Thus does language "other" the "other;" and thus, in reading, is "other than" always in play.

Suffice to say that the problems of "languaging" the context has been integral to this story and to what its telling tells—and does not tell—about the work of power and change.

The Organizational Context of UH

UH manages thousands of units. It collects rent from tenants and receives a financial subsidy from the provincial government; its operating budget is over $100 million. It also provides a rent subsidy to private landlords who house low-income residents in several thousand privately owned units. Other than the homeless, UH residents are the city's poorest citizens. More than a hundred thousand individuals live in UH communities, and many have done so for at least two generations. Obviously, it is dangerous, particularly during a Canadian winter, to live on the streets or in make-shift housing. Yet, unable to find housing and/or resistant to the punitive bureaucratization of their needs, increasing numbers of people, young and old, are living on the street.

UH was conceived of as transition housing for poor families. Most of the buildings were built during a twenty-year period in the 1950s and 1960s, many replacing slum housing with city-core housing tracts. Many critics believe that early construction practices participated in a deeply entrenched system of bribes, pay-offs, and corruption.

Many believe that inferior building materials were used, not only to increase profits but also because of a persistent belief that poor people "deserve" sub-standard housing and that the entitlements of poor people can be bought and sold. Money is to be made from poverty, but not by the poor.

Through years of corruption and inadequate funding for capital repairs, many structures have not received adequate up-keep. The quality of day-to-day maintenance, repairs, and cleaning are regular subjects of resident complaints. Stairwells in many buildings are filthy; garbage is strewn in corridors and on the grounds. There can be feces in the elevators. Cockroaches and mice ("pests" and "rodents" as they are referred to) are a never-ending problem. Experts estimate that it will require millions of dollars to bring the buildings up to standard. Given prevailing government priorities and a blatant disregard for the poor, that money will never be allocated.

Originally, these communities housed poor, white families. During the last twenty years, provincial policy has given housing priority to refugees; thus, the communities have housed more refugees and immigrants. Segregation of "visible-minority" communities is historical and persistent. Most of the communities have become sites of intense internal discrimination, racial conflict, and fighting. Drug trafficking, theft, prostitution, rape, murder, and abuse persist. Police relations are poor.

Many of these communities have also become settings for community activism and development projects, from the innovative to the disastrous.

The lack of coordination in community empowerment has further disen-franchised many residents; it has not broken the cycles of poverty; neither has it enabled adequate recreation programs, facilities, and security.

Raucous resident encounters over the years have prompted UH to con-sider establishing resident councils, seen by some long-standing resident groups as a means to further co-opt dissent. Many community partners and residents experience UH as inefficient, bureaucratic, and non-respectful. Many community partners and residents regard UH as a terrible landlord.

CONDITIONS FOR CHANGE

The Governance Structure until 1994

UH is funded with municipal, provincial, and federal tax dollars; yet it is governed by an appointed board reporting to the governmental parent cor-poration, which also has a Board. Both UH and its parent corporation are, none the less, agencies of a provincial-government ministry, with a histori-cally distant and benign relationship. Until 1994, appointments to UH's Board were usually made every two years, by the federal, provincial, and municipal governments, and confirmed by a provincial Order in Council. (Federal and provincial government terms are a maximum of five years; municipal elec-tions are held every three years.)

The Governance Structure after 1994

In 1994, a year after the general manager was hired, the provincial gov-ernment hired a major consulting firm to undertake a large-scale organiza-tional investigation. Based on the results of that investigation, Board mem-bers were appointed, for the duration of the next Board, exclusively by the provincial minister. The new Chair was to report directly to the Minister, by-passing the Chair, the CEO, and the Board of the parent bureaucracy. This revised structure of UH governance became increasingly important to the change work, as the parent bureaucracy, which I refer to as "the empire," began to exert itself in uncharacteristic ways.

The structural alterations and complex appointment process led to dys-functional and chaotic board practices. Moreover, when the provincial gov-ernment changed, so did the political criteria for appointments; and the ostensible commitment to social housing melted away. During the general manager's tenure, massive changes in Board membership, and conflicting

Board expectations and directions to UH senior staff undercut the possibilities of cohesion and unified focus at UH. The structural chaos also allowed for intractabilities that kept UH operating in predictable ways.

Frequent shifts in Boards and philosophical approaches to social housing have weakened governance and accountability within the organization, particularly at management levels, and ossified it between senior staff and the Board, and between the government and the Board. Boards, chairs, and senior staff have been terminated, regularly and inelegantly; many staff have come to view UH governance as chaotic and irrational; and the agendas of governments, bureaucrats, business interests, and politicians were difficult to detect and affect.

Internal Context   The parent bureaucracy and UH have made countless policy and practical decisions that imply that residents are deserving of deplorable treatment. For example, one decision required all residents to pay for cable television. Staff refused to reconsider the case of a blind resident until the resident elicited media attention. In another decision, a rent calculation error by staff had led to an eviction notice being sent to a resident. Staff decided it would take too much time to correct the error, so the tenant was evicted.

The new general manager quickly identified numerous poor management practices contributing to ineffective operations and poor service delivery: an ineffectual performance-management process; non-competitive remuneration; weak human-resources practices, traditional stratification of employment across gender and race (lower-paying jobs tended to be held by women and visible minorities), serious gender-related and racial tensions (predominantly between white and visible-minority Canadians); inadequate risk-management procedures; ineffective senior-level decision making; poor morale; inadequate property management, including wide-spread contempt and disregard for needs of residents.

UH employs more than a thousand staff: 450 unionized maintenance staff; 170 unionized security and some office staff; and management staff. The bulk of the non-unionized staff do property-management tasks; the rest are senior and middle administrative staff or clerical staff. Most of the maintenance employees are white, male, Italian, or Portuguese immigrants; some staff are or have been residents of UH. More white women have been entering senior, clerical, and administrative positions in the last few years; however, men still dominate in senior and operations areas.

Long service is the norm: many senior staff have worked up and across the organization. Union relations have become weak and acrimonious over the years: one union has had so many internal rifts that fist fights have broken out at their meetings.

In the first year of the general manager's employment, two Board Chairs were terminated; and the general manager was a respondent to a human rights complaint (which took several years to be investigated), provoking criticism of her rhetoric on equity. (The complaint was not upheld.) She uncovered significant inconsistencies in purchasing processes involving goods and services, which led to the firing of several staff members.

The general manager was threatened on several occasions, her home and vehicles vandalized. She was fitted for a bullet-proof vest. Ensuring day-to-day staff security at work and public meetings became increasingly important and difficult.

Was this an organization ready for planned change? Assuredly not. None the less, when I became involved with the strategic planning process, the Board and the government insisted that the general manager "make it happen," a requirement both impossible and not amenable to questioning. Yet the imperative to change—regardless of readiness or capability—may have prevented UH from making any real change and precluded important and difficult discussion about what was and was not possible.

History of Change Interventions at UH

In the ten to fifteen years prior to my experience there, numerous reorganizations and restructurings, many organizational-development undertakings (including flirtations with Total Quality Management and Customer Service) left hints of a presence in pockets of UH, but never really altered work practices. None of these initiatives considered the contradictions within UH or the complexity of the societal context. On the contrary, they tended to erase that complexity, and deadened employees' capacity to think harder about issues of "quality" and raise better questions about the difference between a "customer," a "citizen," a "resident," "the poor." They have left all staff and residents convinced that change would not or could not occur, and skeptical about the net effect and ulterior motivation of employer-initiated participatory-change efforts.

In Fall 1993 I began work for the general manager, with two other consultants, on the Equity Project. UH was experiencing tremendous pressure from the media and residents, due largely to an increasingly dysfunctional Board; and the Chair attracted media attention for alleged unauthorized expenditures and conflict of interest.

The Equity Project   The general manager began this project as a result of the then provincial government's intention to implement Employment Equity Legislation, mandating joint labor-management implementation of equity training, conducting an employment systems review and workforce survey, and developing an equity plan. Employers were to set, meet, and account to the government for specific targets to move traditionally disadvantaged visible minorities, women, persons with disabilities, and native Canadians into, up, and across all organizations affected by the legislation. The equity project at UH tended to focus on race and minority representation due to prevailing urban racial tension, the skills and investments of a black woman consultant, and the deep race-related conflicts at UH.

The Equity Project introduced and consolidated ways of thinking about employment equity at UH that are important in making sense of the Business Planning Project. The equity discourse was shaped inadvertently by the dissonance of equity issues and larger strategic or business-planning concerns, the difficulties of integrating them, and the normalizing discourses that separate them. (Even the Employment Equity Legislation that prompted the Equity Project articulates its interest in individual and group equity only by way of employment targets. It cannot speak to the advantages equity integration can offer organizational service delivery.)

Like the Legislation, the Equity Project focussed theoretically and pedagogically on internal employment issues. We provided training, management coaching, policy development, conflict mediation, and human-resources problem-solving to help senior staff and employees become more aware of the mechanisms and effects of oppression, particularly racism, in employment practices (such as recruitment, hiring, promotion, access to training). In our training sessions, senior staff confronted their inclinations toward racism, and studied the requirements of the impending legislation. Our coaching and problem-solving roles were to help staff use new thinking to alter discriminating practices. "Racism" was understood largely as a "white" practice and form of thinking and feeling that could be rethought, which would lead to structural changes.

The available rhetoric tended both to neutralize difference (as in, we must become the same in employment opportunity), and to rigidify difference (as in, race and skin color are complete and permanent differentiating devices, which must be underlined before they can be discounted).

For some employees, the training we conducted signaled the possibility that their experience of racism (and/or sexism) would no longer be sanctioned, prohibited both by law and by the new knowledge of their white senior managers, colleagues, and staff. For others, the training signaled the inability of management (however well intentioned) to comprehend the complexities and depth of structural racism and discrimination.

The implied promise of a fair and just workplace, escalating expectations, simultaneous skepticism, and chaos made it very difficult to identify and solidify gains or acknowledge real limits. Yet many thought equity work had been "done;" this made it increasingly difficult to examine biased and discriminatory employment practices and day-to-day decision-making that affected all staff.

When the Employment Equity Legislation was rescinded by a new provincial government in 1995, the equity project wound down. Nonetheless, the new Transition Board articulated in their minutes, a commitment to the spirit of the equity legislation:

that diversity exists in the population being served; that four groups are recognized as having employment disadvantage: aboriginal and First Nations persons, persons with disabilities, racial minority persons, and women; that knowledge and accommodation of difference was to be reflected in all processes of communication, decision-making and team-building.

Their commitment to equity was often seen to have accomplished it, while it neutralized the injustices the commitment was meant to challenge. It also had the unintended effect of increasing the difficulty of talking frankly and specifically about the many other serious issues at UH.

Quanta at UH   In reaction to media attention and apparent poor governance at the Board level the government announced that Quanta (a pseudonym for a large international consulting firm) would investigate and make recommendations regarding UH's structure, governance, and service delivery. In Spring 1994, Quanta consultants began interrogating staff, residents, suppliers, and partners. Soon thereafter the UH Board was dismissed; three senior Quanta consultants became the interim Board reporting directly to the Minister. Quanta remained in charge until Spring 1995.

It was an extremely difficult time for staff: forensic investigators examined tendering and purchasing processes for illegal procedures. A resident hot line was established to capture the anticipated onslaught of residents' complaints. The study cost more than $1.2 million, yet little illegal conduct was uncovered and few complaints from residents received. Quanta concluded that UH was very troubled (the fault of no one), and in need of rapid and radical change.

Quanta's intervention mirrored government concern that the situation was urgent, yet their recommendations tended to be cursory and not readily implementable. Their support of the general manager and their recommendation for a "working Board" (albeit with the usual two-year term) propelled the imperative for change. Given this imperative, the equity work in relation to the strategic demands and day-to-day realities of the organization became increasingly tangential.

THE RENEWED MANDATE FOR CHANGE

The Role of the General Manager

My focus on the general manager in this case is twofold: to draw attention to her central role in UH, during her four-year tenure and, especially, during the required change process; and to put her and her role in context, given the history of the organization and the shifting power figures and alternating structures and functions of power that marked her tenure.

The general manager would be perceived as a white, middle-class woman (as would I, albeit differently). These identity categories are relevant to her being the senior person at UH at that historical moment. They suggest contradictory power effects of gender, race, and class particularized at the end of the twentieth century in a North American context. They do not say all there is to say; but unsaid, they disappear as markers. "White," "woman," and "middle class" are not straightforward terms; but act as signifiers by which we see ourselves and are seen, in terms of potentiality and, particularly, of access: to language and, thereby, the power to shape meanings; to positional authority, and thereby, the power to alter organizational structures; to affect meanings and structures; and to affect the conduct of others through persuasion and social discipline. These modes of access to influence do not guarantee individual or organizational change; but without them change work initiated at the top cannot even begin.

Management Intentions

Improving Service through Service Equity and Employment Equity   The direction given the general manager when hired was to improve resident relations; to ensure ethical, economically responsive, and effective business practices; and to rationalize organizational governance.

Her determination to have fairer employment practices was mirrored by her commitment to have staff treat residents more courteously. This gradually became part of more complex requirements of staff to understand how poverty and difference affected residents' conduct and staff treatment of residents. This later came to be understood, problematically, as service equity (as distinguished from but related to employment equity).

As we shall see, both service equity and employment equity created intense conflict and deep disappointment at UH.

Decentralizing Service and Clarifying Accountability

The general manager held the view that relations in the workplace and service to residents would improve by giving responsibility to managers and staff, supporting them to make decisions, holding them to account for decisions made, and following through. What she could not anticipate was how deeply the accountability requirement would mobilize some existing power regimes and coalesce others.

The new Board adopted the central recommendation of Quanta, namely to place decision-making for service delivery closer to the residents: new offices were opened on the properties, staffed by new property managers to oversee the maintenance of buildings and grounds, to collect rent, and to resolve day-to-day residents' concerns. New property managers had to become familiar with and address local security problems and community issues. Most staff were insufficiently equipped for these new skill requirements and required extensive training.

THE PROJECT DESIGN: BUSINESS PLANNING

Background

In Spring 1995, several key events occurred that would shape the required change process: Quanta released their report, and the Quanta-based Board was named by the provincial government reporting directly to the Minister for a two-year period; then the provincial government was defeated by a more conservative government, and the Employment Equity Legislation was rescinded.

In Summer 1995, the new Board directed the general manager to decentralize the property-management function and to adjust the rest of the UH to this structure—in six months!

The Business-Planning Task

In early Winter 1996, UH tendered a consulting project on Decision-Making, Problem-Solving, and Delegation. UH sought a consultant to assist in redesigning organization operations and to support decision-making processes to align with the newly reorganized structure. Decentralization meant entire branches were to shift their focus to supporting either the residents directly or those who worked directly with residents. There were no mechanisms in place, and no useful meeting venues to shape decision-making or to clarify problem identification and solution. I was awarded the tender. The project was to last approximately eighteen months, billed at three days per week.

Early on I facilitated conversations to entice beleaguered and skeptical senior staff and a battle-weary general manager to imagine that the hostile environment might be ordered into problems to be solved, decisions to be made, operations to be undertaken.

Many staff participated only reluctantly in these and many other conversations: they believed that UH was incapable of change, that this general manager would disappear like other general managers, and that my consultant's optimism was ill-founded. As well, they lacked interest in the larger social-justice project, had an investment in keeping things as they were and in protecting one another, and in protecting themselves from yet another disappointment.

There was also a general inability to conceptualize the shift to a de-centralized structure and an accurate assessment that staff skills were insufficient to perform within a de-centralized structure. Between Summer 1995 and January 1996, all positions had been rewritten, and staff were being shifted into new positions; organizational upheaval and staff dislocation and relocation continued until June 1997.

Staff talked about organizational turbulence, but it was so long-standing and persistent that mere talk could not resolve it. Ideally, strategic or business planning comes before downsizing and restructuring; yet UH's Board had directed an all-encompassing reorganization in such a narrow time frame that the Equity/Human Resource Branch could do no more than job reclassifications and job matching. It was also impossible to ready employees so quickly for new tasks and responsibilities.

Business-Planning Goals

The Business Planning Project began in early 1995. I was the sole change-work consultant and staff liaison; I reported to the general manager and worked with senior staff:

1. to develop a business plan, business priorities, and procedures, to be understood by all staff, to ensure equitable work practices and service delivery;

2. to devise simple and straightforward organizational-performance indicators, and to help senior staff gauge the organization's effectiveness, including a simple staff performance-appraisal system;

3. to facilitate shared understanding and agreements about the nature and expected quality of service;

4. to set clear accountabilities and responsibilities for operations and service delivery, and well understood accountabilities for line functions; and

5. to develop mechanisms for integrating all major service and structural activities from the point of service delivery (in this case, the Property Manager's office) "up" the organization to senior staff and "down." My intention, and that of the general manager was to keep "real work" related to equity practices and principles. Though not the only reason for later trouble, this effort was a highly combustible combination.

The Decentralized Imperative   In Canada, a tainted-blood scandal and revelations of irresponsible practices by child-welfare agencies have made organizational liability a focus of public attention. Yet UH's restructuring left intact entrenched ways of dealing with residents, but confused and contradicted roles and responsibilities. For example, the general manager discovered that Fire Code regulations were not being followed; legal orders to comply were lost and her directions to address problems met with constant delay. As senior in the chain of risk management, she was personally liable for the safety of staff and residents; yet she could not effect her responsibility because of structural chaos, individual incompetence, and staff contempt for residents.

The business-planning work with the general manager, directors, and branch staff was designed specifically to produce a "clarification" of new ways of doing business. It was to be a blueprint of how the new organization was to work.

Business Planning   The business-planning process was to link the Board's orientation, training, a new performance-appraisal process, organizational-performance indicators, benchmarking and policy development; and to co-ordinate other consultants. Each of these related activities needed to align conceptually to the planning process. The planning document would provide the overall framework and describe how the pieces "fit"; and articulate the underlying aspiration for these changes and how specific organizational practices could be understood and augmented. It described the business, outlined targets for organizational performance, provided explanations for terms, and reiterated the commitment to equity.

The general manager hoped that a business-planning process could help staff to talk about what was happening and give her an opportunity to increase understanding, alter conduct, and enable UH to "do business differently." The Plan itself would be important, but more so would be conversations with senior staff about their thoughts about UH's work and resulting opportunity for the general manager to shape their thinking and have her thinking shaped by theirs.

The planning document was the result of extensive conversations with senior staff and they with their staff about how UH should "work" *after* the restructuring. I facilitated most of those meetings, wrote drafts of the document for review, prepared process diagrams to accompany text, had one-to-one discussions with most senior staff about how their branch might function in the de-centralized structure, and coached senior staff with regard to their staff-performance issues. My primary intention was to assist senior staff to articulate a framework for the effective management of UH's housing portfolio. The senior operations directors undertook a "steering" role for the business-planning process.

Keeping Equity Tied to the Planning Process   My aspiration, and that of the general manager's and other change-work staff, was:

1. to build a cohesive senior operating group that included the senior staff in property management, asset management, security, and community relations;

2. to distinguish operations from finance, human resources, equity, and technology;

3. to keep equity issues informing the discussion;

4. to increase participation in decision-making; and

5. to link all major change projects (organizational performance and performance appraisal) both conceptually and practically.

Questions of equitable treatment of employees and residents came and went during discussions. Downsizing had resulted in many members of traditionally under-represented employee groups losing their jobs (as they were last hired); therefore, matching UH's staff composition to that of the external environment was impossible. However, the Manager of Training and the coordinator of the performance-appraisal process persistently both pursued with the line staff practical and innovative ways to ensure under-represented employees learned needed skills, were involved in decision-making that affected them, had access to information and opportunities to compete for internal promotions, and were given useful non-discriminatory feedback about their work.

For most senior staff, equity increasingly became either a non-issue when the Legislation was rescinded, or an issue to be resisted. Our efforts now seem like rearranging the deck chairs on the *Titanic*. Senior staff knew the rhetoric of planning and equity and when to produce it, but often did not agree with it and rarely even knew how to put in place agreed-upon practices to achieve it.

ANALYSIS: WORKING WITH QUESTIONS OF POWER

The Assumptions behind the Business-Planning Process

Clearly, UH could not address all critical organizational issues at once. It had altered (or was trying to alter) its structure and method of service delivery, but needed to be able to measure organizational outcomes, to assess success and the need for corrective action. It needed a way to appraise what individuals did, and hold them accountable. Moreover, in terms of employment-equity rights, UH was governed by the Human Rights Code—the rescinding of Employment Equity Legislation notwithstanding.

UH's history with change initiatives had made senior staff very resistant to data collection and analyses. They wanted strategies to arise from issues and problems that they identified in conversation.

Many had, justifiably, disputed Quanta's research claims, and disputed the capacity of data to "tell the truth"; covertly, they did not believe that any consolidating plan could shape meaning and affect conduct. They also had little tolerance for thinking about their current and past situation, and al-

most none for thinking about their thinking. The "Let's get on with it" senti-
ment overtook a more complex view of the situation, often thwarting more
precise assessments of the situation.

A more complex characterization of what was happening inside UH and
how the change process was affecting it was and remains difficult because the
"rational" approach obscures ongoing, contradictory, and powerful workings
of institutions/organizations: our "neutral" ways of talking actually limit what
we can see and know.

Some senior staff, long-time observers, and government officials used
the contradictions produced by the rational planning process for their own
political advantage, while publicly appearing supportive of it. Others, in the
field and far-removed from the nexus of change work, saw no difference.

Our planning process was intended to be continuous, vested in the peda-
gogical idea that we would learn what "worked" as we went along. I reasoned
that the alterations in the organization after the massive redeployment of
staff and reconfiguration of relationships and responsibilities made it necessary to document "who is to do what" before we tried to solve more complex
organizational problems.

While the Board had directed UH to become decentralized, no one shared
the same view of what that meant. Nor did staff share ideas of how "support
staff" would be realigned to support the front-line, property-management
operations staff. Many support staff deeply resented what they experienced
as losing influence.

The early compromise adopted by senior staff was to think of and refer
to the new structure as "coordinated decentralization." Decentralization was
the Board's structural mechanism to achieve fairer and more respectful treatment of residents: this rhetorical and structural compromise signaled the
failure of the aspiration of better treatment for residents that was at the heart
of so much of the general manager's work.

Planning as a Discursive and Relational Activity

The Planning Document as a Discursive Effect   By mid-fall 1996, we produced a draft document, *A Better UH*, which outlined who did what in the
"coordinated decentralization." Our intention had been to create a readable
and accessible discussion text that would "explain" some key organizational
ideas, such as client/stakeholder, equitable service to residents, function,
responsibility, liability and targets/benchmarks for evaluation of "success." It
attempted to describe the new structure, departmental interfaces, and un-

folding ways of working. The document was to be a key means of making and shaping meaning about UH for its staff.

The planning document was edited for clear language, accessibly designed, and filled with photographs of staff at work. I did not anticipate that efforts to "clarify" responsibilities under the new structure would be so perniciously thwarted, nor that "clarifying" might set in motion tactics that would mask the mechanisms that made the change work so difficult.

By January 1997, the general manager and senior staff had hosted meetings throughout UH to discuss the document, the issues, and the problems. However, the Board was in the final months of its two-year mandate and their renewal had become unlikely. The conservative government began speaking more pointedly about privatizing a large number of public-sector functions, including social housing; and the CEO/Executive Chair was lobbying openly in the media for severing UH from its parent governmental organization.

As UH staff were uncertain about job security and the viability of UH, "consolidating" staff thinking became increasingly difficult. Public conversations about the "new" UH and structural and operational changes to keep it viable co-existed with staff worries that nothing could be done to protect jobs or alleviate the situation. Staff continued practices disrespectful of residents and exposed them to harm without acknowledging the disparity between such behavior and the values of the "new" UH.

What was really at stake was social housing as a public responsibility, requiring public funding and public debate; what was at stake was decent service to residents.

Discursive Effects and Relations of Power   In April 1997, all but two Board members, including the CEO/Executive Chair, were not re-appointed. The newly appointed Chair, a member of the previous Board, had a declared conflict of interest in a privately owned property-management company and had had a hostile prior work relationship with the general manager. Two of the new appointments were from the parent-organization's board.

It was clear that a repositioning was taking place. Communication between the general manager, the Chair, and Board members became increasingly difficult. Tight conversations—or none—with the new Board replaced the relative transparency of working with the Interim Board. Intentions now had to be inferred, and could not be queried, undermining and soon completely altering the planning initiatives.

Between April and June 1997 the general manager and I talked often about the potential loss of public housing to private interest, and about how we might continue in the face of it. She had such conversations with a few trusted women in the organization, one of whom dubbed the women "think girls." This later became "tank girls" (from the science-fiction comic), a term of amusing aptness for the general manager.

The tank girls tried to share as much support and information as possible. Each held a major piece of the change process or organizational responsibility: organizational training, overseeing the new performance-appraisal process, human-resource procedures, and policy development. Each tried to anticipate events and "keep" moving. None was prepared to abandon the work. All were exhausted and began to acquire significant illnesses and physical ailments.

Throughout the eighteen months of the planning project, the general manager worked more than sixty hours a week, handled thousands of information documents, attended hundreds of government and community meetings, fielded dozens of resident calls, and conducted countless supervisory and staff meetings. She hosted meetings with virtually every staff person, in large and small groups, to discuss the planning document and the challenge facing UH. She continued to pay attention to the day-to-day problems of inequity. It was not enough.

During this time, I acted as strategic-planning consultant, internal animator, staff person to link the key change projects, and coach to the general manager and a few other senior staff. I produced dozens of reports, facilitated countless meetings, and undertook to think "through" with staff directions to suggest and methods to pursue. This, too, was not enough.

We tried routine organizational-development strategies to "settle" the organization and to lay the groundwork for better ways of managing properties, and meeting residents' needs. However, the internal contradictions and unvoiced resistance among staff, the political and rhetorical context within and outside the bureaucracy and in the urban environment, ongoing staff job insecurity, and the recalcitrant inability of staff to "feel for" residents dissolved the intended consolidation of the planning documents.

Those of us at the center of the change initiatives realized the impossibility of holding any ground we might have won. We sporadically talked about and thought through the implications of the mounting threats to UH, but were unable to devise a methodical strategy that might have salvaged the outcome. Instead, we continued to rely on the change mechanisms in place: to enhance discussion and participation; to shape meaning; to alter the organizational structure; to amend work practices, to increase skill levels; and to provide clear direction and feedback. We were unable to adequately interrogate the ways that other power mechanisms were engaging with, altering, and overriding our own.

I want to begin my analysis by looking at three issues of power and difference:

1. the coalitions and relations of power inside and outside UH, and their effect on meanings consolidated in the planning document;

2. the discursive strategies vested in the planning document as a power mechanism, and its effect on the relations of power; and

3. how those involved most directly in the change work came to bear the marks of the struggles as a direct result of the deleterious effects of power.

Tracing Power Relations

The Empire   The situation at UH was and remains complex: loose but powerful circuits were formed to serve multiple interests by the governments per se, particular government officials, bureaucrats, business-interest groups, some community activists, some key residents, and staff. At the beginning of her work at UH, the general manager built strong allies, among women in the parent governmental organization and the ministry who shared her commitment to equitable service to residents. By the end of her tenure at UH, these allies had all been replaced by men (who might talk about respectful treatment of residents, but whose decisions contradicted any such commitment).

Toward the end of her tenure, neither the general manager, nor I, nor any of the women closest to the change process had sufficient access to, understanding of, or capacity to influence those powerful and complex relations in the bureaucracy "above" us, which directly affected every employee, every resident, and the change process itself. This occurred in part because of structural changes that altered the reporting relations, and diminished contact at the staff level while increasing it at the Board level. It also resulted from replacing allies committed to social housing with individuals committed to private interests, particularly that of the new Chair, who supported the government's privatization agenda. These new people positioned themselves far from the general manager and supporters of her public-focussed agenda.

Eventually, the parent bureaucracy, supported by UH's Board, removed the general manager, thereby derailing the planning process. It did so in a way so punitive as to clearly demonstrate the power of the "empire" to the remaining staff: no questions, no resistance.

Women in the Change Process   The general manager and the women who occupied all consultant and staff positions with the change process were white; some had a feminist analysis that held gender to be a significant social category and site of potential oppression. We were small in numbers but held senior-level connections.

The general manager had significant line control over the work lives of staff. Staff were aware of and fearful of that power. Our influential association with the general manager's central project gave us the power to affect the lives of staff. We became a power network, both influential and to be resisted.

Yet, there were enormous differences in terms of how we understood and enacted the social categories of gender, race, class, ableness, and sexual orientation. That interplay of differences enabled us to initiate relations with others at UH and to affect the power relations in which they were engaged. (Each of us was also affected differently by the gendered tactics of individual men of other regimes. Those who had had considerable experience working in male-dominated contexts were relatively unfazed; those whose experience tended to be in women-dominated organizations found it difficult on occasion to "push back.")

Senior Management Staff   The senior operations staff comprised about half men and half women. All but one was white, and she was later surplused in the restructuring. Many of the senior staff had more than twenty years' experience at UH, but a few were very new. As key players in the process, the senior staff presented the planning document and its efficacy to their staff. Their resistance to the process and their inability to see how planning activity could direct organizational activity strongly affected the planning outcome.

First, we could not "get at" their skepticism about planning as a rational/ meaning-making effort to guide activity. Second, we "talked" about the need for "transparency" in discussions and decision-making, yet senior staff resisted both transparency and new practices.

These were not always deliberate plots but the result of historical sanctions and disciplines that supported resistance, rendered staff fearful of responsibility, taught them make these contradictions invisible, and closed down discussion by impatience with discussion itself. The limits of any planning process to forge agreement and consolidate action in such a context became increasingly apparent.

Senior Women   Most senior staff women did not align themselves with our work "as women." They were, at times, categorically resistant to the project. Several were well-connected to the parent bureaucracy, and experienced the press toward equity as irrelevant or unnecessary. They learned an "acceptable" way of talking about residents (primarily because the general manager introduced sanctions: gentle corrections, persistent questioning, and modeling other ways to talk) but did not change the way they "saw" residents. Only one senior woman radically altered her thinking (or felt the climate more conducive to it). She had a significant impact, in hiring women and visible minorities, and developing extraordinarily thoughtful training and support programs for her staff.

Most senior staff adopted the rhetoric of the planning document: citing the importance of open talk while withholding key information in meetings; declaring the need for performance indicators and individual performance plans and feedback, while presenting their errors as misunderstandings in expectations, or the fault of their staff or one another; agreeing that key functions needed in-depth collaboration, while refusing to manage their staff to work with other staff.

Residents and Front-line Staff   Key residents, front-line staff (some were both), and certain key community-interest groups formed a strong power relation that often resisted senior management staff and consultant interests. We thought we were all challenging the same dominant interests, yet they understood us quite differently. We could not subvert hierarchical organizational structure, union tensions, and class differences to engage directly with those whose interests we understood our efforts to serve.

Knowledgeable residents and activists "saw" private interests move into key government positions. Unionized staff maintained a virulent distrust of all management efforts; experience had taught them that change efforts advantaged only managers. These principal beneficiaries of the change work saw it as inadequate, as they "saw" the power regimes associated with the change work: less money for building and in-suite repairs; more rhetoric about better service; and the same derogatory treatment.

Black and Visible-Minority Employees   Another important set of power relations—though they did not always experience themselves as such—was the loose coalition of black and visible-minority employees, community activists, and some government employees. While supportive of the equity-change process goals, they were often justifiably quick to challenge decisions made by senior staff. Their complaints sometimes resulted in protracted investigations, from which it was difficult to rebuild any sense of trust.

For many, white bodies signified racism. The white-ness of the change agents, the general manager and most senior staff were seen as "proof" of the hollowness of the equity initiative, regardless of its aspirations. They "read" the planning document against this backdrop, and tended to dismiss it.

Summary   These sets of power relations coalesced around the planning process, and structured possible change. The change intervention disturbed some relations in play and put others in play. Without a working theory of power that included an analysis of relations, without practices to trace and bring them into sharper focus, there was no way to critique the change goals. Yet, talking about and questioning these power relations can unmask their workings and, when made explicit, provoke resistance and retaliation. The normative rhetoric of organizational change and equity is ineffectual at addressing the ways discourse affects power relations and vice versa.

Unmasking Discursive Practices as Relations of Power

Change Management and Strategic Planning   The strategic initiatives for change are caught in neutralizing terms: to improve business practices, governance, and resident relations. My consulting goals were directed at the complexities at UH; yet our activities sometimes obfuscated and occasionally exacerbated them.

My work was to "align" with that of the Board and the general manager, and to "align" their work to the goals of better service. I believed that a "transparent" process—"rational," "logical," "empirical" and "explicable"—would help us to achieve these disparate and complex "goals." I think now that our efforts at "clarity" in the planning document were the general manager's undoing, as it articulated, for the "empire" and others, a commitment—to public housing as a public trust—that the private-business interests in the government sought to undermine.

From the perspective of the field staff, unionized workers, and residents, the planning document read as naive or insufficient. In attempting to address their aspirations for more humane workplace treatment and fairer, more respectful service, the document incited their pessimism that "change" would address these issues, or that change offered by management would serve any but management interests.

We used a large number of photographs in the document in the hope that staff would "see" themselves. Yet, the very "presence" of staff in the photographs was read by some as covering over their "absence" from meaningful involvement in decision-making.

We believed that conversation would help staff to "see" where the general manager was hoping to take UH. Many "saw" and refused their own disappearance.

The planning document incited differences in access to power and vested interest to exercises of power; there were no integrated and purposeful mechanisms to counter them.

The Discourse of Equity: Race and Gender Power can pass itself off unnoticed as the normal, rather than as the superior. (Dyer, 1988, p. 45). Whiteness, maleness, ableness, heterosexuality are the unremarkable categories against which we set the "remarkable": blackness, femaleness, differing abilities, homosexuality. It is this "normal" against which all discourses of service and employment equity wrestle.

In order to improve staff interactions with residents, the general manager believed that staff had to "see" residents differently: not as clients in need of care, as in the liberal discourse; not as vagrants and welfare thieves, as in a rightist discourse; not as customers, as in the Quality Management discourse; not as raced bodies from strange places; nor as effects of an impoverished capitalist state. They had to be understood as citizens with entitlements.

However, UH staff could not understand themselves as citizens with entitlements. They had been defeated by successive restructurings, ineffective management of day-to-day operations, government and media criticism that UH was inefficient and costly. They saw the cycle of deteriorating buildings and dwindling budgets for regular maintenance leading to lowered standards of maintenance and cleanliness leading to further deterioration; they picked up garbage, mopped up blood, and cleaned up feces.

Many staff also blamed residents for allowing the buildings to deteriorate, often expressing their frustrations in sexist, racist, classist, and homophobic ways. The employment-equity and the service-equity projects could not alter the way most staff treated residents.

The Discourse of Leadership   The general manager tended to seek input and rely on collective decision-making, a leadership style that relied on exhorting, explaining, and supporting staff to see the work of public housing as important social justice work, not just "good business practice." Even so, some experienced her leadership as line control, judgmental and invasive.

However, as Smirchich and Morgan suggest, leadership can be seen as a "situation . . . in which there exists an *obligation* or a perceived *right* on the part of certain individuals to define the reality of others' (emphasis in original).[1] When leadership is understood as a "process of power-based reality construction,"[2] it necessarily provokes a contesting of that reality construction. Clearly, our efforts sought to shape meanings and thereby define a different reality for the staff, residents, and the parent governmental organization; yet the counter-thinking to that effort made the question of our success questionable.

As well, the general manager's was not the only leadership process at play: there was the role of the CEO, of the Chair, of the media, of the parent organization. There were also many men, in both the parent organization and among field staff, who had little regard for women in senior positions.

Social Housing as a Service Discourse   Interestingly, one of the last issues to be addressed explicitly by the senior management group was how to describe and enact "social housing" as *the* business of UH, to create a shared understanding and enacting of what it meant to be providers of social housing. Differences between "public" housing and "social" housing required clarification, as did understand "housing" itself: Was housing as a basic human right? Did public housing simply mean putting "roofs over heads" or the integrated provision of social programs as well as "roofs?" What was UH's role as a government agent, as a protector of a public trust, and as a provider of housing on behalf of the people of the province?

These central questions could barely be asked, and therefore could never adequately propel decision-making. Operational problems could not be addressed effectively given the lack of cohesiveness among the senior staff, government, and the public.

Throughout these discussions, cost-reduction pressure was mounting, as was the government's interest in privatizing public housing and withdrawing social supports.

Embodiment and Bodies as Discourse   Schatzki and Natter write that bodies are the medium through which social order is maintained. It is, they argue, through the production of bodily energies, activities, dispositions and desires, that social institutions are secured and power resisted.[3] If the body is the site in which UH was secured and power resisted, what can we learn from our troubled women's bodies late in the project

We conducted ourselves as though our deteriorating bodies were a personal failing rather than an effect of the struggle. Our individualizing and rational rhetoric may have made us unable to "see" our gendered bodies as marked and disposable effects of power. Despite back pain that precluded going to work, heart problems, respiratory difficulties, and massive skin rashes we rarely stopped working. We just "kept on"—even as the full force of the empire was unleashed. When the general manager was fired, our determination evaporated: one by one we left UH.

OUTCOMES

The Accomplishments and Limits of Methodology

For the general manager a better outcome would have been entrenched support for social housing as a public trust and responsibility; residents would be better treated. Certainly, a preferable outcome would have seen the huge change effort result in better service and housing for UH residents. Instead, the unstable political environment at UH means that intentional planning cannot "take hold" or mobilize action. UH did not collapse, although privatization has begun.

Some gains were made: resident placement became faster and more efficient; purchasing procedures became more fair and effective; property-management offices were opened across the city to deal more immediately with resident and building issues; and many social programs were protected.

If the starting point for understanding institutions is as the "site of inequalities and resistances where meanings and interpretations are contested,"[4] often obscurely, we have to ask new questions about how we see and think about organizations, how we represent what we see, what we are trying to do as consultants, and what our doing does. We need to ask more complex questions about how power works through individuals and their relationships institutionally, how talk and ideas work as power, how and who consultants are and become. And we have to look carefully at our language and narratives in order to see that we are always implicated in the workings of power.

Reflections and Lessons Learned

About Starting with Power   I began my work at UH with a strong interest in power. An analysis of how power works is an essential beginning point in change interventions that involve challenging the normative discursive and material practices that delegitimize and discriminate against individuals and groups who are "different."

Foucault[5] suggests that power, always an interplay, limits *and* allows for variability. Lamb contends,[6] that power is about new ways of thinking and acting; it induces pleasure, forms knowledge, and produces discourse.

A state of domination occurs, however, when "an individual or a social group manages to block a field of relations of power, to render them impassive and invariable and prevent all reversibility of movement."[7] A state of domination is vested in its own continuance; in a reliance on truth claims and category maintenance[8] that render study, questioning, and rethinking difficult if not impossible. Every relation of power can become a state of domination. We must therefore be able to identify states of domination, thoughtfully and usefully "transgressing" them to effectively oppose them.

Centering Power in Change Work

To put an analysis of power at the center of change work is to attend to the ways power affects what people in the organization think, say, and do—and how it affects what we are able to think, say, and do. Any change intervention strategy invokes and uses power relations to affect what people can think, say and do. Relations of power are always at risk of becoming states of domination.

Foucault argues that the political task:

is to criticize the working of institutions which appear to be both neutral and independent . . . in such a manner that the political violence, which has always exercised itself obscurely through them, will be unmasked, so that one can fight them.[9]

This implies that these effects and the relations that produce them are readily accessible, when it is a technique of power to render them inaccessible; moreover, we are inside and part of the institutions we criticize. Often when trying to uncover the workings of power, either in relationships or in discourse, that "uncovering" is seen as a challenge to power, and invariably produces:

1. low-level denial of its presence or effects, accompanied by discursive maneuvers to prevent further discussion;

2. facile acknowledgment of its workings, accompanied by discursive maneuvers to limit further discussion; or

3. intense denial, from which power maneuvers block discursive openings.

Each of these reactions sets off other effects within the circuits of power. The challenge then is to map how power works, and to keep questions of power at the center of the work. At UH, it was particularly important to center and unmask the power mechanisms by which the organization had been historically structured, and those that coalesced around privatization and the dismantling of the social-support systems. Our own power mechanisms were no easier to interrogate; we need to question ourselves when we "imagine" we are outside of power or can push at it directly without consequence. We also learned to anticipate the violence of "unmasking," and developed better strategies for the battles that might result.

Learning from Writing

Writing in the Face of the Normal   We can "see" individuals *with* power; we can see relations between individuals who *have* power; we can look at institutions *of* power, and some of us (sometimes) "see" systems *for* power, such as gendered oppression. But it is more difficult to see "the normal" as a technique of power relations. The very normal-ness of the normal limits thinking and writing complexly about the techniques of power.

The structures of everyday thinking, according to Senge are ". . . taken-for-granted or tacit, rarely questioned or discussed, but so natural as to seem routine and unremarkable . . . and manifest themselves in concrete work practices, structures, processes and everyday routines."[10]

Merrill-Sands and others[11] argue elsewhere in this text that these deep structures of organizations and the mental models of individuals have particular effects; they serve particular ends.

The ways we try to capture them in language shift and change even as our words try to tie them down.

Writing about Experience to Trouble Talk   A written case study is a particular way of telling a story, of describing and theorizing experience. It typically requires the authority of eyewitness, of qualified researcher, thoughtful interviewer, thorough investigator, and competent intervenor. It invites the reader to see what the eyewitness sees, conclude what the eyewitness concludes.

Yet, the reader brings his or her experience to reading. He or she can refuse the proffered narrative line, ask different questions, and arrive at different conclusions: writer and reader are engaged in a power relation.

In the events that a case study depicts, many people are involved; but the telling is by one or a few people. A number people involved in the change process at UH have reviewed this case study; and my writing has been revised to reflect the views of the reviewers. Yet it remains a story told by one author, from one perspective. As published narrative, it describes a history, authors an autobiography, and acts as collaborative writing.

Every text is in some sense autobiographical. This one reflects my particular situatedness in the world, in a culture, in a gendered, raced, sexed, and classed body. Describing one's situatedness acknowledges difference and begins to make relational sense of the difference that those differences make in how one experiences the world. It opens up the particularity—and the messiness—of experience that neutralizing language tends to obscure. It explores contradictory paradigms, the limits of knowing, the violence and strong feelings that accompany making change happen. It traces how regimes of power work in context to ensure some voices/bodies are heard and others are not.

We need language to convey ideas. However, words derive meaning in contexts: who uses them, with whom, and for what purpose. Words say some things, but not everything about the thing they refer to. Regimes of power shape meanings as truths; asking questions about how "the truth" is shaped questions the regime itself—and can provoke and re-establish the regime. Language is essential to the study of techniques and strategies of power; it is itself a relation of power.

A Return to Discourse

Gender Work and the Notion of "Gender" in "Equity" Work   We need to think harder and talk more about equity as a broad notion, and about gender as a social category within it. The shift of focus from women to gender, broadening the focus to include both men and women, invites men to examine how gender limits them as well as women. But "gendering" as "difference" has different effects on different bodies. We need to pay careful attention to what our terms to differentiate or render similar set into play.

We use the term "gender" to differentiate between men and women; but in "gender- and organizational-change work" it is used to signify similarity. There are differences between men and women; it is empirically possible to trace, in various cultures and at various times, how these differences have come to exert meanings in such a way as to constrain and limit women. At the same time, men are also gendered, and these meanings also constrain and limit them, albeit differently.

Feminism teaches that gender differences produce *differences:* in terms of access to influence and gain; and in terms of freedoms, including freedom from bodily harm. Postmodern theory contends that these differences are regimes of power put in place to produce *differentiation* so self-evident as to be unremarkable and so tenacious as to be difficult to unmask and fight.

When we use "woman" as a simple and immutable empirical fact, we repeat this historical differentiating, if for different reasons. When we differentiate without studying our own regimes of power our techniques of underlining gender differentiation then can become a power regime that eludes the very questioning we brought to the first power moves. There are no simple or complete answers to these differences, only, as Foucault reminds us, the imperative to study and question how they work.

A similar problem occurs in differentiating "minoritized" bodies from "white" ones in a Western context. White bodies unmarked become the "norm," against which all other bodies are differentiated. Remarking, citing, and describing re-iterate the normativity of "whiteness" without calling it into question. We do need descriptive categories—in North America, they have galvanized identity groups for social-justice advances. Yet, as categories galvanize, new meanings come into play that can incite new power relations.

These simple notions are made complex when categories of social difference and traditional disadvantage—such as gender and race—are set into talk. Gender and race were the key social markers of difference at UH. Sometimes the complexity of the effort to differentiate and align just these two notions of difference rendered "equity" meaningless: it might mean race, but not gender, to a "visible-minority" man; gender, but not race, to a "white woman."

The term "equity" also evoked strong and competing interests among people who did not relate to the term by gender or race. The intended Equity Legislation and its language focussed on visible minorities, women, persons with disabilities, and native Canadians; but many gays and lesbians, working-class people, and people from traditionally disadvantaged ethnic and religious groups felt that they should have been, but were not, highlighted by the equity rhetoric. As well, for many, attachment to any term created an explicit differentiation from the "norm" that they were not prepared to take up.

Our rhetoric for change at UH tried to persuade too many groupings of how equity initiatives would serve them; it could not adequately address the political "realities" of the power relations, systems, and discourses, and their often violent effects on the lives and bodies of women and visible minorities.

The "unmasking" of that violence, as Foucault suggests, requires a conceptualization that "fighting" might be required; a plan, a set of tools, a cadre of "fighters"—which we did not have in place, which does not arise out of most organization-development or change work.

The general manager, the senior person and a woman, with multiple and competing agendas, became the site of this struggle. As few of us in the change process were prepared for such a hostile waging of power, we could not develop useful strategies for engaging the enemy.

Against the power now securely vested in the empire, supported by governmental acts eroding social support to the disadvantaged and an international move toward multinational capitalism, the general manager's commitment to social housing, equitable work practices, and better service to residents could not prevail. What difference would it have made to our work (particularly in the later stages) if we had used the metaphor of "war" or oppositional strategies to underpin our planning, rather than the notion of development or enhancement?

Strategic Planning Work and Equity   Is it possible to help organizations work strategically *and* integrate equity into their planning activities? Can some organizations accomplish more than others? Is it possible to keep questions of gender and race centered while an organization attends to its business? It was not solely linking the two that led to the end of the change project at UH; but it certainly set into play multiple power relations that undermined and eventually thwarted the effort to ensure a social orientation to public housing and to build equity into that orientation. The process was also derailed because at the center of the change work was a deeply contested political commitment to public housing as "the real" business of UH.

Moral and political differences were set into more vibrant play by the strategic-planning process and the talk about social housing. We were unable to render these differences explicit without activating various power maneuvers, and more trouble ensued. Conversation became increasingly difficult, because organizational planning as a neutral discourse generally neither encompasses nor describes the investments in play, those multiple, conflicting power regimes and states of domination in whose interests it is to remain inaccessible.

LESSONS FOR PRACTICE

I do not want to represent the empire as the victorious villain, and the general manager as the virtuous heroine. While their effects on UH residents seem discouragingly similar in the short run, I believe they are potentially different. What, then, can we see and think about our own practices from this experience?

1. Keep theorizing power, and how it acts in relationships, in discourse, and on bodies:

    (a) Map individuals' power potentials and relations: hierarchically, within the organization, and organizationally, in relation to other organizations. Assess allies, partners, and detractors; examine how social markers of privilege enhance or dilute power potentials. Attend to the effects of asking questions of individuals and groupings. Inquire about intentions and effects. Anticipate the multiple power regimes at play and build strategies to contend with them.

    (b) Map the organization's power potentials and relations, both in itself and in relation to similar and related organizations. Explore governance mechanisms to see how they limit and constrain individual and organization freedoms Use multiple vantage points for seeing. Anticipate and plan.

    (c) Map how large systems, such as capitalism, "work" across public, government, international, and private interests to shape individuals and organizations to think and see in particular ways. Attend to the effects of efforts to shape conduct and thought. Anticipate and experiment.

(d) Map how bodies are affected in organizations by power maneuvers.

2. Analyze the discursive effects of meanings as we set them into play in organizations, and trace how other meanings interplay. Work critically and ethically to assess the effects of efforts on freedoms for others and ourselves.

(a) Map the discourses in circulation, both the change discourse and those that the change effort attempts to alter and override. Study what happens when these collide. Analyze more fully what is "in" these discourses and where the resistance to talk about talk may occur. Enlist others to grid conflicts and impasses and to devise alternate entry points.

3. Analyze the relationships formed and forming as effects of the discourses put into play. Map the power relationships and movement of meanings.

(a) Care for the self. Working to affect power regimes and states of domination affects bodies. Attentiveness to the body is essential: we are working with power, often unmasking how it works, and waging various maneuvers with it.

Postscript

In the science-fiction film *Tank Girl*, the heroines vanquish the leader of Water Works, a villain who ruthlessly controls access to water. In the popular film, *The Empire Strikes Back*, the villain is likewise defeated, for a time anyway. Our villains are not so easily identified; we are not so virtuous. Our stories do not so neatly conclude. Trouble continues, as do we.

NOTES

1. Linda Smirchich and Gareth Morgan, "Leadership" in Linda Smirchich and Marta B. Calas, eds., *Critical Perspectives on Organization and Management Theory* (Dartmouth: Dartnels, 1994).

2. Smirchich and Morgan (1994).

3. Theodore R. Schatzki and Wolfgang Natter, eds., *The Social and Political Body* (New York: The Guilford Press, 1996).

4. Linda Smirchich and Marta B. Calas, editors. *Critical Perspectives on Organization and Management Theory* (Dartmouth: Dartnels, 1994).

5. Michel Foucault (1983).

6. Andrew Lamb, "Freedom, the Self, and Ethical Practice According to Michel Foucault," *International Philosophical Quarterly* xxxv, no. 4, issue 140, December, (1995).

7. Michel Foucault, "The Ethic and Care for the Self as a Practice of Freedom," interview in *Philosophy and Social Criticism* 12 (1987): 114.

8. Deborah Britzman, "The Ordeal of Knowledge: Rethinking the Possibility of Multicultural Education," *The Review of Education* 5 (1993).

9. Michel Foucault, *The Foucault Reader,* Paul Rabinow, ed. (New York: Pantheon Books, 1984), 6.

10. Peter Senge, Art Kleiner, Charlotte Roberts, Richard Ross and Bryan Smith, *The Fifth Discipline Fieldbook: Strategies and Tools for Building a Learning Organization* (New York: Doubleday, 1994), 235–36.

11. Deborah Merrill-Sands, Joyce Fletcher and Anne Acosta, "A Case Study of Strengthening Gender-Equity and Organizational Effectiveness in an International Agricultural Research Institute" in this volume (1999).

8
—

POSTSCRIPT

DILEMMAS OF THE STRUGGLE

AT THE OUTSET, we stated that our work is organizational transformation, not simply tinkering with organizational margins to suit funding cultures, address the needs of political correctness, or appease organized constituencies. We believe that gender equality can be achieved by organizations only as they transcend the patriarchal and bureaucratic modes of organizing that perpetuate gender inequality. This implies tackling the gendered deep structure—that is, changing inequitable power relations, devaluing heroic individualism in favor of crisis prevention and team work, better work-family balance, and focussing on broad goals rather than narrow targets, both as means and as ends.

As we pursue this demanding and difficult work, we encounter dilemmas and paradoxes to which we have not yet found answers. In this postscript we share these dilemmas in the hope that our collective imagination and actions will lead us to new insights and solutions. As we do so, we bear in mind that we, too, have to be open to change; we must respect other people's boundaries and tread carefully when blazing the trail to change.

A recurring theme in the cases is the complexity of power relations when we move from policy to implementation. Those who have positional power, like the manager at UH or Anita Roddick at The Body Shop, cannot dictate change for gender equity. Yet a view of power-as-energy sets up its own dynamic that makes change neither simple not guaranteed, as these two cases also illustrate. Enfranchising those who have traditionally been excluded does not guarantee that they will speak or act with a "common interest," since competing identities and interests are released in the "empowering" processes described in these cases.

Yet, such change can be fueled by insightful leaders encouraging a process that spawns new directions and results in unexpected benefits. The revival of the BRAC Women's Advisory Committee, which has been expanded to include all senior managers for the purpose of discussing and addressing women staff issues; and BRAC's recent endeavor to engage staff in a discussion of organizational values are examples of such unplanned, positive offshoots of the gender and organizational change process. On the other hand, the change process can be de-railed or dead-ended by powerful insiders and outsiders who see their interests elsewhere or their power adversely affected as a result of the change, as we saw in the case of UH.

In addition, the political context can limit or create a larger space for change than would otherwise be possible. The political climate in the UH case grew increasingly hostile to the value of equity and public housing, while the transition to democracy in South Africa pressed for and supported transformation of all kinds of organizations and institutions.

A second theme, linking institutional change to larger social-change agendas or "business goals" in the case of a for-profit company, is a two-edged sword. It eases access to the organization, as the change process is perceived to be about "something important," not just gender equality, a low priority for most organizations. At the same time, however, as we have seen in all the cases, it can make gender issues decreasingly visible as more familiar, less threatening, management issues, mechanisms and processes gain attention. This is a fundamental dilemma in change efforts aimed at tackling gendered deep structure and evolving new structures and processes for gender equality.

For example, in South Africa, the culture of resistance, finely honed during the struggle against apartheid, permeated organizations such as the NLC, as did a respect for participatory change approaches responsive to its constituency. Nonetheless, putting women on the agenda was still a struggle, as it was viewed as divisive. In CIMMYT, managers' difficulty with the work of the CCC contributed to the lessening of the team's interest in continuing, although it ultimately resulted in a re-engagement of senior managers with the process.

In BRAC, where the organization's agenda easily accommodated a gender and organizational approach, our focus on organizational systems and values looked to many insiders like a management, rather than a gender issue. Take the issue of leave: because women have more family responsibilities, the same minimal amount of leave for women and men is a gender issue. Yet, management's reluctance to allow a non-management group to work on what they saw as their turf was an understandable effort to hold on to power. Careful negotiation was needed; and the gender work in fifty BRAC offices ground to a halt while we resolved this issue.

The change strategy that we have used, either as change agents outside the formal power structure of an organization or as change agents within the organization, is grounded in an action-learning approach to uncovering and changing aspects of deep structure. It is not a coercive strategy that attempts to guilt people into change; it works with the heart, head, and with "doing" work. It creates a learning process that understands psychological resistance to the change of fundamental attitudes. It is both systemic and personal, concerning itself both with systemic changes of culture and norms and with the individual learning of organizational members. It starts from where people are, negotiating strategies and spaces for change. In BRAC, for example, this necessitated working at the outlying fringe of the organization—with area-office staff around the country.

The key tool of the learning process is dialogue; its aim is to build the "field"—those invisible, non-material structures, rather like gravity or magnetism—composed of the organization's principles, values and purpose that allow organizational members, leaders, policies, structures, and systems significant room to adapt.

However, a dilemma we face is whether this paradigm can effectively uncover and change the gender-inequitable aspects of the deep structure of organizations we have identified. Can a participatory approach, building the "field," and starting where people are change power relations and structures of inequality? Or, as Rebecca Tripp believes, is it a war out there? At UH, the tank girls were toppled and the empire struck back. If, as Tripp points out, power masks its tracks, the need for its unmasking may require a strategy of war, not the discourse of development. To what extent does our discourse sanitize the problem? At UH the change agents found their discourse to be at such variance with the organizational members' perception of the nature of the problem and their perceived self-interest that conversation was not possible.

If we do not assume the good will of top leadership, what alternative ways can we build to press for change? In other words, how do we build constituencies for change? The NLC is a good example of building relationships with constituencies as a key element in the process of strengthening internal organizational changes. The permeability of the NLC's boundaries to the political context was seen as a strength. In BRAC, we built an internal change-agent team; but that team was responsible to the existing chain of command. We spent no time building the external, client group to which the organization is ultimately accountable. If working both from the inside, with managers and staff for gender equality outcomes, and from the outside, with constituencies for organizational accountability, are required, is it possible for the change agents to do both at the same time?

For many of the contributors to this book the change process was like a roller coaster ride. What seemed to be a failure or an insurmountable barrier at one moment proved the means of a significant move forward at another. For example, at CIMMYT, fears about gender disappearing from the dual agenda led to a very successful women's leadership initiative. At BRAC when we presented the feedback from our needs analysis, we were told by a key manager that our information was false and misleading; and no decision on whether or how to continue was made for several months. Yet, the internal management discussions about this situation led to an agreement to proceed with an innovative and very fruitful action-learning approach with field offices. At the time of writing, BRAC managers are deliberating on a new phase of GQAL, which would involve strengthening program-impact analysis and evolving a new concept of leadership.

We are aware that the future is buffeted by events beyond the control of individual actors and single organizations. We also acknowledge that our efforts to propel change face a backlash from entrenched interests who calculate that change costs too much. Our goal is to move beyond the short-term interests of the parties to a shared long-term interest in which the way we are, the way we think, the goals we pursue, and the way we organize ourselves to pursue them are transformatory, just, and gender equitable.

In the change process, aspects of deep structure and the focus of the work are not the only issues for negotiation—the change agents are, as well. In trying to effect change, we lead and teach, but we cannot remain untouched; we too must learn and change: hence the term "changing agent." We changing agents express our own ideals and perspectives, and speak in our own voices; yet we cannot remain fixed in our own position, as our role is not limited to that of gender-equality advocate. We need to be aware that aspects of deep structure—perhaps the very aspects we are trying to change— are embedded in our own unconscious. We work to create and achieve new structures and processes, but as gendered (and sexed) beings we are a reflection and a product of the very structures—personal, political and professional—that we seek to change. We need to be open to holding up our values and beliefs for re-examination, just as we ask organizations to do. In addition, as each of us brings our own strengths and vulnerabilities to the process of organizational change, we found it extremely helpful, though at times difficult, to work in balanced and diverse teams committed to critical mutual reflection about their style and content.

Whether as insiders or as outside change agents, our role is a provocative one. We challenge ourselves and others to examine both how we think of ourselves as women and men and how we act upon those understandings. We challenge organizations to examine the ways in which they reproduce gender and social inequities in their work practices and in their systems and in their values. We ask people to explore the volatile terrain of gender relations; and, most important, we ask people to work with us to create new ways of seeing and acting within organizations that will lead ultimately to gender equality. It is from this new collective imagination that the future emerges.

BIBLIOGRAPHY

Acker, Joan. "Hierarchies, Jobs, Bodies: A Theory of Gendered Organizations." *Gendered Society*, no. 4, 1990.

Acker, Joan. "Gendering Organizational Theory." In *Gendering Organizational Analysis*, ed. Alfred Mills and Peta Tancred. Newbury Park: Sage, 1992.

Acker, Joan. "Hierarchies, Jobs, Bodies: A Theory of Gendered Organizations." *Gender and Society*. 4, 1990: 139–58.

Agocs, Carol, Catherine Burr, Felicity Somerset. *Employment Equity: Co-operative Strategies for Organizational Change*. Toronto: Prentice Hall, 1992.

Bailyn, Lotte. *Breaking the Mold: Women, Men and Time in the New Corporate World*. New York: Free Press, 1993.

Bailyn, Lotte, Joyce Fletcher and Deborah Kolb. "Unexpected Connections: Considering Employees' Personal Lives Can Revitalize Your Business." *Sloan Management Review* 38, no. 4, (1997): 11–19.

Bailyn, Lotte, Rhona Rapoport, Deborah Kolb, Joyce Fletcher, et al. "Re-linking Work and Family: A Catalyst for Organizational Change." Working paper, Sloan School of Management, April, 1996.

Bailyn, Lotte, Rhona Rapoport, Deborah Kolb, Joyce Fletcher et al. *Re-linking Life and Work: Toward a Better Future*. New York: Ford Foundation, 1996.

Beer, Michael. "The Critical Path for Change: Key to Success and Failure in Six Companies." In *Corporate Transformation: Re-Vitalizing Organizations for a Competitive World* ed. Ralph Kilmann, et al. San Francisco: Jossey-Bass, 1989.

Block, Peter. *The Empowered Manager: Positive Political Skills at Work*. San Francisco: Jossey-Bass, 1987.

Bradford, Helen. "'We Are Now the Men': Women's Beer Protests in the Natal Countryside, 1929." Seminar Paper delivered to the History Department, University of Witwatersrand: 1984.

BRAC. *Toward Gender Equity: BRAC Gender Policy.* January, 1998.

Britzman, Deborah. "The Ordeal of Knowledge: Rethinking the Possibility of Multicultural Education." *The Review of Education* 5, (1993): 123–35.

Bydawell, Moya. "AFRA Confronts Gender Issues: the Process of Creating a Gender Strategy." *Gender and Development.* Oxfam UK, 5, no. 1, (1997).

Cafati, C., K. Baldini, K. Hoadly, and J. Joshi. "Achieving Parity in Employment Status." *CG Gender Lens.* A newsletter of the CGIAR Gender Program. Boston. The Center for Gender in Organizations, Simmons Graduate School of Management, 1997.

Calas, Marta, B. "Marginal to Mainstream: Scaling Up Gender in Organizational Change Interventions." From the Conference Report. Simmons College, Boston, June 1997.

Chesler, Mark. "Organizational Development Is Not the Same as Multicultural Organizational Development." In *The Promise of Diversity*, ed. Elsie Cross et al. (New York: Irwin, 1994).

CGIAR. *Fourth External Review of CIMMYT.* Washington, DC: CGIAR Secretariat, The World Bank, April 1998.

CIMMYT. *CIMMYT in 1995–96.* Annual Report. El Batan, Mexico: International Maize and Wheat Improvement Center CIMMYT, 1996. "Terms of reference for the Change Catalyst Committee." Internal memorandum, July 25, 1996.

Coleman, Gill and Ann Rippin. "Losing Gender in Collaboration." *Organizations* (forthcoming).

Cole, Josette. Internal background discussion document on NCAR/NLC for the period 1984–93. Prepared for NLC strategic planning process, 1994.

Crawford Cousins, Colleen, Tessa Cousins, and Michelle Friedman. "Participatory Methods." Report from the workshop held for National Land Committee affiliates at Kwazamokuhle, Natal, Feb. 8–14, 1993.

Crawford Cousins, Colleen; Tessa Cousins, and Michelle Friedman. *Holding the Space: Explorations of Power and Control in Training and Development.* Avocado Paper Series 06/94. Olive Information Services, Durban, 1994.

Cross, Catherine and Michelle Friedman. "Women in Tenure: Marginality and the Left Hand Power." Discussion paper for National Land Committee affiliates on tenure issues and gender questions, 1993.

Edwards, M., A. Ewen, W. Verdini. "Fair Performance Management and Pay Practices for Diverse Work Forces." *ACA Journal* 4, no. 2, 1995.

Edwards, M. and A. Ewen. *360° Feedback: The Powerful New Model for Employee Assessment and Performance Improvement.* New York: American Management Association, 1996.

Ely, Robin. "The Effects of Organizational Demographics and Social Identity on Relationships Among Professional Women." *Administrative Science Quarterly* 39, 1996: 203–38.

Ely, Robin and Deborah Meyerson. "Advancing Gender Equity in Organizations: The Challenge and Importance of Maintaining a Gender Narrative." *Organization.* Forthcoming.

Ferguson, Kathy. *The Feminist Case against Bureaucracy.* Philadelphia: Temple University Press, 1984.

Fletcher, Joyce. "A Radical Perspective on Power." In *AWID Trialogue on Power,* ed. Aruna Rao and David Kelleher, 2, no. 2, Spring (1997a).

Fletcher, Joyce. "Relational Practice: A Feminist Re-construction of Work." *Journal of Management Inquiry* 7, (1997b).

Fletcher Joyce. "Relational Practice: A Feminist Reconstruction of Work." *Journal of Management Inquiry* 7, no. 2 (1998): 163–86.

Fletcher, Joyce. *Relational Practice at Work: Gender, Power and the "New" Organization.* Boston: MIT Press, 1999.

Foucault, Michel. *Discipline and Punish: The Birth of the Prison,* trans., Alan Sheridan. New York: Vintage Books, 1979.

Foucault, Michel. "The Subject and Power." In *Michel Foucault: Beyond Structuralism and Hermeneutics,* ed. Herbert Dreyfus and Paul Rabinow. Chicago: University of Chicago, 1983.

Foucault, Michel. *The Foucault Reader,* ed. Paul Rabinow. New York: Pantheon Books, 1984.

Foucault, Michel. "The Ethic and Care for the Self as a Practice of Freedom." Interview in *Philosophy and Social Criticism* 12, 1987.

Foucault, Michel. Power Effects the Body." *Foucault Live.* New York: Semiotext(e), 1996

Fox, M. "Gender, Environmental Milieu, and Productivity in Science. *The Outer Circle: Women in the Scientific Community.* In H. Zuckerman J. Cole and

J. Bruer, eds., New York: W.W. Norton Company, 1991.

Freire, Paolo. *Pedagogy of the Oppressed.* New York: Herder and Herder, 1971.

Friedman, Michelle. Report to the National Land Committee on the Series of Gender Workshops Held with Affiliates 1992.

Friedman, Michelle. "The Rural Challenge: Women and Land. " In Southern Africa Report, January (1994).

Friedman, Michelle. "Breaking the Silence—Women, Gender and Organisational Development: A Case Study of the National Land Committee, Gender Strategy—in Transition." Unpublished paper, 1995.

Friedman, Michelle. "Learning from Doing: Rural Women's Study Tour." *Agenda* 24, (1995): 93–95.

Friedman, Michelle and Colleen Crawford Cousins. "Holding the Space: Gender, Race and Conflict in Training." In *Gender in Popular Education,* ed. L. Manicom and S. Walters. Cape Town: CACE Publications and London: Zed Books, 1996.

Gender Task Group Minutes, 1992, October; 1993, March; 1993, June; 1993, October; 1994, March; 1994, July; 1994, November. Held in the National Land Committee offices in Braamfontein, Johannesburg.

Ginwala, Frene. "Women and the African National Congress, 1912–1943." *Agenda* 8, (1990): 77–93.

Goetz, Anne Marie. "Gender and Administration" *IDS Bulletin* 23, no. 1 (1992).

Goetz, Anne Marie. "Local Heroes: Patterns of Field Worker Discretion in Implementing GAD Policy in Bangladesh." IDS Discussion Paper no. 358, University of Sussex, 1996.

Goetz, Anne-Marie. "Managing Organizational Change: The 'Gendered' Organization of Space and Time." *Gender and Development* 5, no. 1, (1997), 17–27.

Goetz, Anne Marie, ed. *Getting Institutions Right for Women in Development.* London: Zed Press, 1997.

Goetz, Anne Marie and Rina Sen Gupta. "Women's Leadership in Rural Credit Programmes in Bangladesh." Unpublished paper, 1995.

Gormley, W. and Linda Spink. *Exploring Multi-Source Feedback and Assessment Systems.* Simmons Institute for Leadership and Change, Simmons College, Organizational Change Briefing Note, no. 4, August 1997.

Govender, Pregs, in Aruna Rao and David Kelleher (1997).

Graham, Allison, *Essence of Decision: Explaining the Cuban Missile Crisis.* Boston: Little Brown, 1971.

Griffin, Susan. "To Love the Marigold: The Politics of Imagination," *AWID Trialogue on Power,* ed. Aruna Rao and David Kelleher, 2, no. 2, Spring (1997).

Hampden-Turner, Charles. *Charting the Corporate Mind: Graphic Solutions to Business Conflicts.* New York: Free Press, 1990.

Hampden-Turner, Charles. *Creating Corporate Culture.* Reading, Mass.: Addison-Wesley, 1992.

Hirsh, Marianne and Evelyn Fox Keller, eds. *Conflict in Feminism.* New York: Routledge, 1990.

Hochschild, Arlie. *The Second Shift.* New York: Avon Books, 1989.

Hochschild, Arlie. *The Time Bind: When Work Becomes Home and Home Becomes Work.* New York: Metropolitan Books, 1997.

Holvino, Evangelina. "A Vision: The Agitated Organization." In *The Promise of Diversity,* ed. Elsie Cross et al. New York: Irwin, 1994.

Holvino, Evangelina. "Reading Organization Development from the Margins: Outsider Within." *Organization* 3, no. 4 (1996): 520–33.

Itzin, Catherine and Janet Newman, eds. *Gender, Culture and Organizational Change: Putting Theory into Practice.* London: Routledge, 1995.

Jackson B.W. and Evangelina Holvino. "Multicultural Organizational Development." Working Paper 11, Ann Arbor, Program on Conflict Management Alternatives, quoted by Mark Chesler in *The Promise of Diversity,* Elsie Cross et al., New York: Irwin, 1994.

Johansson, U. "Constructing the Responsible Worker: Changing Structures, Changing Selves." Paper presented at the Academy of Management Meeting, Vancouver, British Columbia, Canada, August 1995.

Kabeer, Naila. *Reversed Realities: Gender Hierarchies in Development Thought.* London: Verso, 1994.

Kanter, Rosabeth Moss. *Men and Women of the Corporation.* New York: Basic Books, 1997.

Kardam, Nuket. *Bringing Women In: Women's Issues in International Development Programs.* Boulder: Lynne Rienner, 1991.

Kabeer, Naila. *Reversed Realities—Gender Hierarchies in Development Thought.* London: Verso, 1994.

Kardam, Nuket. In *Getting Institutions Right for Women in Development,* ed. Anne

Marie Goetz. London: Zed Books, 1997.

Kelleher, David, Aruna Rao, Rieky Stuart, Kirsten Moore. *Building a Global Network for Gender and Organizational Change.* Conference Report, August 1996.

Kelleher, David and Kirsten Moore. *Marginal to Mainstream: Scaling Up Gender and Organizational Change Interventions.* Report of a Case Conference sponsored by the Simmons Institute for Leadership and Change, June 1997. Boston. The Center for Gender in Organizations, Simmons Graduate School of Management. Conference Report, no. 1, 1998.

Kemp, Amanda, Noziwe Madlala, Asha Moodley and Elaine Salo. "The Dawn of a New Day: South African Feminisms." In *The Challenge of Local Feminism.* Boulder: Westview Press, 1995.

Kilmann, Ralph, et al. *Corporate Transformation: Revitalizing Organizations for a Competitive World.* San Francisco: Jossey-Bass, 1989.

Kolb, Deborah, Joyce Fletcher, Debra Meyerson, Deborah Merrill-Sands, and Robin Ely. "Making Change: A Framework for Promoting Gender-Equity." The Center for Gender in Organizations, Simmons Graduate School of Management. *CGO Insights* no. 1, October, 1998.

Kolb, Deborah and Linda Putnam. "Through the Looking Glass: Negotiation Theory Refracted through the Lens of Gender." In *Workplace Dispute Resolution*, ed. S. Gleason. East Lansing: Michigan State University Press, 1997.

Kompe, Lydia, Janet Small and Beauty Mkhize. *The Rural Women's Movement. Holding the Knife on the Sharp Edge.* Johannesburg: Transvaal Rural Action Committee, 1994.

Kompe, Lydia. Interviewed in "A Driving Force." *Land Update* no. 17, September/October, 1992.

Lamb, Andrew. "Freedom, the Self, and Ethical Practice According to Michel Foucault." *International Philosophical Quarterly* xxxv, no. 4, issue 140, December (1995).

Lukes, Stephen. In Joyce Fletcher, "A Radical Perspective on Power." In *AWID Trialogue on Power*, ed. Aruna Rao and David Kelleher, 2, no. 2, Spring (1997).

Martin, Patricia. *Men, Masculinities, and Working: From (Some) Women's Standpoint.* Paper presented at Case Conference, Simmons Institute for Leadership and Change. Boston, April 14, 1998.

Mashile Daphne. "Reflections from the Transvaal Rural Action Committee's

Perceptions on Gender Integration at Local Affiliate Level." RSA National Land Committee Report for the GTG Meeting, November, 1994.

McGee Calvert, and V.J. Ramsey. "Speaking as Female and White: A Non-dominant/Dominant Group Standpoint." In *Organization* 3, no. 4, (1996): 520-33.

Meer, Shamim. "Gender Vision for Land Reform." Paper prepared for the RSA National Land Committee Land Reform Vision Process, 1995.

Meer, Shamim. ed., *Women, Land and Authority in Rural South Africa.* Cape Town: David Phillip, 1997.

Merrill-Sands, Deborah. *1997 Human Resources Survey: International Staffing at the CGIAR Centers with a Focus on Gender.* Washington, DC: CGIAR Secretariat, The World Bank. CGIAR Gender Program Working Paper, No. 15. 1997.

Merrill-Sands, Deborah, Joyce Fletcher and Anne Acosta. "A Case Study of Strengthening Gender-Equity and Organizational Effectiveness in an International Agricultural Research Institute." This volume, 1999.

Meyerson, Debra. "Feeling Stressed and Burned Out: A Feminist Reading and Re-Vision of Stress in Medicine and Organization Science." *Organization Science,* 9, (1998): 103–18.

Meyerson, Debra, Deborah Kolb and Robin Ely. "A Framework of Gender Equity and Organizational Change." Invited talk at Lucy Cavendish College, Cambridge University, Cambridge, England, February 1998.

Miller, Carol and Shahra Razavi. *Missionaries and Mandarins: Feminist Engagement with Development Institutions.* London: Intermediate Technology Publications, 1998.

Mills, Albert and Peta Tancred. *Gendering Organizational Analysis.* Newbury Park: Sage, 1992.

Mindell, Arnold. *The Year I. Global Process Work.* Britain: Arkana, 1989.

Mindell, Arnold. *The Leader as Martial Artist. An Introduction to Deep Democracy.* New York: HarperCollins, 1993.

Mintzberg, Henry, Bruce Ahlstrand and Joseph Lampel. *Strategy Safari: A Guided Tour Through the Wilds of Strategic Management.* New York: The Free Press, 1998.

National Land Committee Gender and Research Workshop in Pietermaritzburg, Minutes, June 1992, held in the NLC office in Johannesburg.

Peters, Thomas and Robert Waterman. *In Search of Excellence: Lessons from America's Best-Run Companies.* New York: Harper and Row, 1982.

Plowman, Penny. "Review of the NLC Gender Programme." Final Report to the South African National Land Committee. 1997.

Rao, Aruna and David Kelleher, ed. *AWID Trialogue on Power* 2, no. 2, Spring (1997).

Rao, Aruna and David Kelleher. "Engendering Organizational Change: The BRAC Case." In *Getting Institutions Right for Women in Development,* ed. Anne Marie Goetz. London: Zed Press, 1997.

Rao, Aruna and David Kelleher, "Gender Lost and Gender Found." *Development in Practice* 8, no. 2, Oxfam UK, Oxford: May (1998).

Rao, Aruna and Rieky Stuart. "Rethinking Organizations: A Feminist Perspective." *Gender and Development* 5, no. 1 (1997), 10–16.

Rapoport, Rhona and Robert. N. Rapoport. *Dual Career Families.* Harmondsworth: Penguin, 1971.

Samson, Melanie. "Proposed Process for Developing a National Gender Strategy." Discussion document. August 1997.

Schatzki, Theodore R. and Wolfgang Natter, eds. *The Social and Political Body.* New York: The Guilford Press, 1996.

Schein Edgar. *Organizational Culture and Leadership,* 2nd edition. San Francisco: Jossey-Bass, 1992.

Schein, Edgar. *Process Consultation: Lesson for Managers and Consultants, Volume II.* Reading, Mass.: Addison-Wesley, 1987.

Schuler, Sidney and Syed M. Hashemi. "Credit Programs, Women's Empowerment, and Contraceptive Use in Rural Bangladesh." *Studies in Family Planning* 25, no. 2 (1994): 65-76.

Scott, Joan. "Gender: A Useful Category of Historical Analysis." In *Women's Studies International,* ed. Aruna Rao. New York: Feminist Press, 1992.

Senge, Peter. *The Fifth Discipline: The Art and Practice of the Learning Organization.* New York: Doubleday, 1990.

Senge, Peter, Art Kleiner, Charlotte Roberts, Richard Ross and Bryan Smith. *The Fifth Discipline Fieldbook: Strategies and Tools for Building a Learning Organization.* New York: Doubleday, 1994.

Sheridan, Bridgette. "Strangers in a Strange Land: A Literature Review of Women in Science." Working Paper, No. 17, CGIAR Gender Program,

Simmons Institute for Leadership and Change, Simmons College, 1998.

Shiva, Vandana. *Monocultures of the Mind: Perspectives on Biodiversity and Biotechnology.* New Delhi: Natraj, 1993.

Small, Janet. "A Lesson for Life—The NLC Women's Study Tour." *Speak* no. 66 (1994).

Small, Janet. "The NLC Women's Study Tour." *Land Update.* Republic of South Africa National Land Committee publication, 1994.

Smirchich, Linda and Morgan, Gareth. "Leadership: The Management of Meaning." In *Journal of Applied Behavioural Science* 18, no 3, (1982): 257–73.

Smirchich, Linda and Gareth Morgan. "Leadership." In *Critical Perspectives on Organization and Management Theory*, Linda Smirchich and Marta B. Calas, eds., Dartmouth: Dartnels, 1994.

Smirchich, Linda and Marta B Calas, eds., *Critical Perspectives on Organization and Management Theory.* Dartmouth: Dartnels, 1994.

Sonnert, Gerhardt and Gerald Holton. "Career Patterns of Women and Men in Science," *American Scientist* 84, no. 1 (1996): 63–71.

Staudt, Kathy. *Policy, Politics and Gender: Women Gaining Ground.* West Hartford, Conn.: Kumarian Press, 1998.

Statistics Canada. *Women, Men and Work.* Spring 1995.

Statistics Canada. *Women in Canada.* 1996.

Stuart, Rieky, et al. *BRAC Technical Manual. An Action-Learning Approach to Genderand Organizational Change.* Dhaka: BRAC, 1997.

Thomas, David and Robin Ely. "Making Differences Matter: A New Paradigm for Managing Diversity." *Harvard Business Review*, September-October 1996: 79-90.

Tripp, Rebecca. "Tank Girls, Trouble, and The Empire Strikes Back," in this volume, 1999.

Walker, Cheryl. *Women and Resistance in South Africa.* London: Onyx Press, 1982.

Walker, Cheryl. "Land Reform and Gender in Post-apartheid South Africa." Paper presented to an international workshop: Gender, Poverty and Well-Being: Indicators and Strategies, Trivandrum, Kerala, November, 1997.

Weick, Karl. "Educational Organizations as Loosely Coupled Systems." *Administrative Science Quarterly* 21, (1976).

Weick, Karl. "Small Wins: Redefining the Scale of Social Problems." *American Psychologist* 39, no. 1 (1984), 40–49.

Wiesbord, Marvin. *Productive Workplaces, Organizing and Managing for Dignity, Meaning and Community.* San Francisco: Jossey-Bass, 1991.

Wheatley, Margaret J. *Leadership and the New Science.* San Francisco: Berrett-Koehler, 1992.

Yoder, J. "Rethinking Tokenism: Looking Beyond the Numbers." *Gender and Society* 5, no. 2, 1991: 178–92.

INDEX

ABOUT THE AUTHORS

DAVID KELLEHER is an independent organizational consultant currently involved in a long-term project with Amnesty International in Ottawa, Canada. He has consulted in Canada and internationally with non-profit and governmental organizations, has been a teacher, and is the author of books and articles on organizational change.

ARUNA RAO brings a southern perspective to her work on gender and organizational change, incorporating her experience working for the Population Council's Asia research program on gender and development, as well as her activism in the global women's movement and her research on people's organizations in south Asia. She currently lives in Washington, DC.

RIEKY STUART has worked in Canada, Africa, and Asia, as a program officer, adult educator, manager, and consultant with a range of domestic and international organizations. She is currently Executive Director of Oxfam Canada.

ABOUT THE CONTRIBUTORS

ANNE ACOSTA, trained in education and international agriculture, is the Donor Relations Officer at the Centro Internacional de Majoramiento de Maiz y Trigo (CIMMYT) in El Batan, Mexico. She has been a leader and active internal change-agent for helping CIMMYT create a more gender-equitable work environment.

JOYCE K. FLETCHER is Professor of Management at the Center for Gender in Organizations at the Simmons Graduate School of Management in Boston and senior research scholar at the Jean Baker Miller Institute at Wellesley College. She is a frequent speaker at national and international conferences on women in leadership and has published in both management and education journals. Her forthcoming book, *Disappearing Acts: Gender, Power and Relational Practice at Work,* explores the disappearing of relational work and its implications for women, men, and organizational effectiveness.

MICHELLE FRIEDMAN is program coordinator for the Institutional Transformation Programme at the African Gender Institute at the University of Cape Town, South Africa. A long-time feminist and anti-apartheid activist, she was a contributing editor of *Agenda,* a leading South African feminist journal. She worked for the National Land Committee as gender coordinator and has worked with many NGOs to promote their gender equity efforts.

DEBORAH M. KOLB is Co-Director of the Center for Gender in Organizations at the Graduate School of Business, Simmons College, in Boston. She is a professor of management who has written extensively in the area of mediation and work. She was a principal researcher in the Ford Foundation action-research on project work and family.

DEBORAH MERRILL-SANDS is an anthropologist and Co-Director of the Center for Gender in Organizations at the Simmons Graduate School of Management in Boston. For eight years, she has led a large program on gender and organizational change for the International Agricultural Research Centers supported by the Consultative Group for International Agricultural Research. In addition to her work on gender and on women in science, she specializes in the field of research management.

DEBRA MEYERSON teaches at the Department of Engineering at Stanford University and is an affiliated faculty member with the Center for Gender in Organizations. She is a principal investigator in The Body Shop action-research project.

REBECCA TRIPP is the pseudonym of an independent organizational development consultant based in Canada. She has worked with a large number of government and voluntary sector clients in her practice and has taught at Canadian universities. She has researched and written on gender, bodies, and sport.

Other Books
from Kumarian Press

Gender Analysis in Development Planning:
A Case Book
Aruna Rao, Mary B. Anderson, Catherine Overholt

Designed for gender training, the cases presented are open-ended, allowing students to exercise problem-solving skills. Helps find alternative management strategies as well as planning and evaluation techniques sensitive to gender issues.

Cases $15.95 / Paper: 0-931816-61-0
Teaching Notes $7.95 / Paper: 0-931816-62-9

Policy, Politics and Gender:
Women Gaining Ground
Kathleen Staudt

Staudt identifies and develops connections between women's politics and public policies and practices. She examines the realities of social change from *all* perspectives, reminding us that all institutions, within and outside governments, are sources and sites for struggle.

$24.95 / Paper: 1-56549-079-7
$55.00 / Cloth: 1-56549-080-0

Famine, Conflict and Response:
A Basic Guide
Fred Cuny

Written by the well-known visionary and "maverick" Fred Cuny, this book focuses primarily on responses to what are now called traditional famines or natural disaster. Cuny's approach lives on as innovative and challenging in that his focus on counter famine measures centers on people's livelihoods.

$23.95 / Paper: 1-56549-090-8

Breaking Cycles of Violence:
Conflict Prevention in Intrastate Crises
Janie Leatherman, William DeMars
Patrick Gaffney, Raimo Väyrynen

This timely and clearly-defined book studies how the international community, working with local partners, can effectively prioritize and target resources on key breaking points in societies at risk of violent conflict.

$23.95 / Paper: 1-56549-091-6
$65.00 / Cloth: 1-56549-092-4

The Cuban Way:
Charting Its Own Course to Economic Change
Ana Julia Jatar-Hausmann

Focusing on the experiences of the people who actually reside on the island, this book is an original analysis of the economic policies and trends in socialist Cuba.

$21.95 / Paper: 1-56549-088-6
$59.00 / Cloth: 1-56549-089-4

Defying the Odds:
Banking for the Poor
Eugene Versluysen

This book sets itself apart from the recent literature on microfinance because the author focuses on the growth of microfinance in the context of social and economic changes—and upheavals—in developing countries.

$24.95 / Paper: 1-56549-093-2
$65.00 / Cloth: 1-56549-094-0

Nongovernments:
NGOs and the Political Development of the Third World
Julie Fisher

This definitive work on nongovernmental organizations provides a complete overview of the composition and the types of NGOs that have emerged in recent years. Julie Fisher describes in detail the influence these organizations have had on political systems throughout the world and the hope their existence holds for the realization of sustainable development.

$24.95 / Paper: 1-56549-074-6
$45.00 / Cloth: 1-56549-075-4

Achieving Broad-Based Sustainable Development:
Governance, Environment and Growth With Equity
James H. Weaver, Michael T. Rock, Kenneth Kusterer

This comprehensive and multidisciplinary work provides an excellent overview of economic development and the results of growth. The authors provide a model which looks through economic as well as social, political and environmental lenses.

$26.95 / Paper: 1-56549-058-4
$38.00 / Cloth: 1-56549-059-2

Beyond the Magic Bullet:
NGO Performance and Accountability in the
Post-Cold War World
Michael Edwards, David Hulme

In this volume, experts review the issues of NGO performance and accountability in international development assistance and provide guidance with respect to the process of assessment. Case studies from Central America, Asia, South America, East Africa and North Africa.

$18.95 / Paper: 1-56549-051-7
$38.00 / Cloth: 1-56549-052-5

Promises Not Kept:
The Betrayal of Social Change in the Third World
Fourth Edition
John Isbister

This book develops the argument that social change in the Third World has been blocked by a series of broken promises, made explicitly or implicitly by the industrialized countries and also by Third World leaders themselves.
The third edition takes into account the success stories in the Third World, particularly in East Asia, asking why those experiences have not been more widespread.

$18.95 / Paper: 1-56549-045-2

When Corporations Rule the World
David C. Korten

Shows how the convergence of ideological, political and technological forces is leading to an ever-greater concentration of economic and political power in a handful of corporations and financial institutions. Korten shows how the interest of the corporation is separate from human interest leaving the market system blind to all but its own short term market gains.

$19.95 / Paper: 1-887208-01-1
$29.95 / Cloth: 1-887208-00-3

Mediating Sustainability:
Growing Policy from the Grassroots
Editors: Jutta Blauert and Simon Zadek

This book explores how mediation between grass-roots and policy formation processes can and does work in practice by focusing on experiences in Latin America in promoting sustainable agriculture and rural development. The contributions to this book draw on the work of researchers, activists, farmers and policy makers through concrete evidence and appraisal.

$25.95 / Paper: 1-56549-081-9
$55.00 / Cloth: 1-56549-082-7

Unarmed Bodyguards:
International Accompaniment for the Protection of Human Rights
Luis Enrique Eguren
Liam Mahony

For years international accompaniment has been successfully implemented as a way to protect threatened human rights activists throughout the world. Here the authors succeed in telling a truly inspirational story of the modern establishment of this new tool in human rights protection.

$21.95 / Paper: 1-56549-068-1
$46.00 / Cloth: 1-56549-069-X

Players and Issues in International Aid
Paula Hoy

Provides an overview of the issues surrounding development and assistance and offers multiple perspectives on the complexities of aid. Written for the student or lay person, Hoy discusses official assistance, both bilateral and multilateral, and nongovernmental assistance.

$21.95 / Paper: 1-56549-073-8
$45.00 / Cloth:1-56549-072-X

To order, contact:

Kumarian Press
14 Oakwood Avenue
West Hartford, CT 06119
Phone: 800-289-2664
Fax: 860-233-6072
E-Mail: kpbooks@aol.com
Web: www.kpbooks.com

 Kumarian Press is dedicated to publishing and distributing books and other media that will have a positive social and economic impact on the lives of peoples living in "Third World" conditions no matter where they live.

Kumarian Press publishes books about Global Issues and International Development, such as Peace and Conflict Resolution, Environmental Sustainability, Globalization, Nongovernmental Organizations, and Women and Gender.

To receive a complimentary catalog or to request writer's guidelines call or write:

Kumarian Press, Inc.
14 Oakwood Avenue
West Hartford, CT 06119-2127
U.S.A.

Inquiries: (860) 233-5895
Fax: (860) 233-6072
Order toll free: (800) 289-2664

e-mail: kpbooks@aol.com
Internet: www.kpbooks.com